REVISED

No Place for Abuse

BIBLICAL & PRACTICAL

RESOURCES TO COUNTERACT

DOMESTIC VIOLENCE

Catherine Clark Kroeger
& Nancy Nason-Clark

IVP Books

An imprint of InterVarsity Press
Downers Grove, Illinois

InterVarsity Press
P.O. Box 1400, Downers Grove, IL 60515-1426
World Wide Web: www.ivpress.com
E-mail: email@ivpress.com

Second edition ©2010 by Catherine Clark Kroeger and Nancy Nason-Clark
First edition © 2001 by Catherine Clark Kroeger and Nancy Nason-Clark

InterVarsity Press® is the book-publishing division of InterVarsity Christian Fellowship/USA®, a movement of students and faculty active on campus at hundreds of universities, colleges and schools of nursing in the United States of America, and a member movement of the International Fellowship of Evangelical Students. For information about local and regional activities, write Public Relations Dept., InterVarsity Christian Fellowship/USA, 6400 Schroeder Rd., P.O. Box 7895, Madison, WI 53707-7895, or visit the IVCF website at <www.intervarsity.org>.

Scripture quotations, unless otherwise noted, are from the New Revised Standard Version of the Bible, copyright 1989 by the Division of Christian Education of the National Council of the Churches of Christ in the USA. Used by permission. All rights reserved.

Design: Cindy Kiple
Interior Images: Jim Jurica/iStockphoto
Cover Images: Jeffrey Coolidge/Getty Images

ISBN 978-0-8308-3838-7

Printed in the United States of America ∞

InterVarsity Press is committed to protecting the environment and to the responsible use of natural resources. As a member of Green Press Initiative we use recycled paper whenever possible. To learn more about the Green Press Initiative, visit <www.greenpressinitiative.org>.

Library of Congress Cataloging-in-Publication Data

Kroeger, Catherine Clark.
 No place for abuse: biblical and practical resources to counteract
domestic violence / Catherine Clark Kroeger and Nancy Nason-Clark.—
Rev.
  p. cm.
 Includes bibliographical references (p.   ).
 ISBN 978-0-8308-3838-7 (pbk.: alk. paper)
 1. Church work with dysfunctional families. 2. Family
violence—Religious aspects—Christianity. I. Nason-Clark, Nancy,
1956- II. Title.
 BV4438.5.K76 2010
 261.8'327—dc22

                                                                  2010019869

P   18   17   16   15   14   13   12   11   10   9   8   7   6   5   4   3   2   1

Y   25   24   23   22   21   20   19   18   17   16   15   14   13   12   11   10

Contents

Preface

On Thursday, April 28, 1757, during a visit to Liverpool, John Wesley made a single entry in his journal.

> I talked with one who, by the advice of his Pastor, had, very calmly and deliberately, beat his wife with a large stick, till she was black and blue, almost from head to foot. And he insisted, it was his duty so to do, because she was surly and ill-natured; and that he was full of faith all the time he was doing it, and had been so ever since.[1]

Although other entries detail the give-and-take of conversations with those whom Wesley counseled, this observation is not accompanied by even a word of comment.

There was no denying the act of savagery that had been committed or the pious satisfaction that had been derived from it. How could anyone reconcile the gospel of love and light with the pastoral advice that had instigated the attack? How could Wesley insert himself into so delicate a situation?

Wesley was caught between the desire to honor the ministry of another pastor and his own sense of social justice. Remarkably he apparently attempted some sort of spiritual counseling with the offender—an effort that is infrequent among modern spiritual leaders. Often all the words of advice are directed toward the victim.

Two hundred and fifty years have passed since Wesley made that entry, and the dilemma remains. Sometimes we have denied that domestic violence exists within the church; at other times we have resorted to simplistic formulas that we hoped would rapidly fix the problem, or at least swept it under the rug. How are we to develop an understanding of a phenomenon that seems to be burgeoning all around us?

Wesley himself was no stranger to the misery of domestic abuse. A visitor once peered into the window of his cottage before knocking at the door. There he could see Mrs. Wesley dragging the unfortunate revivalist about by the queue in which gentlemen of the era braided their long hair. John Hampson, one of Wesley's preachers, declared, "More than once she laid violent hands upon him, and tore those venerable locks which had suffered sufficiently from the ravages of time."[2] An entry from April 1771 in Wesley's diary reads:

> For what cause I know not, my wife set out for Newcastle, purposing "never to return." *Non eam reliqui; non dimisi; non revocabo* [I did not forsake her; I did not dismiss her; I shall not recall her].[3]

Even great spiritual leaders are not immune. Neither now nor then can we bury the problem in Latin or in any other pious speech. As the people of God, we must face the reality and "think Christianly" about the evil that lurks within our own hearts.

HOW THE FIRST EDITION OF THIS BOOK BEGAN

At a general assembly of the World Evangelical Fellowship (WEF), an African woman rose and asked, "When will this organization address violence against women? There are men in this very room who abuse their wives."

The response was a standing ovation.

God's people were ready to examine the great wound in the

churches and to apply healing balm. The Women's Commission of the WEF was asked to form a task force on violence against women and to consider how the evangelical church worldwide could offer compassion and healing to victims. What is the extent of the problem of abuse? How are evangelical churches responding to the suffering caused by violence in the home? What theological principles can help the church offer hope in the midst of crises, to families both inside and outside the fold?

The International Task Force[4] began its work by developing a theological statement concerning abuse and a series of principles to reveal how God has spoken out about violence through Scripture. We were asked to write a book-length statement addressing the prevalence of abuse, together with a sustained biblical argument condemning violence and with practical strategies for churches as they respond to the needs of victims and their families.

WHY A SECOND EDITION?

Ten years have passed since the first edition of this book was released. It has been used around the world in many contexts, but in those ten years, much has changed in that world. New statistics have become available that cause us to face new realities. There is a great deal of new thought about domestic violence. In some areas, significant progress has been made; in others, the situation is even worse than before.

Nancy not only supplies us with a new and astonishing array of hard facts from around the world, but also lets us hear the voices of human beings caught in the tragedy of domestic abuse. Her continuing research gives us glimpses of the manifold situations and circumstances in which abuse occurs. She leads us through a remarkable resource that she has developed to inform and equip ourselves for Christian action. She even provides us with a step-by-step walk through the RAVE (Religion and Violence e-Learning) Project website. Such a resource could not have been dreamt of ten years ago.

In the past decade, Cathie has been able to interact more freely with secular caregivers, to gain a deeper understanding of the vital role they play and to discuss how elements of spirituality may be made available to those whose souls cry out for spiritual help. We are entering a new era of communication.

John Stott used to say that believers need to engage in double listening: with one ear to what is going on in the world and with the other ear to what the Word of God tells us. It is Cathie who brings a biblical understanding to the table. She seeks to deal with the many considerations that conscientious Christians must face as they launch into the deep of a very stormy issue. Like the prophets of old, we must observe and reflect, pray and bring God's Word to bear upon the evil—and then recruit others to move forward with appropriate action.

In our work together, Nancy offers the expertise of a trained sociologist; Catherine, the insights of a biblical scholar. Together we bring a variety of perspectives to bear on this complex problem. We are citizens of two different nations, trained in different disciplines on two sides of the Atlantic, born in different generations, worshipping in different evangelical traditions. But we share a united conviction that Christian churches today must recognize and respond to the suffering created by family violence.

The first four chapters of No Place for Abuse will demonstrate the prevalence of violence worldwide and its presence in evangelical homes. Until we catch a glimpse of scenes of horror from around the world, we will never have eyes to see violence in the neighborhoods where we live and in the churches we attend. It is always more difficult to deal with shame in one's own backyard.

Secular knowledge alone is insufficient. Women and men alike voice another concern: When will people talk about abuse in theological language? When will they tell us what the Bible says? When will the church speak to people of faith about matters of abuse in the home? When will Christians heed the message of Scripture and begin to obey its principles? To address this need, nine chapters present biblical reasons that Christians must acknowledge the global crisis of abuse of women. We argue that believers must respond to this evil wherever it occurs, both within and beyond the fold of faith.

Equipped with the latest data and best practices, as well as the biblical imperative to speak out against this evil in our midst, the reader will find in the last chapter of *No Place for Abuse* a guide to taking action. A step-by-step tour of the RAVE Project website (www.theraveproject.org) outlines the resources available for putting into action the call to hear and respond to the cries of those impacted by domestic violence. Working in unison, churches and their leaders can combat violence against women and proclaim the message of hope and healing.

This book is intended to speak to people holding differing views on the dynamics of marriage and family life. There is no room for gender politics. The time has come for believers to unite efforts and obey God's command to deliver the oppressed from the hand of the violent. We need to be faithful in remonstrating with oppressors and seeking to guide them into new patterns of behavior. We must be tender in the care of those who are afflicted. The healing balm of Gilead needs to be applied.

The Bible consistently calls for God's judgment on those who use their power to inflict suffering on others. Conversely, great blessing is promised to those who use their power to alleviate the oppression and suffering of others. How will we—God's people—respond to this challenge?

For too long, sacred and secular caregivers have worked in isolation from one another. By blending sociological studies and biblical insights, this book sounds a call of compassion and justice to God's people around the world. It also calls to those working in secular contexts: Do not forget that many people—men and women alike—have deep religious convictions. The journey toward accountability for perpetrators and healing for victims has spiritual dimensions that cannot be denied.

As you read our book, it will become clear that it is written in two different voices—separate and distinct, but of common purpose and vision.

✳ ✳ ✳

We acknowledge helpful companions in our journey of researching and writing *No Place for Abuse.*

I (Nancy) thank those who have funded my research program over the past twenty years: the Louisville Institute for the Study of Protestantism and American Culture, the Social Sciences and Humanities Research Council, the Lawson Foundation, the Women's Program of the Canadian federal government, the Constant Jacquet Research Award from the Religious Research Association, the Fichter Research Award from the Association for the Sociology of Religion, the Muriel McQueen Fergusson Centre for Family Violence Research, and the University of New Brunswick. Participating denominations have also provided financial support as well as in-kind donations of time or resources.

Recently, the Lilly Endowment provided a four-year grant that enabled the development of the RAVE Project on which chapter fourteen is based. Through their generous support, an idea for a worldwide resource for pastors and congregations became a reality, and for that I will be forever grateful. Since the RAVE Project website was first launched in October of 2008, over one thousand distinct IP addresses (that is, individual computers) access its resources *each week.* In fact, it had over 500,000 hits within the first couple of weeks of "going live."

Over the past twenty years, I (Nancy) have come into contact with thousands of women and men, laity and clergy alike, who have opened their lives and told their stories to our research team. Thank you for the privilege of listening to your pain and your hope. Along the way, I have worked with many wonderful graduate students who have become cherished colleagues and friends. For a very long time, Barbara Fisher-Townsend has worked diligently with me on a score of research initiatives. She is the very best research associate anyone, anywhere, could ever hope for. More recently, Cathy Holtmann, Steve McMullin and Leah Cunjak have been part of the RAVE team. All of these amazing people brighten the halls of our shared working space, creating intellectual synergy, lively interchange and lots of hard work, not to mention laughs over lunch and needed distraction over coffee. Working with smart, dedicated, creative people is something I truly enjoy but never want to take for granted. Thanks so much for choosing to work alongside me.

There are many others to thank: Terry Atkinson, Lori Beaman, Amanda Henry, Christy Hoyt, Tricia Jarratt, Charlotte McIntosh, Sheila McCrea-McCallum, Tracy McDonald, Lois Mitchell, Julie Owens, Lanette Ruff and Michelle Spencer—women and men who have played an important part in some phase of the research process or in the accounting of its funding.

On a personal note, I wish to acknowledge the *tremendous* support of my family: David Clark, my life partner, a clinical psychologist and prolific scholar of depression and anxiety disorders; and daughters Natascha and Christina, now university students with increasingly independent lives, who enrich my waking hours in ways too numerous to count. Living a peaceful, fulfilled life at home enables me to focus in my research and writing on those robbed of this experience.

There are many to whom I (Catherine) must express gratitude: victims, shelter workers, pastors, laypeople, counselors, leaders of batterers groups, therapists, law enforcement personnel and even some batterers themselves. I am grateful to them for telling their stories and those of their friends—for revealing their spiritual struggles, the responses they were given by churches and individuals, and their soul-wracking questions about human agony and biblical teaching. We have sought to share their perspectives while protecting their identity, to let others know what evangelicals suffer and what they perpetrate. These nameless stalwarts have led us to look at the Bible more closely and ultimately to dare to voice our convictions.

Together we are grateful to James Hoover of InterVarsity Press for first endorsing a book that addresses evangelicals around the world about a very unpopular subject and then inviting us to prepare a second edition. We thank God that Jim could understand the importance of sharing the devastating truth as well as the resources that are available for healing. We also thank those who have worked with us over the years, including the members of the first World Evangelical Task Force on Abuse and the board of PASCH (Peace and Safety in the Christian Home) for their ongoing vision, assistance and encouragement. We pray our feeble efforts will bring hope and healing to those whose lives have been touched by the devastating consequences of domestic violence and other forms of abuse.

> Creator God:
> We ask, O Lord,
> that you would open our eyes to see
> the suffering of women around the world.
> Give us ears to hear their cries
> and hearts that will not rest
> until we have done our part
> to apply the healing balm of Gilead to their wounds.
> Amen.

1

The Prevalence and Severity of Abuse Against Women

Our purpose in updating *No Place for Abuse* is to provide pastors and church people with the most recent information on domestic violence and to outline best practices by which they can respond to those who suffer from its consequences. In 2001 InterVarsity Press published the first edition of *No Place for Abuse*—our message to congregations and their leaders about the prevalence and severity of abuse, and strategies they might employ as they attempt to respond to the issue and those impacted by it.

In some ways, not a lot has changed since 2001: the problem is as real today as it was then, the suffering for victims and their families is as profound and the need for churches to speak out against abuse just as compelling. In other ways, however, a great deal has changed in the ten years since we completed the research and writing that led to the first edition. The Internet has altered the way we look for information and resources; the networking opportunities and capabilities of pastor and parishioner alike has expanded exponentially; and there is mounting evidence of the pervasiveness of the problem and the long-term consequences for survivors, for those who act abusively and for the children who witness or experience violence in the home.

In the pages that follow, there are updated statistics, the integration of new research and insights and our ever-developing thinking on these issues from both a biblical and sociological perspective. During the years we have been working together, we have not wavered in our belief that churches and their leaders are essential—lifegiving and spirit-empowering—components in any community-based response to domestic violence. Thus we believe the quest to offer resources that are informed by research and prompted by a passionate commitment to promote—and live—peace and safety within all our homes is as important now as it ever was.

Our purpose in writing No Place for Abuse was to challenge the evangelical Christian community to listen to the voices of women from around the world—including those in their own backyard—talk about the violence they have suffered. We wanted to address the problem straightforwardly: to offer information so that church people and pastors would be ignorant no longer, to offer advice on effective biblical ways to respond to victims and their families and to offer a challenge that congregations and their leaders take up positions among community and national groups committed to eliminating violence in our midst, encouraging violence-free family living and responding with the mind and heart of Christ to those who suffer violence.

While the message and the purpose remain much the same, the need for spiritual resources and practical advice is now harnessed in the knowledge provided on the Web. As a result of our ongoing development of web-based resources, this revised and expanded second edition of No Place for Abuse utilizes these and offers an integration of Web and print capabilities for raising awareness on domestic violence and responding compassionately and with best practices to those who suffer.

Over the past ten years, we have received a lot of feedback and support from readers. We have learned how pastors, youth leaders and small-group facilitators have used our materials. We have talked to victims, survivors and pastors who have been challenged to search the Scriptures by first accessing those references we offered. The statistics have been consulted by seminary students for their papers and pastors for their sermons. Survivors and family members have found help and comfort in the stories, in the strategies for safety and empowerment, and in the words of prayers to be offered and potential sermons to be preached.

In this edition, we have tried to augment the resources by tapping into the RAVE website, a project that offers more direct biblical material. For Christians who have been impacted personally by domestic violence, the Scriptures offer both a call to live differently and a comfort for those who suffer. Paying attention to what the Bible says about abuse ought to interest many believers.

Christians also should not be ill-informed about the nature, prevalence and severity of abuse that characterizes our churches, our neighborhoods and our world. We believe that most Christian people, when provided with both the biblical teaching condemning violence and the social-science data about its consequences, will want to do something about it. We do not believe that the Spirit-filled life should include abusive acts, nor should it turn a blind eye to the suffering of another.

Violence against women exists in every country of the globe, among all people groups. Abuse occurs within every faith community. And it knows no socioeconomic boundaries. Rich women, poor women, black women, white women, educated women, illiterate women, religious women, beautiful women—all women are potential targets of violence, and all women are at some degree of risk.

Governments around the world are recognizing the devastating consequences of violence against women, and researchers and healthcare professionals are being called upon for expert advice and guidance for both community-level actions (such as emergency response teams) and national policy initiatives. Large sums of money are now being directed toward research on the elimination of violence, reforming the judicial system to respond to the needs of victims and perpetrators, and ensuring that health and other social services offer effective coordinated responses to the needs of abused women and their dependent children.[1]

There is immense documentation, from academic researchers, women's organizations, policy analysts, health-care providers and victim support groups, of the prevalence and severity worldwide of violence against women and the girl child. Since 1995 and the Fourth World Conference on Women in Beijing, many nation-states have sought to take seriously the challenge to reduce women's risk of physical or sexual assault. Professional organizations like the American College of Obstetricians and Gynecologists have responded with protocols for their members. Umbrella organizations like the World Health Organization have held consultations, created task forces, produced training materials and conducted research among their member groups. The World Bank has documented the enormous cost of violence. Some political parties in power, or in opposition, have sought to address violence against women through policy statements, zero-tolerance declarations, directives, government grants and community initiatives.

Amid growing world recognition of the problems women face, their everyday fears, the bruises and battering they experience and the needs of their children for safety and security, where are the churches? Why have religious groups been so slow to recognize violence against women and so slow to respond to victims' cries for help? Indeed, amid the ever-increasing number of men and women worldwide who recognize the severity of woman abuse and have personal and professional commitment to work toward its elimination, where are God's people, called in God's name to bring healing in the midst of suffering?

By and large, a "holy hush"[2] pervades religious organizations. Violence is ugly, and most churches and their leaders feel uncomfortable talking about it and ill-equipped to respond to its victims. The issue is very sensitive, and many laypeople and pastors alike would prefer to sweep it under the church carpet. Moreover, violence touches many people at the core of their being, because they either recognize in themselves the tendency to control others or have suffered humiliation at the hands of someone else.

Let's face our reluctance head-on: the reality and consequences of violence make most Christian people—indeed most any people anywhere—very uncomfortable. As the people of God, we would prefer to think abuse does not occur in our churches' families. So we act as if it were someone else's problem, something we do not need to contend with ourselves.

But violence is everyone's problem. It is an issue that is not going away. It is prevalent in our churches and in the communities our churches serve. We need to admit that we have been hiding from the problem—and sometimes contributing to it—and that we are not very committed to being part of its solution.

Many voices declare that the church has caused men to be violent toward their wives or at least provided fertile soil for men's mistreatment of power within their families. They argue that since the church is part of the problem, it cannot be part of the solution. Thus when violence against women is being discussed, God's people are seldom consulted. Since we speak out so infrequently about violence, our collective voice is hardly ever heard on this issue. Generally speaking, leaders in religious organizations and those involved in community pastoral care are rarely invited to participate at the secular consultation table. The silence of our churches and our leaders is often interpreted in the public square as complicity with violent acts.

It is assumed—we think erroneously—that Christian people do not have a biblical response to the suffering of women worldwide. It is assumed—we think erroneously—that the healing journey of a victim has nothing to do with her walk of faith. It is assumed—we think erroneously—that pastoral care has nothing unique to offer and could be damaging to a woman's search for health and wholeness.

The time has come to challenge the contemporary evangelical church to wake up to the prevalence of violence in its midst, to take up its role as part of a community-based response and to offer the

healing balm of Gilead to those who suffer the devastating consequences of abuse. Men and women filled with devotion to God can
play a vital role in proclaiming this message: every home a safe place,
every home a shelter. There is no place like home. When abuse strikes,
there is no home.

We believe the time has come for a renewed prophetic voice to
emerge from the pew and from behind the pulpit—voices that want
to change our communities, to challenge our people and to offer new
strategies to ensure that our world is a safer place in which to live.
Christian people ought to be men and women of hope and of vision,
binding up the broken-hearted and showing all people everywhere a
more excellent way. It is in that spirit of hope that we share our vision—a vision where the evangelical church worldwide would join
hands to condemn all types of abuse, to recognize in particular the
suffering of women and its consequences for children, and to commit
our time and our passion to work toward the elimination of all forms
of family violence—with God as our guide, Jesus as our companion
and the Holy Spirit as our comforter. We need God's direction, the
companionship and blessed example of Christ, and the Spirit to both
strengthen us in the struggle and to apply the healing balm.

In the pages that follow, we present the data (individual narra-
tives, country-by-country summary statements about violence against
women and national statistics on its prevalence), followed by the
challenge to change the world, one home at a time. Let us not forget,
the home is no place for abuse. Neither let us forget, *the church is no
place for silence.*

WOMAN ABUSE ACROSS THE WORLD

Violence against women is a worldwide problem. Although abuse
takes many forms, happens in many places and affects women differently, the first step in understanding the magnitude of the problem is
to look at its frequency and the many, varied forms it takes and responses that are required. Researchers from all corners of the globe
have demonstrated that domestic violence threatens the physical and

mental health and security of millions of women. A woman living in the developed world and the developing world is more likely to be injured, raped or physically threatened by a current or former intimate partner than by a stranger or any other person. That is why many women's organizations have claimed that violence is the number-one fear or reality of women worldwide.

The statistics are startling. Violence against women is a pervasive problem in North America, Europe, Africa, Australia, Asia and South America. In every country where woman abuse has been studied using a large-scale sample and consistent measures, at least one in ten women reports that she has been physically abused by an intimate male partner. These figures *do not* include verbal abuse, sexual assault or threats of violence. As such they are very conservative estimates of violence against women. Moreover, data like these rely on women's self-reports of victimization. The abuse of women who are unwilling to admit to themselves what has happened or unwilling to disclose their pain to an outsider simply goes unreported.

Physical abuse includes behaviors such as kicking, biting and punching. Sometimes an object is used to inflict harm, such as a knife or gun. It is not uncommon for women to sustain serious injuries at the hands of a partner; sometimes they die as a result. All victimized women feel shame, betrayal and fear. Some try to hide the secret of their abuse; others gather up enough courage to escape.

We have provided information in two different forms. First, we offer a snapshot of violence against women around the world. Here we refer to studies collected by the World Health Organization; the United Nations; the World Development Bank; national research offices, such as Statistics Canada and the U.S. Department of Justice; and large studies conducted by various university researchers, with collaborations between and within several countries.

To someone with little prior exposure to violence or abuse, this country-by-country exposé is an "eye-opener"; it challenges the thinking that domestic violence, or abuse against women, is isolated and sporadic. In most cases, these data cannot be compared across countries; they have not been collected in ways that allow comparison. They are the result of the individual efforts of various researchers or organizations. But the message they offer cannot—and should not—be ignored. Violence against women and children is a pervasive problem worldwide.

Later in this chapter, we will offer a table outlining prevalence rates more specifically. But first, we provide a look at the issue in many individual countries around the world. As you read these statistics, we encourage you to ask yourself a few questions:

- What do these figures reveal about intimate relationships around the world?

- What should the response of God's people be to such suffering?

- Is there a role for my congregation, or for me?

Afghanistan

- In Afghanistan, the average woman is married before the age of sixteen. According to a 2005 report by Amnesty International, some girls are married by nine years of age.[3]

- Based on information published in 2007 by the Integrated Regional Information Networks, one in three Afghan women had experienced physical, psychological or sexual violence.[4]

Australia

- Across Western Australia, females were victims in 91.4 percent of domestic violence cases, and males in 8.6 percent of cases.[5]

- Based on information published by the Australian Bureau of Statistics in 2006, an Aboriginal person was 45 times more likely to be a victim of domestic violence than a non-Aboriginal.[6]

Bangladesh

- It is claimed that Bangladeshi women are the most battered in the world, where survey results reveal that 47 percent of adult women have been physically assaulted by an intimate partner.[7]

- Amnesty International reported in 2005 that women accounted for the large majority of acid attack victims. Reasons for most attacks: disputes between families or refusal by women of marriage or sex.[8]

Brazil

- According to a report by the World Health Organization in 2005, 12 percent of all women in São Paulo and 9 percent in Pernambuco reported sexual abuse before the age of 15 years. The majority of this violence was perpetrated by a male family member.[9]

- In research reported by the World Health Organization in 2005, approximately one in two battered women in studies in São Paulo and Pernambuco were beaten before their first pregnancy and one in three disclosed that the beatings got worse during pregnancy.[10]

Cambodia

- In Cambodia, poverty and abuse often drive children to live on the streets. In fact, domestic nongovernmental organizations estimated in 2002 that there were more than 10,000 street children in Phnom Penh alone who were easy targets for sexual abuse and exploitation.[11]

- According to the 1996 Household Survey on Domestic Violence in Cambodia, 16 percent of women had experienced physical violence by a current partner; 8 percent reported being injured.[12]

Canada

- According to Statistics Canada in 2005, 653,000 Canadian women reported being a victim of spousal violence in the past five years, with 26 percent of these women being assaulted more than ten

times. The violence experienced by women tended to be more severe—and often more repeated—than the violence experienced
by men.[13]

- According to the 1999 and 2004 Canadian General Social Survey,
  Aboriginal people were three times more likely to be victims of
  spousal violence than those who were non-Aboriginals.[14]

Chile

- According to a United Nations Populations Fund report in 2007,
  most laws remained woefully inadequate in protecting abused
  women or in imposing sanctions against those who abuse them. In
  Chile, divorce was illegal, even in cases of extreme domestic violence.[15]
- A 1998 World Health Organization report said that battered
  women in Chile experienced a 40-percent increase of abuse during pregnancy.[16]

China

- In 2008, "China Daily" reported that more than 12,000 anti-
  domestic-violence centers had been installed across China to protect people, especially women, from domestic violence.[17]
- Figures from the All-China Women's Federation in 2007 showed
  that about 30 percent of Chinese families, some 80 million, had
  experienced domestic violence. About a quarter of the 400,000
  divorces registered each year resulted from family violence.[18]

Colombia

- According to the U.S. Department of State, Country Reports on
  Human Rights Practices, 2005, the Institute for Legal Medicine
  and Forensic Science reported that only 5 percent of the 19,251
  cases of domestic violence against women in Colombia between
  January and June of 2005 were reported.[19]

- Amnesty International detailed in 2004 that survivors of sexual violence in Colombia also faced a further, debilitating battle with their families and communities: they were ostracized and stigmatized. Survivors could be subjected to harsh social and cultural norms that blamed the victim for the attack.[20]

Croatia

- The Open Society Institute reported in 2006 that there were ten shelters that could accommodate 211 women victims and their children in Croatia. This was a marked increase from that reported by the Coalition for Work with Psychotrauma and Peace in a 2004 report, which noted 19 shelter beds for abused women in Croatia. Stop Violence Against Women identified four shelters in their 2005 report.[21]

- In a 2003 report, 83 percent of abused women in Croatia said that they never called the police in the aftermath of domestic violence, and 90 percent reported not contacting a shelter.[22]

Egypt

- According to the United Nations in 2000, 80 percent of women surveyed in rural Egypt said that wife beatings were common—and often justified—particularly if the woman refused to have sex with her partner.[23]

- Official statistics collected in Egypt indicated that murders committed in defense of honor accounted for 5.4 percent of all the murders committed in 1997. In a four-month study in 1998, 14 murders were allegedly motivated by honor.[24]

Ethiopia

- According to a 2005 report of the World Health Organization, entitled "WHO Multi-country Study on Women's Health and Domestic Violence Against Women," nearly 35 percent of all ever-partnered women in Ethiopia experienced at least one severe form of physical violence by an intimate partner (for example, being kicked, dragged or burned on purpose, or having a weapon used against them).[25]

- According to the same report, of women who had ever been pregnant in Ethiopia, 8 percent reported physical violence during at least one pregnancy. Of these, 28 percent had been punched or kicked in the abdomen, almost always by the father of the child.[26]

Finland

- The Prosecutor-General's Office of Finland in 1994 estimates that between 6,000 and 10,000 rapes are committed annually; almost 30 women die every year as a result of domestic violence.[27]
- The Union of Shelter Homes maintained 23 shelters for victims of domestic violence, including children, according to a 2004 report. According to researchers, most women seeking shelter from violence were women between 25 and 35 years of age and either married or in a common-law relationship, and nearly one-third were immigrants.[28]

Germany

- According to the German Family Minister in 2004, higher rates of intimate-partner violence were experienced by those women in Germany planning to leave their partner.[29]
- German women with Eastern European or Turkish parents (or grandparents) were among the most affected by domestic violence. Around half of the immigrant women said they had experienced sexual or physical violence at the hands of their partners.[30]

India

- According to a 1998 report, two in five Indian women (42 percent to 48 percent) in Uttar Pradesh and 36 percent to 41 percent in

Tamil Nadu said they had suffered beatings from their husbands.[31]

- University researchers in Bombay found that a relatively large proportion of women who experienced fetal loss believed the miscarriage or stillbirth was the result of a violent assault inflicted on
them by their husband.[32]

Iran

- In 2008 Amnesty International reported that women in Iran faced
far-reaching discrimination under the law. They were denied equal
rights in marriage, divorce, child custody and inheritance. A girl
under the age of 13 could be forced to marry a much older man if
her father permitted it.[33]

- In Iran, 81 out of 100 married women experienced domestic violence in their first year of marriage, according to Women's Forum
Against Fundamentalism in Iran, in 2004.[34]

Ireland

- In a 2003 report, Amnesty International said there were 45,000
help-line calls in Ireland to rape crisis centers, 89 percent of which
were from females. In 97 percent of the cases, the perpetrators
were male.[35]

- In a 2002 report, four out of 10 women who had been involved in
a sexual relationship with a man experienced violence.[36]

Israel

- A 2007 article on the Yad Shara Family Center website reported
that there were 15 shelters throughout the country for battered
women, among them one shelter for Arab women and two for Or-
thodox and Haredi women.[37]

- According to the Association of Rape Crisis Centers in Israel, in
2004, 32,737 calls were received at the national hotline of the rape

crisis centers. Of those, 8,049 calls were from victims who reported their assault for the first time.[38]

Jamaica

- Statistics from the Sexual Offense Unit of the Jamaican Police indicated that, in 1997, 1,857 cases of sexual offenses were filed, of which 40 percent involved rape and bodily harm. Between January 1 and November 15, 1998, 760 cases of rape and 455 of physical abuse were reported.[39]

- Data provided by the Emergency Unit of the Kingston Public Hospital indicated that every day in 1997 approximately 20 women were treated on an outpatient basis for wounds requiring stitches and 90 percent of those situations were the result of domestic violence.[40]

Kenya

- According to a 2005 report by Amnesty International, the most recent Kenyan Demographic Health Survey indicated that more than half the women in Kenya had experienced violence since the age of 15. It reported that husbands inflicted 60 percent of the beatings.[41]

- While the law in Kenya in 2006 formally prohibited female genital mutilation, it was still practiced, particularly in rural areas. According to the United Nations Children's Fund (UNICEF) in 2006, almost one in three women had been subjected to FGM.[42]

Malaysia

- According to the Women's Aid Organisation, Shahrizat Jalil, then minister for Women, Family and Community Development in Malaysia, told a gathering of women that the number of rape cases in the country had nearly doubled, from 1,217 in 2000 to 2,341 in 2006.[43]

- It was estimated in 2007 that 39 percent of Malaysian women had been abused by their partners, making domestic violence a significant, but often hidden, social problem in Malaysia.[44]

Mexico

- According to UNICEF México, in 2001, four in 10 women reported acts of spousal violence committed against them, and only three of those commenced legal proceedings. Men were the perpetrators in 90 percent of family violence cases.[45]

- Based on a population-based study conducted in Mexico from June to September 1998, among 1,535 women aged 15 to 49 years, the prevalence of low-moderate-level violence was 35.8 percent, and severe violence was 9.5 percent. The lifetime prevalence of reported rape was 5.9 percent.[46]

Netherlands

- In a 2004 study in the Netherlands, 100,000 children a year witnessed domestic violence between their parents, and 40 percent of them were considered to be at great risk of developing behavioral problems.[47]

- According to the Council of Europe, 2003 reports from the Netherlands estimated that the costs entailed by domestic violence against women amounted to more than 200 million Euros per annum.[48]

New Zealand

- In a 2005 study that asked men in New Zealand about their use of violence, 35 percent of men admitted to being physically violent with their partner in their lifetime, while 20 percent of men reported physically assaulting their female partner during the past twelve months.[49]

- During December 2005 and January 2006, New Zealand police attended nearly 11,000 instances of reported family violence—about one incident every eight minutes.[50]

Nicaragua

- A study on women conducted by two Nicaraguan nongovernmental organizations in conjunction with a Swedish university found that 52 percent of Nicaraguan women had been victims of violence from a spouse or partner at some point in their lives.[51]

- Of the cohort of 2,570 women experiencing domestic violence, 29.3 percent noted that this had happened five or more times within the past 12 months.[52]

Nigeria

- The 2003 Nigerian Demographic and Health Survey revealed that 64.5 percent of women and 61.3 percent of men agreed that a husband was justified in hitting or beating his wife for reasons that included burning food and not cooking a meal on time.[53]

- In a 2004 study, the law permitted husbands to use physical means to chastise their wives as long as it did not result in "grievous harm," which was defined as loss of sight, hearing or power of speech, facial disfigurement or life-threatening injuries.[54]

Norway

- According to a 2006 Amnesty International report, there were 50 shelters for women in Norway, and more than 2,500 women sought out these shelters every year. A predominant and growing number of the inhabitants were women of immigrant background.[55]

- According to a Parliamentary Assembly report in 2002, each year 10,000 women in Norway (out of a population of 4 million people) sought medical treatment because of physical injuries due to domestic violence.[56]

Paraguay

- A 2007 report by the U.N. Development Programme found that 50 percent of the cases of violence against girls in Paraguay involved sexual violence; in more than 30 percent of cases, the abuser was known to the victim.[57]

- In 2007, there were no state institutions providing shelter for women who experienced wife abuse in Paraguay. This made it virtually impossible for women to escape violent relationships and put many women and their families at ongoing risk.[58]

Peru

- According to a 2005 report of the World Health Organization, 49 percent of ever-partnered women in Lima and 61 percent in Cusco reported physical violence by a partner at some time in their lives. The rates of sexual violence by a partner were 23 percent in Lima and 47 percent in Cusco.[59]

- According to a 2005 World Health Organization report, 15 percent of ever-pregnant women in Lima and 28 percent in Cusco experienced physical violence during at least one pregnancy. Of these, one third in Lima and over half in Cusco were punched or kicked in the abdomen. In virtually all cases, the perpetrator was the unborn child's father.[60]

Philippines

- According to the 2000 Philippine National Police surveys, there were 4,545 registered cases of wife battering in the Philippines. This figure represented an increase of 27 percent from the 1999 statistics.[61]

- The number of registered victims of rape in the Philippines was reported as 1,575, 16 percent higher than the 1999 surveys.[62]

Puerto Rico

- According to national statistics, in 2007 there were more than 21,000 domestic violence incidents per year. The number of incidents had been increasing each year since 2002.[63]

- Victims of domestic violence tended to be women (86 percent) and younger people (44 percent are between 20 and 29). In eight out of 10 cases, the incidents took place in the home of the victim.[64]

Russia

- A survey conducted by Moscow State University between 2002 and 2003 involving 2,200 Russian respondents found that 70 percent of women claimed they had been abused by their husbands, while 90 percent of all respondents claimed they had either experienced or witnessed abuse between their parents.[65]
- Every 40 minutes, a woman in the Russian Federation is killed by domestic violence, according to a 2008 Amnesty International report.[66]

Rwanda

- According to 2004 research statistics, 71 percent of women who had been beaten by their husband in Rwanda believed that he was justified in doing so.[67]
- In a 2005-2006 report, nearly one in three women in Rwanda had experienced physical violence since age 15.[68]

South Africa

- According to nongovernmental organizations in 2006, an estimated 25 percent of women in South Africa were in abusive relationships, but few reported it.[69]
- Interviews conducted with 1,394 men working for three Cape Town municipalities found that approximately 44 percent of the men were willing to admit that they abused their female partners.[70]

Spain

- According to a 2008 Amnesty International report, 2 million women faced domestic violence in Spain, and every four days a woman was killed by her spouse or ex-spouse.[71]

- According to that same report, of 600,000 women in Spain who suffered aggression at the hands of their partners, only 21 percent placed an official complaint.[72]

Switzerland

- Based on a national survey and official statistical data from various sources in 1999, using a 12-month prevalence rate of 11.3 percent, the cost of domestic violence to the Swiss government was estimated to be 260 million Euros annually.[73]

- In 2002, 989 women sought temporary shelter from abusive partners, representing an increase of 20 percent since 2001.[74]

Tanzania

- In the Kibondo refugee camps, there were 613 documented cases of domestic violence in 1998 within four of the camps: Kanembwa, Mkugwa, Mtendeli and Nduta. In 1999, there were 764 documented cases.[75]

- In both Dar es Salaam and Mbeya about 15 percent of women reported that their first experience of sex was forced.[76]

Thailand

- According to a 2006 World Health Organization report, 41 percent of women in Bangkok and 47 percent in Nakhon Sawan had experienced physical or sexual violence by an intimate partner.[77]

- Of women who had experienced physical violence, 50 percent in Bangkok and 44 percent in Nakhon Sawan had been injured as a result of the physical violence by their intimate partner. About one-third of women who had serious injuries never sought medical treatment.[78]

Turkey

- In 2005, a legal provision came into force in Turkey for municipalities with more than 50,000 inhabitants to open at least one
shelter for survivors of domestic violence. By 2007, Amnesty International claimed that not a single municipality had established a
new shelter, because of limited budgets or lack of political will.[79]

- According to a 2003 report, the Turkish government continued to
allow virginity testing to determine if a woman had lost her virginity, thereby damaging the honor of the family. In extreme cases,
women were killed to protect the honor of the family.[80]

Uganda

- Based on a 2005 report from the Family Violence Prevention Fund,
research in Uganda showed that abusive men often intentionally
infected their partners with HIV.[81]

- According to a 2003 report of the World Health Organization, a
survey in Rakai, Uganda, found that 70 percent of the men and
90 percent of the women thought wife-beating was all right in
some circumstances. Of the 5,109 women of reproductive age
surveyed, 30 percent had experienced physical threats or abuse
from their current partners. Of those, the majority had suffered
three or more specific acts of violence during the preceding
year; almost half experienced injuries as a result of the
abuse.[82]

United Kingdom

- According to a 2002 Home Office report, every minute police in
the United Kingdom receive a domestic assistance call—yet only
35 percent of domestic violence incidents are reported to the
police.[83]

- There were an estimated 635,000 incidents of domestic violence in
England and Wales; 81 percent of the victims were women and 19

percent were men. Domestic violence incidents also made up nearly 22 percent of all violent incidents reported by participants in the 2002 British Crime Survey.[84]

- According to the Home Office in 2007, domestic violence cost in excess of 23 billion pounds a year and claimed the lives of two women each week.[85]

United States

- In 2000, intimate-partner homicides accounted for 33.5 percent of the murders of women but less than 4 percent of the murders of men.[86]

- The health-care cost of intimate-partner violence against women totaled 5.8 billion dollars yearly, according to the Centers for Disease Control and Prevention in 2004.[87]

- For 30 percent of women who experienced abuse, the first incident occurred during pregnancy, according to the U.S. Department of Justice in 1997.[88]

It is powerful—and often convicting—to consider how pervasive and how serious domestic violence continues to be in our world. It occurs in every corner, in every kind of family, in every faith tradition. Scores of women and children suffer at the hands of those who act abusively. And abusers suffer too. There is pain, and there is much devastation. Usually, there is very little hope and much despair.

While these summary statements offer a snapshot of the suffering in many different places, the data contained in table one below offers a starting point for assessing the magnitude of the problem. As table one reveals, in every country where reliable data has been collected, large numbers of women have been physically assaulted by a male intimate partner.

Table 1.

Country	Statistics	Source
Afghanistan	Of violent acts committed against women, 73.5 percent were perpetrated solely by one person.[89] The most common perpetrators were family members, including intimate partners (82 percent).[90]	United Nations Development Fund for Women, Violence Against Women Primary Database Report, 2006
Bangladesh	According to government statistics, one woman was subjected to violence every hour.[91] Acid attacks remained one of the most barbaric acts against girls and women in Bangladesh, where three to five young women a week were being burned with acid and the numbers were increasing at an alarming rate. By throwing acid, men not only destroy a women's face but also her future.[92]	Bangladesh Common Country Assessment, 2005 University researcher, Majumdar, 2002
Brazil	Among ever-partnered women, 27 percent in São Paulo and 43 percent in Pernambuco reported having experienced physical violence.[93] Among women who had been pregnant at least once, 8 percent in São Paulo and 11 percent in Pernambuco reported physical violence during a pregnancy. Among these, 29 percent of women in São Paulo and 30 percent in Pernambuco were hit or kicked in the abdomen.	"WHO Multi-country Study on Women's Health and Domestic Violence Against Women," 2005
Cambodia	Although comprehensive statistics were not available, a local nongovernmental organization claimed 244 cases of domestic violence and 174 cases of rape during the preceding year.[94]	U.S. Department of State, Country Reports on Human Rights Practices, 2002

Country	Statistics	Source
Canada	Statistics Canada (2005) reports that younger age poses a higher risk of experiencing spousal violence with women between the ages of 15 and 24 reporting the highest one-year rates of spousal violence. Reporting rates of spousal abuse have increased significantly since 1995, with 37 percent of female victims and 17 percent of male victims reporting the incidents to the police in 2004.	Statistics Canada, 2005
Chile	A 2004 National Women's Service (SERNAM) study reported that 50 percent of married women had suffered spousal abuse—34 percent physical violence and 16 percent psychological abuse.[95] In a sample of women from Santiago, 26 percent of women reported at least one episode of violence by a partner, with 11 percent disclosing at least one episode of severe violence.[96]	U.S. Department of State, Country Reports on Human Rights Practices, 2005 UNICEF, 2000
China	Thirty-four percent of women and 18 percent of men had been hit during their current relationship; the prevalence of hitting resulting in bleeding, bruises, swelling or severe pain and injuries was 12 percent for women and 5 percent for men.[97]	University researchers, W. L. Parish et al., 2004
Colombia	The Institute for Legal Medicine and Forensic Science reported 19,251 cases of domestic violence against women in the first half of 2005.[98] The number of women killed for conflict-related reasons outside of combat increased by 20 percent between 2000 and 2002.[99]	U.S. Department of State, Country Reports on Human Rights Practices, 2005 2003 UNDP Human Development Report on Colombia, El Conflicto, Callejón con Salida/ Solutions to Escape the Conflict's Impasse

Country	Statistics	Source
Croatia	In 2004 there were 908 reports to the prosecutors' office of the offense of violent behavior in the family; 627 criminal charges were brought to court; 377 were convicted.[100] One in three women reported being a victim of physical aggression by a marital or extramarital partner.[101]	Autonomous Women's House Report, 2003
Egypt	An estimated 67 percent of women in urban areas in Egypt and 30 percent in rural areas had been involved in some form of domestic violence at least once between 2002 and 2003.[102] Of women above age 14, 47.4 percent had experienced domestic violence.[103]	2003 survey by the Center for Egyptian Women's Legal Affairs The 2005 Egypt Demographic and Health Survey
Ethiopia	Nearly half (49 percent) of ever-partnered women in Ethiopia experienced physical violence by a partner at some point in their lives, and 29 percent during the 12 months before the study.[104] Fifty-nine percent of ever-partnered women experienced sexual violence at some point, and 44 percent during the previous 12 months.[105]	"WHO Multi-country Study on Women's Health and Domestic Violence against Women," 2005
Finland	The number of calls to police concerned with domestic violence was estimated at 10,000 to 12,000 annually.[106] Violence or threats by their ex-partner were experienced by 50 percent of all Finnish women who had lived in a relationship that had been terminated.[107]	Teuvo Peltoniemi, chief information officer of the A-Clinic Foundation
Germany	In Germany one in five women suffered physical or sexual violence at the hands of her partner.[108] Every fourth woman in Germany had been sexually or physically assaulted by her partner.[109]	DW-World.DE, 2005 German Family Minister Renate Schmidt

Country	Statistics	Source
India	Women reported tortured in 1994: 25,946.[110] Women who committed suicide based on a dowry dispute in 1994: 1,613.[111]	Women in India: A statistical profile, 1997 University researchers, Ramasubban and Singh, 1997
Iran	For the vast majority of Iranian women, married life was linked to pain and humiliation; 81 out of 100 married women had experienced domestic violence in their first year of marriage.[112] According to the Islamic regime, a woman's main purpose in life is to marry and have children. Single or divorced women have neither prestige nor social status and suffer discrimination in many areas.[113]	Women's Forum Against Fundamentalism in Iran, 2004 United Nations High Commission Report, 2002
Ireland	Of women who had been involved in a sexual relationship with a man, two out of five experienced violence; 46 percent reported being injured.[114] In 2006, 3,132 barring orders were applied for, and 1,357 were granted.[115]	University Researchers: Bradley et al., 2002 Courts Services Annual Report, 2006
Israel	Between 1992 and 2001, the total number of women murdered was 197.[116] An estimated 200,000 women suffered from violence each year, and 600,000 children witnessed violence at home.[117]	"L.O. Combat Violence Against Women," 1992 Yad Sarah Family Center: "Undoing Domestic Violence," 2007
Japan	Of ever-partnered women, 13 percent reported having experienced physical violence at some time in their life at the hands of an intimate partner.[118]	"WHO Multi-country Study on Women's Health and Domestic Violence against Women," 2005
Kenya	In a study reported by UNICEF, 42 percent of 612 women surveyed in one district reported having been beaten by a partner.[119]	"Domestic Violence Against Women and Girls," 2000
Malaysia	According to the police commission in Malaysia, there were 3,101 cases of domestic violence reported in 2004, up from 2,555 cases in 2003.[120]	U.S. Department of State, Country Reports on Human Rights Practices, 2005

Country	Statistics	Source
Mexico	Domestic abuse occurs in one of every three homes in Mexico.[121]	U.S. Department of State, Country Report, 2001
	Four in 10 women reported acts of spousal violence committed against them, and three of those commenced legal proceedings.[122]	Canadian Immigration and Refugee Board Issue Paper, March 2003 UNICEF México, 2001
Netherlands	Of all women aged between 20 and 60, 21 percent reported an act of physical abuse and 11 percent an act of severe physical assault.[123]	WHO, 2002 Ministry of Social Affairs and Employment, 2007
	More than 40 percent of women had experienced domestic violence at some point in their lives. Of these, 10 percent reported some form of physical, sexual or mental abuse on at least a weekly basis.[124]	U.S. Department of State, Country Report, 2006
New Zealand	Of ever-partnered women, 33 to 39 percent had experienced at least one act of physical or sexual assault from a partner during their lifetime; severe physical violence was experienced by 19 to 23 percent of women.[125]	New Zealand Family Violence Clearinghouse, 2005
	Between November 20, 2005, and January 3, 2006, six women were killed by their partners or ex-partners, and 19 children were left motherless.[126]	UNICEF New Zealand, July 2006
Nicaragua	A study on women conducted by two Nicaraguan nongovernmental organizations in conjunction with a Swedish university found that conjugal or domestic violence constituted 75 percent of cases of violence against women in Nicaragua.[127]	University researchers, Ellsberg and Peña, 1996
	Of women in Nicaragua, 30.2 percent had been beaten by a spouse or intimate partner, with 13.2 percent reporting being beaten in previous 12 months.[128]	"Profiling Domestic Violence: A Multi-Country Study," 2004

Country	Statistics	Source
Nigeria	One in every three women had been beaten, coerced into sex or abused in some other way—most often by someone she knew, including her husband or another male family member.[129]	"Domestic Violence Against Women—a Story of Community Prevention Strategies from Two States in Nigeria: Enugu and Ondo," 2005
	An estimated two-thirds of the women in certain communities in Lagos State experienced physical, sexual or psycho-logical violence in their family, with husbands, partners and fathers responsible for most of the violence.[130]	U.S. Department of State, Country Report, 2006
Norway	One out of six Norwegian women was a victim of men's violence at one time in her life.[131]	Amnesty International, 2004
	In a 2004 survey, almost half of all incidents of violence toward women, and less than 20 percent of incidents of violence toward men, were domestic violence or took place in residential areas.[132]	Statistics Norway, 2004
Paraguay	Of women, 19 percent had been assaulted by an intimate partner.[133]	United Nations, 2004
Peru	Of ever-partnered women, 49 percent in Lima and 61 percent in Cusco reported physical violence by a partner at some time in their life.[134]	"WHO Multi-country Study on Women's Health and Domestic Violence against Women," 2005
	The rates of sexual violence by a partner were 23 percent in Lima and 47 percent in Cusco.[135]	
Philippines	Physical abuse, which included wife battering, registered at 48 percent of all gender-based crimes against women in 2000.[136]	2000 PNP Surveys
	There were 1,575 reported cases of rape representing 16 percent of all gender-based crimes.[137]	

Country	Statistics	Source
Russia	Every day 36,000 women in the Russian Federation were beaten by their husbands or partners.[138] Every 40 minutes, a woman was killed by domestic violence. Official figures state that domestic violence is part of the life of every fourth Russian family.[139]	Amnesty International, 2008
Rwanda	In Rwanda, approximately 19 percent of women experienced physical violence in the previous 12 months.[140]	Rwanda: Demographic and Health Survey 2005, 2006
Samoa	The law prohibited abuse of women, but social customs tolerated their physical abuse within the home, and such abuse was common.[141] Many cases of rape went unreported because tradition and custom discourage such reporting; spousal rape was not illegal.[142]	U.S. Department of State, Country Report, 2006
South Africa	One study surveying 1,306 women in three South African provinces found that 27 percent of women in the Eastern Cape, 28 percent of women in Mpumalanga and 19 percent of women in the Northern Province had been physically abused in their lifetimes by a current or ex-partner.[143]	University researchers, Jewkes et al., 1999
	In 1999, 8.8 per 100,000 of the female population aged 14 years and older in South Africa died at the hands of their partners. This is the highest rate ever reported in research anywhere in the world.[144]	University researchers, Mathews et al., 2004
Spain	The number of women killed by their partner or former partner reached 71 in 2007.[145]	Amnesty International, 2008
	People sentenced for domestic abuse in Spain between 2005 and 2007: 49,968.[146]	Spain News: National, 2007

Country	Statistics	Source
Switzerland	In a study of nearly 1,200 ninth-grade students in Geneva, 20 percent of girls revealed they had experienced at least one incident of physical sexual abuse.[147]	United Nations Development Fund for Women, 2007
	In a study in 2005, 40 percent of women in Switzerland said that they had experienced physical or sexual violence at the hands of a partner, ex-partner, acquaintance, family member or stranger in their adult life.[148]	Swiss Federal Office for Gender Equality, 2005
Tanzania	Of ever-partnered women, 41 percent in Dar es Salaam and 56 percent in Mbeya had experienced physical or sexual violence at the hands of a partner.[149]	"WHO Multi-country Study on Women's Health and Domestic Violence against Women," 2005
Thailand	One-third of women who had serious injuries requiring hospital care following abuse never sought medical treatment.[150]	Voices of Thai Women, Foundation for Women, 2003
	Twenty-three percent of women in Bangkok and 34 percent in Nakhon Sawan reported physical violence by their intimate partner at one time in their life.[151]	
Turkey	A survey of middle- and upper-income families in 1996 found that, when initially questioned, 23 percent of women said their husbands were violent toward them but this figure rose to 71 percent when they were asked questions about specific types of violence.[152]	"Violence against Women in Turkey," 2003
	Many women reported that their husbands beat them on their wedding night.[153]	

Country	Statistics	Source
Uganda	One in three women living in surveyed rural areas experienced verbal or physical threats from their partners, and 55 percent sustained physical injuries as a result of domestic abuse.[154]	U.S. Department of State Country Reports, 2006
	According to Amnesty International, in northern Uganda, girls were being abducted and forced into marriage. Men were "given" women and girls as rewards for "good behavior," for example, following orders to kill prisoners of war and capture villagers.[155]	"Stop Violence Against Women, Rape as a Tool of War: A Fact Sheet," 2005
United Kingdom	One in four women will be a victim of domestic violence in their lifetime.[156]	Council of Europe, 2002
	On average, two women per week were killed by a partner or former partner and between 6 to 10 percent of women suffered domestic violence in a given year.[157]	University researchers, Stanko et al., 1998
	The British Crime Survey estimated that approximately 754,000 women had been raped on at least one occasion since age 16.[158]	
	British Crime Survey found that there were an estimated 12.9 million incidents of domestic violence acts against women and 2.5 million against men in England and Wales in the preceding year.[159]	University researchers, Walby & Allen, 2004
	Researchers report that every minute police received a call from the public for assistance for domestic violence—an estimated 1,300 calls each day, or over 570,000 each year.[160]	University researchers, Stanko, 2000
	According to the British Crime Survey, 40.2 percent of actual domestic violence crime was reported to the police.[161]	University researchers, Dodd et al., July 2004

Country	Statistics	Source
United States	The Centers for Disease Control and Prevention report that nearly 5.3 million incidents of interpersonal violence occur each year among U.S. women aged 18 and older, resulting in nearly 2 million injuries and 1,300 deaths nationwide each year.[162]	World Health Organization
	Battering injuries are reportedly the cause of more women requiring treatment in emergency rooms than muggings, rapes and traffic accidents combined, and are the leading cause of injury to women between 15-44 years of age.[163]	United States Senate Judiciary Committee
West Bank/ Gaza	Fifty-two percent of women reported being physically assaulted by a partner during a 12-month period.[164]	Researching Violence Against Women: A Practical Guide for Researchers and Activists, 2005
	A Palestinian Central Bureau of Statistics survey found that 23.3 percent of married women in the West Bank and Gaza had been victims of domestic violence in 2005.[165]	Violence against Palestinian Women and Girls, 2006

Studies may differ in their funding base, their research design, the exact wording of the questions or how the research instruments are administered, but the overwhelming evidence of physical abuse of women worldwide cannot be ignored. Though the names of the researchers differ, as do their countries of origin and their training, the data gathered from the lives of ordinary women present consistent findings that women from every nation suffer physical violence at the hands of men with whom they have exchanged marriage vows or shared intimacy and residence.

RAPE AND SEXUAL ASSAULT

While large-scale studies investigating rape and sexual assault are rare, those that do exist reveal the high proportion of women and girls who have experienced a rape or attempted rape at some point during their lifetime.[166] Within both developed and developing nations around the globe, rape and other forms of sexual assault are an ever-present fear for scores of females of all ages.

Although sexual assault may be committed by a stranger, in the vast majority of cases the victim and the aggressor know one another.[167] A sense of betrayal, then, is a central feature of the violence. When the sexual violence is perpetrated by a father, uncle, brother, grandfather or another adult male relative, the victim must sort out myriad feelings, ambiguities and contradictions. She may feel both love and hate. She may be dependent economically on the abuser or fear reprisal should her tale of abuse be voiced. Other times the violator is not a family member but a trusted adult—a coach, teacher or religious leader. Here too betrayal occurs: the sense of trust has been broken, and the victim's vulnerability is marked.[168]

Moreover, thousands of women worldwide are coerced or abducted into forced prostitution or sold through other forms of human trafficking.[169] Domestic workers and migrant women are especially vulnerable to rape and violent attack by their employers, who may withhold not only their wages but access to important personal documents, such as passports.

The desire to keep rape or sexual assault a secret is especially powerful in cultural contexts where a woman's virginity is a sign of personal and family honor, not to mention a prerequisite for marriage. Since shame is attached to rape, the victim may wish to protect both her future and the honor of her family by keeping a rape secret.[170]

To deal with the multitude of pressing problems that surface after sexual attack, organizations within many countries have set up rape crisis hotlines and rape crisis centers. In some jurisdictions, there are special rape crisis emergency rooms at local hospitals or uniquely trained teams of women officers and health-care workers who deal with victims of such trauma.

Violence against women and children is also a by-product of armed conflict and can include random acts of aggression—including sexual violation—by both enemy and "friendly" forces; sometimes mass rape is even a strategy of war.[171] Where there is displacement of large numbers of women and children as refugees, suffering can take the form of the demand of sex for survival—a woman may be forced to exchange sexual favors for food or shelter or the protection of her children. Gang rape (more than one perpetrator per woman or girl child) and forced pregnancy are also common situations involving armed conflict and military personnel. Sometimes women are seen as "territory" to be conquered or plundered; the violation of women and girl children is meant to exacerbate men's humiliation and pain.

There are many forms of exploitation directed toward women and girl children, including female genital mutilation (FGM)[172] and son preference.[173] Victims of FGM are estimated at between 100 million to 140 million girls and women around the globe, with a further 2 million at risk of this practice.[174] In several areas of the world, boy children are more highly valued than girls. In extreme cases, this may lead to violence against girl children or female infanticide; less extreme cases include less access to food, health care or education for girl children.

WOMAN ABUSE IN THE CHURCH

Statistics are an important component in the story of abuse worldwide. But narrative accounts of the lives of ordinary women give context to those statistics, enabling researcher and reader alike to visualize real women living in a specific time and a specific place amid very real problems. We present accounts of the lives of four women, all evangelical Christians, all victims of violence. Their stories reveal parts of a complex web of faith, family, fear and violence. As in all the stories told in this book, names and identifying information have been changed to protect the identity of the women; the details of their abuse, however, have not been altered.

Janice and her family moved to Sydney, Australia, from western Europe when she was a child. Her missionary parents settled into a nomadic existence, working among Aboriginal peoples. In time she met a newly converted Aboriginal man, and some years later they were married. With a thriving ministry, life was very exciting for them.

An unplanned pregnancy began to exacerbate some of Janice's husband's problems with anger. Whenever he got angry, he hit her. Janice knew there was a cultural component to her abuse, for often she had bathed wounds of aboriginal women who had been battered by their husbands.

Before long, a six-week cycle developed: calm, growing discontent, violent outbursts, an apology—and the cycle began again. Life was growing very difficult for Janice; she suffered a cracked skull from beatings to the head and broken ribs from blows to the chest.

Authorities within the hierarchy of the couple's denomination were called to give counsel. There was much prayer but no firm reprimand for the husband's violent ways. On one occasion, Janice gathered her six children and fled her home, fearing he was going to kill her. Eventually he was temporarily removed from church leadership when his threat to murder her was voiced in front of influential church leaders.

While her husband is no longer in pastoral leadership and the frequency and severity of the violence have begun to decline, Janice has never received the supportive services she needed from either local police or community organizations, and the church family has let her down. The violence she suffered has never been condemned, nor has healing been offered to her broken body and spirit.[175]

Macy had a heart for God and had worked in a Christian mission organization most of her adult life. Trained as a nurse and later as an administrator, she felt moved by suffering around the world and responded by offering her time and her talents. For years Macy struggled with depression and low self-esteem. Finally she decided she needed to find a more caring church family, to help address some of her malaise and offer her more opportunities to use her gifts.

Macy was drawn to a small fellowship with a set of programs for seniors in low-cost housing. She quickly established herself as a hard worker and a committed follower of Christ. Before long, the pastor and his wife, both in their fifties, took a special interest in her life. But the pastor's interest developed in ways both unanticipated and unwelcomed. He engaged in sexual indiscretions with her, then weeks later raped her, taking advantage of her loneliness and the emotional vulnerability she had expressed to him during counseling sessions. Because he was highly respected in the community, no one was willing to believe Macy's story of sexual abuse, and no one offered to help her seek healing and wholeness in its aftermath.[176]

The stories of Janice and Macy exemplify violence against Christian women around the globe. No multinational studies have collected statistics *specifically* on the prevalence of woman abuse among evangelical believers. But as we shall see, there is growing evidence that violence is all too common in the lives of women believers within ordinary evangelical and mainstream churches.

What we do know is that violence against Christian women has an impact on the spiritual journeys of individual women and their families,[177] and often on the life of the congregations to which they belong. While abuse may be committed behind closed doors, its shock waves extend well beyond the family context. Like their secular sisters who have been battered, religious victims of abuse bear the scars of physical and emotional pain. Janice's physical and emotional abuse and Macy's sexual abuse have brought long-term consequences for both women, their ministries and their families. But their pain has spiritual overtones as well. Each woman has been silenced by elders in her faith tradition. Each woman has learned that her spiritual leaders care more about the reputation of the abuser than the scars of the abused. When each woman gathered the courage to tell her story of betrayal, she was dismissed by those who might have helped to chart her healing journey.

In *Domestic Violence: What Every Pastor Needs to Know,* the Reverend Al Miles says that two themes emerged from his nonrandom survey of over one hundred pastors: the importance they attach to saving marriages at all costs and the pastoral temptation toward quick-fix solutions for abusive men and abused women.[178]

In a small study of 187 American women who qualified as being abuse-free for at least one year, Anne Horton, Melany Wilkins and Wendy Wright found that 54 percent of religious victims and 38 percent of nonreligious victims sought help from a religious professional in the aftermath of violence in the home.[179]

During the fall of 1989, the Christian Reformed Church in North America conducted a survey among a random sample of one thousand adult members attending their churches. Of the 643 respondents, 28 percent had experienced at least one form of abuse. A total of 12 percent reported physical abuse, 13 percent sexual abuse and 19 percent emotional abuse; as these percentages reveal, many had experienced more than one form of abuse. Converting these prevalence rates to the actual number of people victimized, the Christian Reformed Church estimated that between 48,000 and 62,000 adult members had experienced physical, sexual or emotional abuse.

A research initiative involving evangelical clergy in the Atlantic Provinces of Canada[180] revealed that pastors perceived violence rates among married couples in their current congregation to be 19 percent, just under one in five.[181] These same pastors estimate the rate of violence in the secular culture to be about 29 percent, a full ten percentage points higher than in their congregations. This is despite the fact that researchers in the field of family violence have consistently argued that abuse crosses all religious boundaries and that the rates inside and outside the walls of the church are similar.

Violence among families of faith reflects the cultures they inhabit,[182] but interweaving the narrative is their faith and religious identity. The role of religion in helping women find their voice is both curious and critical.[183] Macy and Janice had the courage to speak the words that named their experience, though their cries for help fell on deaf ears. Some women do not live long enough to disclose their abuse, and others are prevented by a lack of social, economic or religious power.

Susan Pickles never had the chance to tell her story. Death robbed her of life and voice. An American paper told the details of her death to the world: Scott Pickles, a former lawyer in his early forties, took the lives of his wife and two children in New London, Connecticut. According to the *Norwich Bulletin* of October 28, 1999, the guilty man, a born-again believer, apologized in court to the victim's family, his family and his clients. But his remorse could not bring three dead bodies back to life. Apparently Pickles had been experiencing severe debt, limited professional success and fear that his wife would leave him. In a final act of control, he had determined their fate.

Before Pickles was handcuffed and taken away, the father of the slain woman asked the judge to deliver a message to the man who killed his daughter and grandchildren: "Tell him I don't hate him. . . . I do forgive him." With his voice cracking, the elderly man gazed heavenward and said that he would look forward to joining his slain family members—all of whom were evangelical Christians—someday in heaven.

For many American Christians, it is inconceivable that an evangelical man in their country would be found guilty of murdering his wife and children. For many non-evangelicals, it is inconceivable that the father of a slain woman and grandfather of two slain grandchildren would want to give a message of forgiveness to the murderer. Most people around the globe would find it hard to understand why someone with so many resources and opportunities at his fingertips would feel so hopeless. It is a multilayered story, to be sure—the desperation, the control, the faith and the consequences. As we shall see in later chapters, the issue of forgiveness is central to understanding the complexity of the relationship among religion, abuse and the healing journey.

According to Anne Horton and Judith Williamson in *Abuse and Religion: When Praying Isn't Enough,* more abuse victims, perpetrators and family members seek help from ordained ministers and other religious leaders than from all other helping professionals combined.[184] Rotunda, Williamson and Penfold (2004) reported that 43 percent of victims sought help from their clergy, as did 20 percent of male perpetrators, and the majority of each of these groups indicated satisfaction with the help they received. Clergy responses to domestic violence were also examined by Ware, Levitt and Bayer (2003), who report that the multifaith leaders in their research reported limited experience assisting victims.

In 1988 Lee Bowker reported the results of two studies of religious abuse victims and the help they reported receiving from ordained ministers. One-third of the women who responded to his survey in *Woman's Day* magazine reported that they had been the recipient of some form of pastoral counsel. In terms of effectiveness, the women rated the assistance from clergy as less helpful than that from other sources of support.[185] A research team interviewed 178 clergy in New York and Connecticut and found that less than half of their respondents had training in pastoral care, were not confident in their ability to respond to those impacted by domestic violence and rarely consulted with other professionals about this type of problem.[186]

For almost twenty-five years, Nancy and her team of graduate students and research colleagues have been attempting to understand what happens when a woman, man or couple looks to their congregation or its leadership for help in the aftermath of domestic violence. Listed below are a few key findings that emerged from these studies.

- Based on a pilot project exploring tensions, contradictions and collaborations between religious leaders and community-based shelter staff in twelve different sites, there are several obstacles to sacred and secular workers partnering to assist religious women who have been abused.[187]

- In a study of 343 conservative Protestant pastors in Canada, it was revealed that the majority were called on several times a year to respond to a woman who was being abused by her current husband/partner; a man who had acted abusively toward his wife/partner; or an adult who was coping with issues of abuse from the past.[188]

- Through personal interviews with 100 conservative Protestant clergy ministering in churches of varying sizes, they learned that the average pastor spent 16 percent of his or her professional time providing relationship or marital counseling (two afternoons a week); 85 percent reported that the demand for pastor counseling had increased and that it was one of their greatest stresses.[189]

- Focus groups held in 28 churches (involving 247 women) representing rural, urban and small-town contexts revealed that one of the best-kept secrets of church life is the amazing support network women offer each other under the umbrella of their congregation or faith network.[190]

- Religious women suffering abuse who look to their pastors for help are often disappointed to find that there is limited awareness and understanding of domestic violence by their leaders, modest knowledge of the resources available and a lack of ability (or discomfort) in providing help that is explicitly spiritual in nature (for example, prayer, Bible readings).[191]

- Based on survey and interview data with almost one thousand clergy from a variety of Protestant traditions, it was identified that some clergy are reluctant to refer abused women and other family members who seek their assistance to professionals in the community or community-based agencies. Where referrals are needed most (among those religious leaders who have little or no training in issues of domestic violence), they are least likely to occur.[192]

- Interviews and focus groups with large numbers of men who have acted abusively, women who have been abused and those friends and clergy who have walked alongside them reveal that when clergy preach a message condemning family violence, discuss abuse in their premarital counseling, offer support, give referral suggestions, provide ongoing encouragement and hold those who act abusively accountable for their actions, the impact is profound.[193]

Vimla's story was told only to a researcher; otherwise it was sheltered from public knowledge by secrecy, shame and silence. Vimla is the wife of an evangelist, a man who travels throughout southeastern Asia spreading the gospel. They met at a church youth gathering when they were in their teens. According to Vimla, they married out of love, feeling an initial attraction to each other and the sense that God would bless their home. During the early years of their marriage, Vimla reported, her husband was very kind, and during this time she bore him two sons and one daughter.

His ministry began to flourish, but his treatment of his own family began to deteriorate. For several years Vimla had been the victim of repeated beatings. "He is very kind and good to people outside the home, but not to us," she confided. "Somehow he does not beat me up in the presence of our children, which I appreciate." She felt frightened and very alone.[194]

While there are many features in common between Vimla's life and the lives of battered religious women in other contexts, there is a cultural reality that we need to consider. Recently four hundred evangelical women participated in data gathering in India and other parts of Asia concerning woman abuse. Three of every four women reported some form of physical abuse by their husbands. Women whose marriages were arranged by parents were less likely to report physical violence. One reason for this seems to be the higher level of involvement by the extended family when a marriage is arranged.[195]

In an informal discussion session held in India among religious leaders from many faith communities and a variety of nations, it was disclosed that one reason Asian men beat their wives is that men do not like women to be assertive or articulate or to answer back to their husbands or other elders in the family.[196] While the cultural contexts vary, the devastating consequences bear a marked similarity: the body is harmed, emotions are damaged, the relationship dies and the spirit is crushed.

A few years ago, Nancy conducted fieldwork in Jamaica and Croatia to examine more fully the relationship between religion and domestic violence in other cultural contexts. Through focus groups, individual interviews and surveys, she had formal contact with more than one hundred survivors, clergy and other professionals, supplemented by informal contact through workshops with several hundred more. In Jamaica there is a high degree of awareness among pastors and other religious leaders of the prevalence and severity of abuse that occurs within the family context. Yet pastors in the Caribbean are more sympathetic to the plight of children than of women and are reluctant to hold men accountable as the primary aggressors in intimate partner violence. In Croatia, on the other hand, there is a low degree of awareness among pastors and other religious leaders concerning abuse. Operating here is a pervasive view that violence permeates all sectors of society and therefore abuse within the family is predominately a reflection of the region's historic conflicts.

As we consider statistics from countries around the globe, let us remember that the lives of Janice, Macy, Susan and Vimla represent other evangelical women, some with voice, some without voice, bearing the marks of violence and suffering its consequences.

THE DYNAMICS OF ABUSE

Let us address some of the frequently asked questions related to violence against women and other forms of family violence. For those who have not experienced abuse themselves or witnessed it in their family of origin, it is often very hard to understand why abuse occurs, why victims do not leave abusive homes and why the cycle of violence is so often repeated in the next generation. While our treatment of these issues cannot possibly be exhaustive, we believe it is very important for Christians to become as informed as possible on abuse, its manifestations and its consequences.

Why do so many men abuse their wives? Three main sources of data help researchers learn about abusive men: in-depth interviews with abused women who report on the behavior and personal characteristics of the men who battered them; regional or national surveys (like those reported in table 1), in which men self-identify their abusive behavior; and statements from those who are participating in programs for men who abuse their wives or girlfriends.

In their book *Behind Closed Doors,* Murray Straus, Richard Gelles and Susan Steinmetz argue that the greater the gap between the eco-

nomic and prestige resources of a husband and a wife, the greater the
man's tendency to maintain his dominant position in the marriage
and the family by resorting to force.[197] As a result, abuse may be more
likely to occur during a man's problems with work or a period of un-
employment.[198] Abusive husbands are more likely to perceive their
wife's behavior as threatening their sense of self, so men who have
low self-esteem to begin with have a greater tendency to use force
when they perceive their power challenged.[199]

Other researchers claim that higher levels of general aggression in
abusive men interact with certain features of their families of origin,
like violence, poor communication skills and a lack of self-confidence.[200]
Estimates suggest that between 50 and 75 percent of the men who
batter their wives experienced or witnessed abuse in their own childhood home.[201] One family research laboratory has argued that young
boys who have watched their father beat their mother have a
1,000-percent greater likelihood of violence in adulthood than boys
who never undergo this painful childhood experience.[202] There is
compelling evidence that violence is learned behavior, and most
often it is learned in the home.[203]

In a small-scale study conducted in the Boston area, James Ptacek
explored how abusive men themselves understand and account for
their violence.[204] Participants in a program for men who batter ratio-
nalized their violence through both excuses ("It was the booze") and
justifications ("She bruises easily").[205] According to Ptacek's research,
abusive men resort to violence to silence their partner or to punish
her for failing to be the "perfect" wife.[206]

Our research team was involved in the first-ever attempt to document empirically the characteristics of men who sought assistance
from a faith-based batterers' intervention program.[207] In the north-
west United States, we analyzed over one thousand closed case files
and found that, compared to men in secular programs, those we studied had a higher proportion of men who had witnessed or experienced abuse in their childhood homes, while rates of alcohol abuse
among the men and their criminal histories were similar to those in

secular programs. Men in the faith-based program we studied whose attendance had been mandated by a pastor to attend had higher rates of program completion than those whose attendance had been mandated by a judge.

While there is evidence that some couples initiate violent acts equally,[208] in the majority of cases it is the man, not the woman, who controls whether there will be abuse in the home.[209] According to Larry Bennett, a professor of social work, many violent men claim that their wives can be violent at times too, but none of the violent men he counseled had ever reported that they "were afraid to go home at night."[210]

The role of alcohol is often overestimated in explanations of why men batter. While many abusive husbands blame their battery on excessive drinking, actually the husbands who batter when drinking also batter when sober.[211] In fact, contrary to conventional wisdom, in more than 50 percent of abuse cases, there is no consumption of alcoholic beverages at all,[212] and there is no evidence to suggest that alcohol dependence is linked to coercive behaviors that are part of the pattern of domestic violence.[213]

Why do women remain with partners who abuse them? Whether we are teaching in the university classroom, delivering a paper at a scholarly conference, offering a workshop for clergy or social-service providers, speaking at a women's retreat or preaching in a Bible-centered church, people always ask why women stay in abusive relationships. Sometimes the question is asked in a public setting; sometimes it is voiced in private. Those who have never experienced violence personally find it hard to understand the ties that make it difficult for women to extricate themselves from an abusive environment. On the other hand, the question on the minds of those who have direct experience is voiced like this: "How can a woman ever muster the courage to actually leave?" Thus personal experience of abuse frames one's understanding dramatically.

For any individual woman, of course, the reason it is difficult to terminate a violent relationship (temporarily or forever) is complex.

In just a few paragraphs it is impossible to cover all the reasons staying put seems more beneficial than leaving. We are not necessarily advocating that all women must or should leave an abusive marriage permanently, but we would *never* suggest that a woman *ought* to remain in a context that puts her life at risk or threatens the safety of her children. But why is leaving even on a temporary basis such a difficult decision?[214]

Fear is the number-one reason women do not leave abusive husbands and violent homes.[215] A battered wife fears for her future, fears further violence and fears for the lives of her children. In fact, fear permeates her life and is often experienced as a paralyzing terror, ruling her day and destroying her sleep through nightmares. Fear makes women lie about the reality of the abuse ("I bruised my face when I fell down the basement stairs"). And fear hampers women's ability to see the choices they might make to enhance their personal safety. So they spend what energy they have left trying to keep the secret rather than trying to escape.

Finances—economic dependency—keep many women from perceiving that there are options besides life with their violent husband. Many abusive men are good providers of the food, housing and clothing their wife and children need. A woman's lack of personal or economic resources, coupled with the fact that she might never have been employed in the labor market, means she cannot see any alternatives. How would she provide for her children without money or a job? How could she obtain employment if her skills have been used primarily at home since the children were born? Where could she flee and who would offer her refuge? Thus some battered women believe that the violence they experience is their "payment" for food, housing and their children's schooling. Added to this, many abused women feel so poorly about themselves that they actually consider that they deserve their husband's battering. Family violence researchers have argued that a woman's level of economic dependence on her husband is a major factor in whether she will remain in an abusive environment, or return to a violent husband after a temporary respite.[216]

The fantasy of change, or the hope that someday the violence will cease, keeps many women with violent husbands for years or for a lifetime.[217] After abuse, there may be remorse. After the violence, there may be pleas for forgiveness. After the pain, there may be promises of change. Although the evidence suggests that few batterers do alter their abusive ways,[218] many women cling to that hope, that fantasy, year after year. Religious women are especially likely to cling to the belief that their violent husband wants to and will change his behavior.[219]

As Nancy has argued in *The Battered Wife: How Christians Confront Family Violence,* religious batterers often manipulate pastors and other Christian people by employing religious words, including Scripture, to ensure that there is reunion between their wives and themselves, the violated and the violent.[220] The minister with little counseling experience or training in responding to abuse may find it difficult to distinguish between the inauthentic plea of a manipulative man and the genuine repentance of a husband sorry for the violence of his past and committed to altering his ways.

In essence, women remain with the men who abuse them because they are fearful, because they lack the economic or social resources to leave and because they cling tightly to the hope that someday he will change. In addition, some religious women feel that God does not permit them to leave, that marriage is forever, no matter how cruel their husband's treatment, that this is their cross to bear or that perpetual forgiveness of their husband for his repeated behavior is God's expectation. For women such as these, it is often very difficult to sort out the difference between long-suffering in honor to Christ and to their marriage vows and actively contributing to putting their own lives in danger.[221] The wise pastor will help such a woman navigate these troubled waters.

2

Beginning to Respond

Mildred[1] and Russell Jennings lived one life on the outside and another at home. They had five grown children, all of whom had been very successful in their chosen careers. While this older couple was sliding further and further into debt, to outsiders it appeared they had everything they needed and wanted. The truth was that Russell hungered after power and status, and satisfied his longings with purchases, like new cars and other flashy gadgets. He gave little thought to Mildred or her needs.

Mildred, whose mother lived with them, was shy and retiring by nature. She was very involved in her church and at home overly concerned to please her husband. Russell was a controlling man, and Mildred's response to his control was to try harder and harder to please him. In fact, she felt caught between the very real needs of her aged mother and her husband's unrealistic demands. He tried to control every detail of her life, including where she went and with whom. When she resisted his control, he would adopt one of two strategies: start yelling and belittle her, or turn silent. On one occasion he flew into a rage and tried to kill her.

But Mildred was very forgiving of Russell, trying to live a life where she exemplified the scriptural imperative to forgive seventy times seven. Not surprisingly, Mildred suffered from low self-esteem. This was compounded by a childhood experience of watching her father treat her mother poorly—a pattern that had occurred between her maternal grandparents as well.

Mildred sought pastoral assistance when Russell kicked her out of their house, together with her eighty-three-year-old mother. In fact, these two older women were given two hours to leave the family home forever. In desperation she contacted her pastor because she had nowhere else to go. The pastor found temporary shelter for the women with another family from the church who owned a large farmhouse.

In the aftermath of the crisis, Mildred had so many unanswered questions: Where was God at her point of need? Would she ever be forgiven for leaving her husband? Should she forgive him one last time? Through counseling, the pastor recognized Mildred's spiritual needs and her misguided religious convictions related to forgiveness and suffering. He helped her to see that God was not asking her to ignore the pain and the abuse of the past, but rather to hold Russell accountable for his actions. Then the pastor helped legal counsel understand why Mildred was so forgiving of the abusive acts of her husband. In Mildred's case, the pastor acted as a mediator between her spiritual questions and her practical problems. Her erroneous religious thinking he tried to challenge, and he offered a needed spiritual supplement to what others in the community offered her in terms of safety and respite.

For more than two years, the pastor had regular contact with Mildred—sometimes by phone, sometimes in person. Her spiritual journey toward healing and wholeness was augmented by a religious leader who was willing to listen, offer practical advice and hear her cry for spiritual help.

As was the case in many of the hundreds of stories of abuse we have heard over the past twenty years, told by survivors and those who have walked alongside them, Mildred's spiritual needs were primary on her road to personal well-being. Like a shattered window, she felt her life as she knew it had been blown apart. Yet the pastor and other community-based professionals, such as her lawyer, helped Mildred to pick up the pieces of her broken life and reclaim strength and safety.

Mildred placed the intact family in high regard. Like so many highly committed religious women, she was reluctant to leave her husband and to seek alternative solutions for her personal safety and emotional health. For she had promised to love and honor her husband until death. In a fashion similar to other abused religious women, she felt it was her responsibility to keep on forgiving, to keep on trying to salvage the marriage and never to give up hope that her husband might change.

Through our research we have found that most religious women who are abused do not consider themselves to be battered wives. In fact, Julie Owens, a nationally recognized domestic violence trainer and herself a survivor, tells of how, after her husband had been charged with murder and sent to prison, she heard about a program for battered wives in the state of Hawaii and called to see if she might come. She told the advocate on the telephone, "I am not a battered wife, but my husband tried to kill me."[2]

The resources that religious women seek in the aftermath of domestic violence in part differentiate them from other abused women. They are often very reluctant to seek secular, community-based sources of support, preferring to look to others of like-minded faith for assistance—clergy and lay alike. Since many faith communities place the intact family on a pedestal, religious women are especially prone to blame themselves for the abuse, believe they have promised God to stay married until death and experience both the fear and the reality of rejection at church when attempts to repair the relationship fail.

After reading the story of Mildred and Russell, and reflecting on the statistics and data from the last chapter, you might be asking yourself some questions: What can one person do? Might I be able to reach out to someone in my community or church? Or the question might be framed in a broader context: What can one congregation do? Could I raise this issue at a board meeting or discuss it with my pastor or alert my Bible-study group to the prevalence of violence in the home? Could my congregation catch a vision of supporting victims of violence and condemning abusive acts in our community? Or the questions could be framed from a global perspective: What would happen if evangelical churches around the world joined in condemning violence and supporting its victims?

The United Nations Secretary General's Campaign to End Violence Against Women notes that women who have suffered as victims of interpersonal violence experience a range of health problems, diminishing their participation in public life.[3] World Health Assembly Resolution 49.25 proclaims violence to be a public health issue. It calls for concerted action by health-care workers around the globe and commits the World Health Organization to the publication of guidelines and standards to address this urgent issue.

The American Academy of Family Physicians[4] and the American Association of Colleges of Nursing[5] have gone on record stating that violence is a major public health concern. In 2003, in an address titled "Family Violence as a Public Health Issue," the U.S. Surgeon General stated, "I am part of the President's team dealing with family violence as a serious public health issue threatening women and children, and sometimes men, of every age and from every racial and socio-economic background in America."[6] Domestic violence is indeed a public health issue. It is also an issue with spiritual dimensions.

We think that alliances of churches around the globe need to consider violence against women a *religious* issue, an issue demanding thoughtful and immediate response from denominations and ministry organizations right down to the grass-roots level—the local congregation. Many denominations have prepared a position statement on domestic violence or created policy documents to which pastors or administrative staff can refer. These are a wonderful and welcome beginning to the dialogue. But more needs to be done—and quickly.

HEARING THE VOICES

While a global perspective is important—indeed imperative—for giving us a vision of the need of victims and the immense problem of violence against women, individual acts of kindness and support begin on home territory. Here we present some voices—of victims, of care-givers and of clergy—that paint a picture of what congregations can accomplish when hearts are stirred by the suffering of women around the world and in their own churches.

Voices of victims.

> But when I became a Christian, I was thankful to the Lord be-cause I had a pastor who . . . knew what I'd been through, and he didn't judge me. And he was the type of pastor who was working with women who had been through . . . abusive mar-riages.[7]
>
> I spent 15 years in a violent home with my first husband and I think that at one point I wouldn't have wanted interference, but then again if I had a sense that it was there, I might have been able to get help.[8]

Voices of women helping women. Cheryl was a young woman—not yet thirty—who lived in a coastal community. She bore the scars of re-peated episodes of abuse from her common-law husband, a large-framed, ex-military man. Cheryl herself did not belong to any particu-lar community of believers, but her relationship with the local evangelical church was mediated by a faithful member, a neighbor named Sue.

Cognizant of Cheryl's fear and her husband's intimidating ways, Sue organized a team to help Cheryl move to a safe new location. One Sat-urday morning, with Cheryl's husband occupied at his job, Sue's volun-teers packed up Cheryl's belongings and transported them to a new apartment, miles away in another town. Sue's husband drove his pickup truck, and several church members helped to load furniture and other items belonging to Cheryl. As Sue shared this story, she emphasized how impossible it would have been for Cheryl to escape the abusive environment without the support of men and women of faith.[9]

Voices of clergy.

> I thank the Lord that I'm a great big two-hundred-pound guy because . . . I've had a husband who was violent against his wife haul off and hit me, and all I could think about was these glasses cost me two hundred dollars and I don't want to get them broken. . . . I see the violence against women and it makes me mad, and there's a lot of it going on.[10]

> Choosing the path of least resistance. That's probably her way of contributing to the conflict in that [violent] relationship . . . by staying.[11]

STRATEGIC THINKING

How might the evangelical church—its leaders and its people—help bridge the chasm between the pain of victims and the hope of the gospel? Appropriate response to an individual can never be determined in advance of hearing the pain she has endured and the practical help she seeks. Yet we will suggest some basic ground rules that may enable congregations and individuals to augment the healing journey of victims.

It is very important to hold offenders accountable for both their past abusive behavior and their promise of changed actions. Ultimately all believers need to promote violence-free family living by modeling appropriate and healthy reactions to disappointment and disagreement. The role of church leaders and church programs in teaching, encouraging and mentoring such behavior is vital and should never be underestimated.

Congregations and church leaders need to begin a soul-searching process related to violence against women and other forms of family violence. While change is always difficult, the gospel tells us that we do not need to be the same people we were in the past, that the old person and the old ways can be altered by God's transforming power, that with new insight, powered by God's Holy Spirit, our actions tomorrow can be more in keeping with the life and compassion of

Christ than our behavior was yesterday.

This message rings true at both the individual and the corporate level. Sometimes as individuals we need to acknowledge our mistakes and repent. Sometimes as congregations we need to acknowledge our failings and repent. Sometimes as organizations we need to admit our shortcomings and repent. To respond with the mind of Christ to the suffering of abuse victims worldwide, we will need to search our individual, congregational and organizational souls. This process will be painful, but without it, change is impossible.

There are many men and women around the globe who have never been violent toward a partner or a child. We rejoice in that fact. But often these same people have never felt compassion toward victims of violence, because they have no eyes to see their suffering or ears to hear their cries. This book aims to address that lack. We believe that once people of faith and church leaders have been confronted with the reality of the prevalence of violence, they will want to do something about it.

RHETORIC VERSUS REALITY

Martha[12] and her husband, Daniel, were key laypeople in First Presbyterian Church of Birch Grove, a picturesque bedroom community to which large numbers of men and women retreat after a long working day in the nearby industrial city. She worked in the denominational headquarters as an office manager, and he held the elected position of Sunday school superintendent in the church. Together they sang in the choir, and their home served as a comfortable location for many church executive meetings. They were any pastor's dream couple—attractive, talented, relatively affluent, hardworking people who wanted to contribute to the weekly routine of church life. But Martha and Daniel had a secret: he was an abusive husband and she was a battered wife.

The abuse started when Martha was three months pregnant with their first child. They had gone out for a social evening at a friend's home. In the car on the way home, Daniel accused Martha of talking to some of the men at the party. Caught by surprise, Martha retorted that they were longtime friends of all the couples and that during the evening she had talked to everyone who was present. When they got home, he called her a whore and hit her across the face.

Martha and Daniel lived the lie for years; eventually they had four young children and resided in a large, two-story house in an enviable neighborhood, but every time she considered leaving, Martha was reminded that her salary alone could not support food, rent for an apartment and the children's music and sports activities, let alone money for church projects. She felt trapped, alone and afraid.

Sometimes life was good, and Martha was lulled into believing that Daniel had changed. He was often repentant after an abusive episode, and in the early years of their marriage, she clung to the hope that someday he would be less abusive and that she would be a better wife. Years passed, and the children entered high school. Then an incident occurred that caused Martha to call the police, fearing that Daniel was going to kill her.

They had gone several weeks without speaking to each other, and she broke the silence one evening as she stood at the sink, he at the stove, both preparing supper. Her voice and her words about the vegetables threw him into a rage. Daniel grabbed her and started pounding her head into the kitchen cupboard, making an effort not to bruise her face so as to call forth the sympathy of others. As Martha told me her story, tears streamed down her face, but then she smiled a little. "My head made so much noise banging those cupboards that Carla, our teenage daughter, came downstairs." When Carla entered the kitchen, the banging stopped.

It was difficult for Martha to recount exactly what happened in the aftermath of this violent outburst. But the police were called, an arrest was made, and Daniel was escorted temporarily from their home. To her astonishment, the clergyman for whom she worked did not believe her story, despite the fact that Daniel was in jail for the weekend. In a nutshell, Daniel was simply too nice a man—a fine Christian man at that—to ever harm anyone, especially his wife.

Martha disclosed the story to no one else.

Her life was now surrounded by a new lie: she and Daniel had irreconcilable differences, and they were going to seek a divorce. Her denominational employer was fearful of what people might think about a divorced woman as office manager; her pastor was afraid of what congregants might think about a divorced Sunday school superintendent. No one seemed to fear for the safety of Martha and her children.

The healing process was slow, much slower than Martha had hoped. While the children were supportive, even they did not understand the full extent of Martha's pain or its long history. It was too difficult to tell them; in fact, she wanted them to harbor predominantly pleasant childhood memories, memories where the abuse was still hidden. It was important to Martha that they remember their childhood as one characterized by the words *happy Christian family.* For her, though, such a family existed only in her dreams.

EVANGELICALS AND THE FAMILY

Evangelicals feel very passionate about the family and speak warmly and enthusiastically about the importance of "family values." In many parts of the world, religious people are deeply committed to particular notions of the family and often bemoan the fact that the family is under attack by secular forces in contemporary culture. With the Scripture close at hand, evangelicals teach that God planned for men and women to choose lifelong partners and to share the joys and burdens of parenthood until death drew their work to a close. Socializing the young, teaching them spiritual truths and offering them a skill and knowledge base from which to live is at the core of what Christians claim to be doing in a family setting.

The mechanics of how this is accomplished, though, differ according to the surrounding culture and a family's social location within it. Time also has an impact, for our culture and its norms are ever-changing. Though God is not limited by time, how we humans express our love and devotion to others and what skills and knowledge we believe are essential for our children differ according to the place and age in which we live. Understandings of the family do not remain static; they are always changing as we respond to new information about our health, the economy or political realities.

Christians need to realize that, while passion for family living and family values may feel timeless, how these are communicated and carried out in any place or any given generation will differ. We must be on our guard to ensure that nostalgia for the traditional family, however that is defined, does not prevent us from ministering to the real needs of our communities. In fact, one person's nostalgia may be another person's nightmare: the white picket fence, the 2.5 kids, the dog and the family van are not universal or sacred. They are laden with cultural and class values, not necessarily godless in themselves, but not necessarily emanating from the heart of God. In other words, the image is not meaningful for everyone, nor does it produce warm fuzzies for all.

How do these nostalgic images and evangelical musings on the traditional family link to violence? The answer is straightforward. We teach and preach that the family is sacred, ordained by God, honored by Christian people. The family may be sacred, but sometimes it is not safe.[13] In our enthusiasm to support the family, we often overlook that important fact. Statistically speaking, women, men and children are more likely to be harmed or threatened or injured within their own family home than outside it. When we place the family on a very high pedestal, the result is a chasm between those whose experience of family life—in their childhood or adult life—differs dramatically from the picture we paint in our Sunday-morning sermons or teach through our Sunday-school curriculum.

We must recognize the reality of families in crisis and in pain. There are many women and children who arrive in our churches on Sunday and return home to an environment where their physical and mental health cannot be ensured. For those of us who claim the family as a central building block in our nations and our churches, it is essential to take responsibility for responding to families in crisis.

The rhetoric may draw on images of happy family living, but the real experience of many men, women and children is very different. Taken too far, the notion of "happy family living" blinds people to the plight of those who suffer in the family context. Taken too far, "happy family living" excuses some family members from living and acting as responsible, caring people. Taken too far, the family becomes a battle zone where the rules of culture do not apply.

While ensuring healthy and safe family living should appeal to all humans everywhere, it should be especially crucial for those of us who claim the label *Christian*. We preach and teach that the family is very important to God, but we often act otherwise. Does our church programming take into account that many women, men and children do not live in an intact nuclear family? Do we offer support and assistance for families in crisis? How do we teach our families to cope with disappointment and anger? Where can families connected to our faith communities turn when they need resources or counsel? What happens when an abused woman looks for help in your church?

We say we believe in the family, but sometimes our programming suggests that it is only certain kinds of families we hold dear. We say it is important for children to grow up in a loving environment, but do we offer assistance to mothers and fathers who are in turmoil? We say that family happiness is a gift from God, but can women who fear for their lives at the hands of their violent husbands find support and respite in our congregations?

What are some ways that churches around the world might respond to the level and severity of violence against women evidenced in chapter one and illustrated above? There are both healthy and unhealthy responses.

UNHEALTHY RESPONSES

Lack of awareness.

- If wife abuse was really that common, I would have heard much more talk about it before now.

- It might be occurring in other parts of the world, but it is not happening much in my local area and certainly not in my church.
- I can't think of a single man who would raise his fist against his wife.
- Some people deserve the terrible things that happen to them.
- I wonder what women do to make their husbands that mad at them.
- I have never heard my pastor talk about it, so it can't be a problem in my church.

Resistance to condemnation of abuse.

- What happens in someone else's family is none of my business.
- If it was that bad, she would just leave.
- How can I condemn abuse when I don't understand all the circumstances?
- There's nothing I can do to stop another person's abuse.
- Talking about these issues may make matters worse.

Lack of education.

- No one will come to my Bible study again if I raise the issue of violence.
- I am not going to talk about it; it makes me feel uncomfortable.
- Men do not like to hear the pastor say things like this.
- It would embarrass people in the congregation.

Lack of prevention.

- If it is going to happen, there is nothing anyone can do about it.
- Some people are born to be violent, and there is no way to help them.
- Talking about violence will turn people away from the church.

Lack of empathy.

- I could never help anyone who is a victim of violence.

- I don't want to know if someone in my church acts that way.

- People should keep their troubles to themselves.

- I have enough of my own problems; I don't want to know about the problems of others.

- I might say the wrong thing if I were to try to help someone.

Lack of referrals.

- The church has no business helping in the community.

- Some of the agencies in the community are very negative about the church, so we should keep to ourselves.

- Women who are abused do not need legal help or social assistance.

- Violence within church families must be hidden from the surrounding community.

Such responses are wrong; they don't work and don't bring credit to the cause of Christ. We must find our way to much healthier responses, discovering ways that churches around the world can respond to the suffering created by violence against women.

HEALTHY RESPONSES

Awareness.

- Be committed to increasing the awareness of pastors and church people about abuse.

- Recognize that family violence and wife abuse exist in every nation around the world.

- Help congregations see that violence exists among church families as well as families living in the neighborhoods where churches are located.

- Use posters and information packets to alert church attendees to the seriousness of violence in the home.

- Offer training materials to pastors and lay workers in local church settings.
- Use illustrations in sermons and other teaching materials that make it safe for someone to come forward to disclose violence in her own life.

Condemnation of abusive behavior.

- Speak out about abusive behavior whenever an opportunity presents itself.
- Let governments and nongovernmental agencies alike know that the church stands firm in its opposition to spouse abuse and violence in the home.
- Make it clear to church people that God does not condone men battering women or women battering men.
- Whenever possible, ensure that Christians and the church are counted among those opposed to wife battering or any form of family violence.

Education.

- Make sure that Bible colleges, seminaries and other training centers for pastors include in their curriculum information on spouse abuse and family violence.
- In Sunday-school teaching and in Bible studies, emphasize how important it is for men and women to deal with their frustrations and disappointments in nonviolent ways.
- When counseling couples preparing to marry, emphasize resolving conflict without abuse.
- When training teachers and other non-ordained workers in the church, alert them to the prevalence of violence and offer them help in responding to victims.

- Ensure that the difference between healthy and unhealthy relationships is discussed in the youth-group setting, where young men and women are beginning to be involved in critical interpersonal relationships.

Prevention.

- Model loving, nonabusive behavior in the families of pastors and other church leaders.

- Be explicit in helping families know where they can turn for help.

- In youth activities, encourage young men and women to treat each other well and to respect each other's abilities and points of view.

- Help newly married couples to resolve differences and seek help when necessary.

Empathy.

- Help men and women learn to listen to each other and to be interested in the lives of other people in the church and in the community.

- Offer safe places to talk about life's disappointments and problems (for example, small-group fellowship, women's Bible study, men's prayer breakfast).

- When you promise someone confidentiality, ensure you mean it and keep your promise.

- Practice acts of kindness that help others know you care about them.

- Learn to rejoice with those who are happy and to weep with those who are sad.

Referrals.

- Be aware of the resources in your area for helping hurting families.

- Know the name of the local shelter for battered women and how to access help there.

- Volunteer church resources to assist community initiatives dealing with domestic violence.

- Think about what particular gifts and ministries the church has to offer victims of family violence.

- Publicize the church's mission to abuse victims in local shelters or other community agencies.

This list of healthy responses to problems of violence is simply meant to get Christians thinking about all the ways pastors and the people in their congregations can encourage and model healthy living, and provide resources and help to those who suffer from violence. Later we will provide a more in-depth discussion of strategies for responding to abuse; for now it is important to realize that only as we become aware of the nature and extent of the suffering of women, children and families can we be motivated to do something about it.

Up to this point, we have only hinted at the Christian call to compassion and the scriptural injunction to rescue those who live in fear. Having established that violence against women in our world is a pervasive reality, we turn to God's Word for guidance, instruction and comfort.

Hear the Word of the Lord!

3

Growing in Compassion

A PASTOR RESPONDS TO DOMESTIC VIOLENCE

Robert Wilkins[1] is the pastor of a midsize church in a bedroom community, sandwiched between a growing industrial city and farmland. Approaching forty, he has been in the pastorate long enough (thirteen years) to realize that the demands of the ministry can sometimes be overwhelming and his level of preparedness woefully inadequate.

Robert estimates that perhaps 30 percent of his pastoral work involves relationship or marital counseling; in an average week he sees five different adults seeking his counsel for relationship or marital problems. At least half of those who come for counseling do so for several sessions, and the most frequently cited problems are the breakdown of communication in the home, the impact of shift work on the family and coping with disruptive children.

Unlike many pastors, Robert is willing to refer many of those who seek his counsel to a nonclerical counselor if he feels the situation is beyond his field or level of expertise. As a former army chaplain, he is comfortable working in a multidisplinary team, but he hesitates to refer members of his congregation to a secular counselor unless he is well acquainted with the counselor personally. He prefers to make his referrals to other Christian counselors, individuals with a strong faith connection. His reluctance is based on his experience: "I find that most secular counselors are not open to the spiritual," he says.

Robert reports that the demand for his marital counsel is increasing, a factor he believes is related to the mobile, transient community in which he lives and the rampant individualism in the Western world. When asked to recount a story of a woman who sought his assistance in the aftermath of domestic violence, he tells the story of Joan.

Joan came to Robert fearing for her life and the lives of her two children. Her husband, William, had grown up in an abusive home himself, and they had been married eighteen years. Robert says sadly, "It had not been a happy relationship, but tolerable. He has pushed and shoved her from time to time." Then he continues the story: "But his scare tactic is to take his hunting rifle out and lay it on the bed and say, 'Okay, I'm gonna shoot myself, I'm gonna shoot myself and somebody else.'" Joan had endured this kind of abuse for years. In the aftermath of his abuse, William would be remorseful, buy her presents and promise to change. But change never came.

Robert found himself in the awkward situation of counseling Joan to leave the marriage, to find respite and safety for herself and the children. In his words, "It's kind of strange that a pastor would do this, but if the situation is abusive like that, I don't counsel the woman to go back, unless he is willing to secure some good counseling. But he wasn't."

Joan came to church regularly, and William came on special occasions, like Christmas and Easter. Robert saw the couple in their home, met with Joan separately in his office and referred them both to separate counselors for more intensive assistance. Joan followed through on the referral suggestion and met intermittently with Robert thereafter to update him on her therapeutic progress. William was not willing to seek any help for himself: from his perspective, there was nothing wrong, nothing that needed repair. At the time of our interview with Robert, this couple was still living together, and Joan would seek respite at her parents' home (approximately twenty-five miles away) when she was too afraid to be near William.

In summing up his perspective on counseling situations involving abuse, Robert says, "I would never say to a couple or to a woman, or to a man, 'You've got to stay in this relationship because God says you've got to stay in this relationship.' I think that's hogwash." Like many pastors, Robert sees the chasm between the high value many Christians place on the intact family and the reality of domestic violence in cases like Joan's. As a pastor, he says he tries to assist in any way he can. "But I am not a miracle worker; I work for the miracle worker. Unless he intervenes in a dramatic way, some relationships dissolve and all I can do is apologize for that, but I can't change it."

From our studies of religious leaders, we have learned how difficult it is for pastors to see their intervention as successful if the marriage ends in divorce. Many clergy feel pressure to keep families together and marriages intact. In this way, pastoral counselors frequently find themselves in a very difficult double bind: they are stalwart supporters of family values, including reluctance to see any couple divorce, yet many of the families who seek their counsel need to separate to ensure the safety of all. With limited training and a lack of resources at their disposal, some clergy have not yet learned to identify that it is the relationship that has failed, not their advice.

Translating the rhetoric of "happy family living" into practical help for women, men and couples in crisis is no easy task. It is time consuming and emotionally draining for the pastor and often discouraging. There are few simple answers, and the rewards can seem to be in short supply. As a result, pastoral counselors sometimes feel they are caught in the crossfire between the ideology of the family that their denominations and churches hold dear and the nature, severity and persistence of male aggression and abuse.[2]

Carol[3] and Joe struggled just to survive. There was never enough money to pay the bills, never permanent employment, never marital harmony. Moreover, Joe tended to drink excessively. And their oldest child, a boy who had been diagnosed with ADD (attention deficit disorder), was having problems at school. Always Carol and Joe feared that the future would be worse than the present. Because money was scarce, there were few family outings, few unexpected treats for the children, and very few evenings or weekends of fun.

To be sure, Carol and her children had happy moments, when her mother would invite them to the country and the children could run free, or when Joe would be called in to do mechanic work on the weekend and the extra money would enable him to take their son to McDonald's and bowling, allowing Carol and the girls a break from all that noise and activity. And there were times when all five of them would go to the park on a Sunday afternoon. But for the most part, Carol and Joe did not enjoy each other's company, and they found the children burdensome.

Carol's father had been abusive toward her mother and one of her brothers. Joe himself had been a victim of child abuse; as a man he bore the physical and emotional scars of poverty and violence. Both Carol and Joe suffered from low self-esteem and from hopelessness and powerlessness. Joe had "done time" in a local jail and "time in a rooming house," when he had been given a court order to live apart from Carol.

At the time I became aware of Carol and Joe's story, a particular church community had taken them under its wing. Carol was participating in a young-mothers group; Joe was receiving individual counsel from the pastor; Carol was offered the services of a Christian counselor (paid for by church sources); the children had been integrated into age-appropriate programs in the church. Moreover, church women were supporting the family through ongoing contact and acts of kindness, such as child care and gifts of clothing and food. According to Carol, Joe had been nonabusive for over a year, and she was working part time at a garden center. Life was far from easy, but it was looking much better than it ever had in the past.

The violence was condemned, the fear was acknowledged, and the couple were offered choices. According to Carol, most of her church contacts (including the pastoral staff) had encouraged her to leave Joe and begin a new life free from the violence of the past. But because she was reluctant to do that, the faith community was working to help the family reach the goal of abuse-free family living.

The support had been ongoing for more than two years at the time I first met Carol. By her own account, church women took her places, brought groceries and came to look after the children while she was at work, and the missionary group had raised money for her at Christmas. One woman had taken her on a weeklong vacation while another sister in the faith had cared for the children.

While the story offers no dramatic turnaround or quick solution to the relational and economic difficulties Carol and Joe faced, it is clearly an example of support for an abused woman and her children—and the perpetrator of that violence as well—within a church congregation. And if change is to occur within Carol's family, that support from the faith community will need to continue for a very long time.

CALLED TO COMPASSION

"Who is my neighbor?" a teacher of the law asked Jesus. In response Jesus told the parable of the good Samaritan, then he asked, "And who was the neighbor?" The answer was painfully obvious: the one who saw the need, bandaged the wounds, transported the traveler and paid for extended care and lodging.

Our social action, or response to what we see around us, derives its motivation and vision from the practical ministry of our leader, Jesus of Nazareth. Let us consider three examples of Christ's earthly ministry that we might wish to imitate as we respond to victims of abuse and violence.

Jesus nourished the crowds by offering them both spiritual and physical food. By particular acts of kindness on our lifelong journey of compassion, we earn the respect of others and the right to witness to God's love in our hearts and lives. Throughout Jesus' travels with his disciples and the women among the entourage, he showed concern for the physical well-being of his followers; when they were hungry, Jesus fed them; when they were weary, he offered them rest; and when the disciples were frightened, he calmed the seas.

Jesus washed the disciples' feet. As the heart of our Lord was being prepared for his own imminent suffering, Jesus planned one last meal for the disciples to have together. And he welcomed each one by washing their feet. What an interesting model for us! Even when his betrayal and death were close at hand, Jesus ministered to those needier than himself. Can we put aside our own needs and desires long enough to see the needs of others? Where and with whom do we have washing that needs to be done?

Jesus wept over the death of Lazarus. Jesus' compassion for those around him was remarkable. Not only did he realize their need, but he took on their pain. Why did Jesus weep over Lazarus when he knew that life could be breathed into that dead body? Because Jesus cared for him. Because he loved Lazarus and was emotionally involved with him and his two sisters, Mary and Martha. Jesus wept over Lazarus not because of his death but because of the pain and sadness it created. When we love people, we too will weep for them, even as we know that their circumstances can be altered and that we can play a role in that transformation.

When we imitate the life of Christ, we are involved in feeding, washing and weeping. How? First by validating the pain of someone who is hurting. Listening is powerful—that is what survivors tell us. It is a form of validation. Studies conducted by our research team over the past twenty years have revealed that one of the most helpful ways women of faith have assisted abused women has been through the offer of a listening ear: "Taking children, being a listening ear, a grocery person, taxi driver. Just seeing a need and doing it before they have to ask, just to make . . . life easier."[4]

When we listen to others' stories, we validate their experience. Our silence and our attention says, *What has happened to you is important to me: I am willing to listen.* We can tell people until the cows come home that we are interested in them, but if we never listen intently to what they say, our words are like a "noisy gong or a clanging cymbal" (1 Cor 13:1).

Listening to a person's story is not the same thing as evaluating it or judging its accuracy—that is the responsibility of legally trained professionals and the justice system. People in pain report that the first step toward healing and recovery is simply to have someone to hear them out, someone who is empathic and sensitive, slow to speak and eager to listen. Though listening can be hard work, it doesn't take special training or advanced skills. A good listener shows interest in the person and in the information she is sharing. It's speaking and advice-giving that require advanced education and wisdom.

The Christian call to compassion is first and foremost a call to meet people where they are, to see the reality of their plight, to hear the cry of their heart and to attempt to understand their pain. Somewhere in the healing journey it may be necessary for someone with professional training to sort through the dynamics of the suffering person's past and present, and to evaluate the accuracy of her story, the long-term impact of what she has suffered and all the precipitating factors. Though such a process is important, the first need of abuse victims is for someone to listen, empathize and assist them in locating the practical and emotional help that they need to continue living.

MENDING BROKEN HEARTS

Bonnie suffered terrible verbal and sexual abuse from her husband, James, a man who was successful in business but preoccupied most of his waking hours with matters of sex. He dreamed of being a pimp, someone who could fulfill his own sexual fantasies at the same time that he was coordinating the sexual activities of several young women.

Jim wanted Bonnie to dress provocatively to seduce any man she met at church or in the community. He insisted that she dress without underwear; to accomplish this unreasonable request, he would often hide her undergarments. For five years she endured constant discussion of her body and daily behavior that made her uncomfortable in private and in public. During the latter phase of her life with Jim, his goal was to transform her into a prostitute.

Since Bonnie and Jim were evangelical Christians and attended a nondenominational church known for its active discipleship, she sought help and guidance from the leaders. Despite her frequent pleas for assistance, no one was willing to take the sexual abuse seriously or to challenge her husband on his behavior. From time to time she was encouraged to be loyal to him, but never to seek refuge or respite from the badgering she endured.

As a childhood victim of physical abuse and molestation, Bonnie was well acquainted with the survivor role. Consequently, it took her many years and the ongoing support of a Christian therapist to finally extricate herself from such an unhealthy environment. Describing the marriage as the worst chapter of her life, she confided that even now, many years later, the sexual abuse still torments her. Her broken heart is in need of ongoing repair.[5]

The most basic form of Christian service is love in action—mending broken hearts. Christians will be identified by their love for one another (Jn 13:35). The task of mending suggests repair, fixing things that are broken. Isaiah 61 speaks of binding up the brokenhearted, comforting those who mourn, replacing mourning with gladness, offering a garment of praise in place of a spirit of despair. And how will this be accomplished? When God's people go up to Gilead and apply its healing balm to the wounds of those who suffer (Jer 8:20-22; 46:11).

God has a passion for mending brokenness. Scripture is filled with passages in which the God of the universe shows compassion for the weak of this earth, like a hen that gathers her chicks under her wings (Mt 23:37). This is the picture of the Christian God: a deity who has the hairs of our head numbered, who cares about the feeding patterns of sparrows and the enduring beauty of lilies in a grassy meadow (Lk 12:7, 27-28). How much more valuable, sister in Christ, brother in Christ, are you? How much more valuable indeed!

While there can be little doubt of God's interest in the heart-mending business, individuals must recognize their need of repair and congregations must be prepared to assist in the tasks of mending.

God's mending does not occur as in a factory, where hundreds of machines and machine operators sew clothing in a standard fashion. God's mending occurs one heart at a time—sometimes at the altar, sometimes at the kitchen table, sometimes during a walk in the woods, sometimes prompted by the words of another woman of faith, always prompted by the still small voice (1 Kings 19:11-12).

As people of faith, we need to learn to recognize brokenness in ourselves and in those around us. We have to acknowledge our need to have the healing balm of Gilead applied to our afflictions—physical or emotional or spiritual. The God we serve, who loved us before we could love in return, is in the business of mending hearts, shattered dreams and broken bodies. To put it in the language of the day: the market niche of God's Spirit is heart repair. But how is the healing balm of Gilead applied? That's where you and I come in. That is the role of congregational life.

God chooses earthly vessels, jars of clay, ordinary people to assist in responding to the brokenness around us. There are many models of menders offered in Scripture: think of Dorcas, Phoebe, Priscilla and the unnamed stretcher bearers, each a conduit to the healing touch of Jesus.

The story of Dorcas is recorded in Acts 9. A woman named Tabitha, translated as Dorcas, lived in Joppa. She was constantly doing good and helping the poor and needy, especially widows. She would use a needle and thread in her upstairs room to sew garments for poor women who had nothing to wear. Clothing needy widows was her market niche.

But Dorcas fell ill and died, and the church in Joppa begged Peter to redirect his travels so that he could come. Somehow the Christian community in Joppa was convinced that its ministry opportunities would be thwarted without the talents and gifts of this elderly woman. Peter came. The church widows showed him the handmade garments Dorcas had crafted. Peter prayed. Dorcas arose.

In the tradition of Dorcas, some today use domestic talents in service of Christ. This woman used unsophisticated tools—a needle,

some thread, a pair of scissors—to offer hope to needy women. Her
ministry of clothing worked to mend some of the rips and tears that
years of living had created. She was a sister of mercy before the name
was adopted by Catholic nuns. And congregations can become sisters
of mercy to families in crisis.

Phoebe's service to God and to the growing Christian community
is recorded in Romans 16. Paul commended to his readers this
woman, whom he calls a servant (or a deacon) of the church in
Cenchreae, asking that they receive her in a manner worthy of the
saints, offering her help and remembering her labor. How exactly did
Phoebe serve the church? Among other tasks, female deacons in the
early church prepared women candidates for baptism[6] and visited
women and girls in their homes, which was not always appropriate
for men to do. While Dorcas was stitching broken hearts, Phoebe was
washing them.

When the Christian church sets about bathing our lives, we do not
feel dirty or shameful any longer. The old nature, replete with heart-
ache and pain, is replaced with a new nature fashioned in likeness to
Christ. The past is washed away. God's Spirit beckons us to start
over—to mourn no longer, to rise and go forth, to put our hand to the
plow and not look back.

While Dorcas stitched and Phoebe cleansed, Priscilla offered wise
counsel. A tentmaker by trade, Priscilla and her husband, Aquila,
began a house ministry in Ephesus after being commissioned by Paul
to leave their homestead in Corinth for the sake of ministry. Their
family story, recorded in Acts 18, suggests that Priscilla used her talents both inside and outside the home to share the gospel and to
reason in the synagogues—and often she and Aquila sold their goods
in the marketplace. She used her intellectual prowess to convince
others of the efficacy of the gospel of Christ. She offered hope to the
hopeless by words of wisdom, reason and truth.

The unnamed stretcher bearers who brought their friend to Jesus
were also ministers of healing balm (Mk 2). Four buddies had a para-
lyzed friend, and since they were unable to offer direct assistance for

his malaise, they decided to take him to the Jewish rabbi known for healing powers. When the friends carried him on a stretcher to the house where Jesus was staying, they found it so crowded that it was impossible to make their way inside. Undeterred by the obstacle of overcrowding, they climbed onto the roof, dug through it and lowered their friend into the room where Jesus was teaching. As a result of his encounter with Jesus, the man stood up and walked home, healed and forgiven.

This is a very interesting story of acknowledged human limitations and the power of spiritual strength, of perseverance in the face of obstacles, of what happens when people pool their resources to help someone in need. If our congregations are filled with friends like these—undeterred by obstacle because they are convinced of the necessity of getting close to Jesus—imagine how many will be touched by the healing balm of Gilead.

BEING A SPIRITUAL SHEPHERD

As table two reveals below, clergy are not strangers to family violence. A large proportion of ministers are called on to respond to women, men and children whose lives have been affected by violence within the family.

For the purposes of our discussion, let's consider the data related to woman abuse and the most common counseling situation for pastors: a woman with an abusive partner. Table two reveals that 83.2 percent of Canadian pastors reported that during their ministry they had been called on to intervene in a situation involving a victimized woman and an abusive man, most often her legal husband. Further analysis of this data revealed that approximately 10 percent of Canadian clergy report that they respond to at least five battered women each year, with the majority of pastors having regular, but less frequent, experiences of counseling battered wives.

And their experiences were not with abused women alone. Seventy percent of Canadian clergy claimed to have counseled an abusive man. This figure is noteworthy in its own right, for there are very

Table 2. Percentage of Canadian Clergy Who Have Ever Counseled in These Situations Involving Violence

A woman who has an abusive husband or partner	83.2
A woman who was abused in childhood by a parent	77.2
A couple whose relationship is often violent	74.0
A man who is abusive toward his wife or partner	70.4
A child/youth who has been abused by his/her father	67.7
A father who is abusive of his children	57.0
A man who was abused in childhood by a parent	53.3
A woman whose husband is abusing the children	49.7
A child/youth who has been abused by his/her mother	47.7
A mother who is abusive of her children	46.3
A teenager who has an abusive boyfriend	44.1
A woman who is planning to marry an abusive boyfriend	43.6
A man who has an abusive wife/partner	39.8
A woman who is abusive toward her husband/partner	38.3
A woman who is being abused by her son/daughter	30.9
A man who is planning to marry an abusive girlfriend	12.5

Adapted from Nason-Clark 1997: 69.

few community-based services for men who batter their wives, and what services do exist seem to be poorly funded.[7] Thus pastors are among the few resources available to assist perpetrators of abuse.[8]

In 2009, one of my graduate students, Joanne Galbraith, completed a thesis that investigated the experience of Protestant clergywomen in responding to women who had been abused.[9] She found that most of the women pastors were called upon regularly to respond to the needs of abused women, a fact that many of these pastors attributed to their gender. All of these pastors endorsed the safety of the abused over the preservation of the marriage. Interestingly, it was often their "ministry of presence" that provided opportunities for both parish-

ioners and community women to see these female pastors as a safe
haven—a person willing and able to listen to a life story and walk
alongside on the journey toward healing and hope.

The Canadian data in table two above supplement the very limited
data worldwide detailing the experiences of ministers in responding
to women or men abused by family members.[10] These findings suggest that a minority of evangelical clergy have substantial experience
in this area, while most ministers report limited but ongoing counseling of abuse victims. It is critical not to exaggerate or minimize the
counseling experience of clergy in the area of family violence. While
clergy experience is clearly no match for the prevalence of need in
this area, pastors are an ongoing resource to battered women and
abusive men, something those outside the church often fail to recognize. But how do these clergy respond? What help do they offer?

A quick look at some social-work literature and contemporary
feminist writing would suggest that clergy are nearly always unhelp-
ful and advise women to return to abusive home environments that
threaten their physical or psychological health.[11] From this vantage
point, clergy minimize women's pain and fear and teach their congregations the necessity of keeping the family together at all costs. Yet
the data from scholarly research are far more complex than this partially informed view would suggest. Opinions regarding how pastors
respond to battered women who seek their counsel are marked by a
lot of passion[12] but are informed by very limited empirical study.[13]

A research project in which over one hundred evangelical ministers were interviewed found that *counseling* means something quite
different to those trained in theology and those professionals with
social work, psychology or psychiatric degrees.[14] Ministers are less
likely to set therapy goals, assess progress, evaluate interventions
and refer to other community-based resources than workers who
have secular credentials. On the other hand, clergy are more likely
to be willing to see men and women at any time of the day or night,
to schedule appointments at very short notice, to visit men or women
in their own home, to tell about their own struggles and to feel guilty

when contact with a family does not lead to marked improvement. Somewhat surprisingly, clergy are often reluctant to offer specifically *spiritual* interventions, like Scripture reading or prayer. Perhaps they minimize its effectiveness to an abuse victim, or, more likely, they need guidance in how to read with, or pray for, a woman suffering abuse.[15]

While our research offers scant evidence that clergy admonish women to return home to unchanged abusive husbands, pastoral counselors are excessively optimistic that violent men *wish* to change their abusive ways and *will* cease their abusive behavior. Ministers often blame themselves for failing to engage a violent man in counseling or failing to bring reconciliation between a perpetrator and a victim. Since most clergy cling to the belief that violent relationships should be transformed, they feel discouraged and defeated when a violent relationship is terminated permanently. While evangelical clergy as a group are reluctant to recommend divorce, most do advise legal action when it becomes clear that an abusive man will not change his violent ways and when a woman's safety, as well as that of her children, is continually compromised.

Victims frequently report that simply hearing their pastor or religious leader condemn the abuse they have suffered aids in their healing. Sometimes such words are spoken in private as a pastor speaks words of comfort to a battered woman. Other times they are public words, preached in a sermon or taught in Sunday school. We suspect that if pastors realized how powerful their spiritual support for abused women actually could be, they would offer support more freely and more frequently. The dual impact of words of comfort for victims and words of condemnation for violent acts brings the healing balm of Gilead to people of faith who suffer abuse.

Offering several comforting Bible passages to a bruised woman validates her experience of pain and reminds her that God does not condone the violence she has suffered. She may feel that she deserves abuse. She may believe that this is her cross to bear. She may feel that she is not worthy to be treated like a human being. A wise pastor understands the extent of a victim's low self-esteem and applies the healing balm to her wounds just as the good Samaritan did to the hurt traveler. Validate her pain. Offer practical help. Soothe her broken spirit with God's words of comfort to her and God's words of rebuke to the perpetrator.

As a spiritual shepherd, a pastor is uniquely positioned to bring comfort and offer challenge. But first he or she must understand the pain of the victim. Whether it is an abused woman seeking help on her own or a couple coming together, the knowledgeable pastor will ensure that the woman tells her own story in her own words, out of the presence of the man who intimidates her or has violated her body. Even if the couple arrives together, a pastoral counselor should ensure that in the assessment phase, each person has a private opportunity to recount his or her version of events.

The experienced minister will ask appropriate questions, thereby making it safe for a woman to disclose in private her pain and vulnerability. She may initially say she has come for help because she is desperately unhappy. Asking a variety of questions about her life at home and work, the minister may hear her disclose violence or verbal abuse. While it is important not to assume violence in the life of every unhappy couple or unhappy woman, it is also critical not to assume the absence of violence simply because it has not been disclosed.

For most couples, religious or not, violence is a strongly guarded secret.[16] The woman may feel embarrassed, guilty, responsible for keeping her husband happy, responsible to keep the family together. She may have religious beliefs that inhibit her from saying anything unpleasant about her husband.[17] She may believe that the violence is her punishment for unkind words, spiritual immaturity or sinful actions. She may assume that since she married him, she must accept whatever he does to her. She may believe that God expects her always to turn the other cheek.[18] Sometimes she may feel that her life is next to worthless.

A wonderful opportunity awaits the pastoral counselor who is sensitive to the suffering of a battered woman and knowledgeable about religious and secular resources to address her pain and malaise. The woman may need ongoing therapy that is beyond the pastor's expertise to provide. She may need legal counsel. She may need to flee to the safety of a transition house or other shelter.[19] She may need money or help with the children. Most certainly she needs a caring church community and a pastor who offers spiritual and emotional support, wise counsel and appropriate referral suggestions.

In a research study of evangelical youth ministers and their youth groups, teenagers claimed that their youth pastor could be described as a friend par excellence. They sought out this pastor to help them sort through the sometimes conflicting demands of their parents, church and peers. Youth pastors themselves claimed that it was their interpersonal skills more than anything else that drew young men and women to them for counsel. They established credibility by being a friend—listening a lot, speaking a little. Many church youth reported that they rarely if ever discussed dating violence or family abuse within meetings held in the church. This is unfortunate, since many disclosed that their families had engaged in abusive behavior or that their dating relationships had at times been abusive.

The challenge to spiritual shepherds, of adults or teens, is simply to acknowledge that violence in families is a pervasive problem and to offer help and healing for victims, model violence-free behavior and make their study a safe place for a person to disclose the pain and humiliation of battery.

* * *

In chapter fourteen, we introduce pastors and others who walk alongside victims and perpetrators to a vast array of resources that they can harness as they begin to think about how to raise awareness in their churches on these issues and how to respond to those who have been impacted by them. These resources are linked to our ongoing RAVE [Religion and Violence e-Learning] Project, a Lilly Endowment-funded endeavor to offer web-based training and practical assistance available free of charge at <www.theraveproject.org>.

Our website includes lists of helpful Scriptures; sermons on domestic violence; answers to frequently asked questions; voices of survivors, those who have acted abusively and pastors who have intervened; critical questions to ask a woman in crisis (including a safety plan); ways to identify essential community resources, including shelter contact information; and suggestions for how a congregation can get involved in helping address violence in the home. We include the voices of a variety of pastors who speak directly to a woman at her point of need, "Words of Hope" regarding the issue of domestic violence and our innovative Dating Game, a cartoon-enhanced resource to help youth identify healthy and unhealthy dating relationships.

Below, we provide some critical questions that a pastor needs to ask when a woman seeks help in the aftermath of violence at home.

QUESTIONS TO ASK YOURSELF
WHEN RESPONDING TO AN ABUSED WOMAN

Keep this reference guide in your top desk drawer or in the file you use when making notes during an interview session. You can glance at it to ensure that all the critical areas have been addressed in your response to a victim of wife abuse.

- Am I sure that it is safe for this woman to return home?
- Have I presented guidelines for what to do if her home is unsafe at any time?
- Have I helped her develop a safety plan?
- Have I validated her pain without being a judge?
- Have I offered therapeutic options?
- Have I made it clear that the church wants to be a safe place to disclose abuse?
- Have I made it clear what resources are available in our church?
- Have I made it clear what resources are available in our local community?

- Have I condemned the abuse she has suffered using spiritual language?

- Have I offered some spiritual help that is grounded in Scripture?

- Have I prayed with her in a way that does not suggest that being a victim is her fault?

- Have I offered practical help and support by seeking to understand what she needs at this point in her life?

- Have I made it crystal clear that she is welcome to come back whether or not she takes my advice?

- Have I talked about what confidentiality means? Am I committed to keeping it?

- Have I discussed the limits of pastoral confidentiality (for example, mandatory reporting of child abuse)?

- Have I determined whether the children are at risk? Whether the abuser is at risk?

- Have I determined whether I, the pastoral counselor, am at risk?

4

Steeple to Shelter

Paving the Pathway

SHELTER STAFF RESPOND TO
ABUSED RELIGIOUS WOMEN

Karen Mudd[1] is the executive director of a women's shelter in a large city. With accommodations for over thirty women and their children, plus outreach services to abused women still in their own homes, she has a very demanding schedule, and she sometimes feels the weight of the world on her shoulders. Her staff is often overworked, and though she is a very reasonable employer, the needs of the community—especially women and their children who have been violated—are ever present on her mind. She is caught between the demands of the work, her social-work background stressing the importance of boundaries with clients and her knowledge of the value of self-care for herself and those with whom she works. Karen tries to model the balanced life, but as with many professionals, that is easier to talk about than to practice.

On the job, there are always fiscal concerns. Most of the money for the daily operations of the shelter comes from government grants and other "soft" money. Capital costs, when they can be obtained, usually come from a foundation, where a board of directors has placed the issue of violence against women and children as a top priority for funding for a specified period (usually one year). So Karen finds herself always chasing money—for needed repairs (and sometimes improvements) to the facilities, for program enhancements for abused women and their children, for adequate pay and ongoing training for her staff and for community dialogue and workshops for other professionals. To be blunt: there is not enough time or enough money to fill all the demands.

In the urban downtown where the transition house is located, there are a growing number of immigrant families, and the diversity of women at the shelter reflects these societal changes. It is important to Karen that the shelter is respectful of all women's cultural and religious experiences, but this is difficult at a practical level. Most of her staff do not have specific knowledge or life experiences that would enable them to talk authoritatively to Muslim or Jewish women, or Mormons, or Pentecostals. In fact, highly religious women of any tradition are difficult for the workers at the shelter. Sometimes individual workers blame the religious backgrounds of the women for the abuse, but Karen has been diligent in helping her staff see that there are many religious leaders—representing a variety of faith traditions— who speak out against violence in its many and varied forms.

Despite her optimism, Karen knows firsthand that not all religious leaders are willing to work with the shelters. Over the years, she has met many women who have been told to endure the abuse in the name of Christ. Other pastors ask abused women not to go to secular agencies for help when violence threatens peace at home. Still others tell women that they will lose the support of their religious community if they tell an outsider what is happening within the walls of their home.

To be sure, some of the blatant disregard for secular shelters has lessened in recent years, but as executive director of a large facility, Karen does not see religious leaders often asking her how they can support the work of rescuing women and children. Rather, it is the women's organizations within those faith communities that are most likely to reach out, volunteer to help or give financial or in-kind donations. Sometimes, there are women pastors who are particularly open to involvement with Karen and her staff, and some of the shelter staff themselves are members of various faith communities in town. In Karen's experience, there is usually one woman who builds a bridge between her church and the local shelter—and then others come on board. And sometimes they are very successful in forging initiatives with the religious leader or women's group or other ministries within that congregation.

As a result of some of these initiatives, Karen has become friends with several women connected to various faith communities around the city. This has opened doors for networking and has helped Karen to understand more fully some of the challenges for building bridges between community agencies and congregations. Now several of those contacts will call Karen to solicit her advice when an abused woman comes to the congregation for help. She also receives invitations to send brochures and other materials on abuse to faith leaders so that they can disseminate these to their congregants.

Karen's contact with many religious leaders has made her far more comfortable relating to those very religious women—of whatever faith tradition—that come to her agency seeking shelter and respite when they flee a violence intimate partner. She would like to have a list of local religious leaders who are willing, and trained, to assist women who would like spiritual counsel in the aftermath of domestic violence. Whether this dream can ever become a reality, only time will tell.

✳ ✳ ✳

Several older women make their way slowly from the parking lot toward the auxiliary door of the church building. It is Tuesday afternoon, and fifteen women have gathered to quilt, have a snack and pray for the women who are living in the local transition house. For several years now, these seniors have donated the quilts they produce to the children who come with their moms to seek refuge at the shelter, often having fled from an abusive home with little preparation time. The quilters' goal: to ensure that every child who enters this publicly funded facility leaves with a handmade quilt. As a boy or girl cuddles in its warmth or gazes at its colorful patterns, the message will ring loud and clear: women who love God also love you.[2]

Victims of violence experience a multitude of practical and spiritual questions and dilemmas. They need multifaceted support—religious and secular, emotional and practical.[3] Yet workers trained in very different disciplines and ways of thinking often find it hard to cooperate to achieve a single goal.[4] It is not surprising, then, that secular workers, like staff in a transition house or social workers at a community agency, do not often refer religious clients to clergy. Why? They fear that the counsel offered in a pastoral study will thwart their clients' healing journey. Simply put, they do not trust the advice of ministers. They believe that it will negate any progress achieved through therapeutic intervention. They think clergy would do more harm than good.

It is also not surprising that clergy are very reluctant to refer their parishioners to secular sources of help. They fear that the counsel offered in a community health setting will break up the family and thwart the woman's spiritual development. They do not trust the advice of social workers or others trained in a discipline not specifically based on the Bible. They believe that the intervention of transition house staff will prevent reconciliation of an abusive man and his battered wife. They think secular social workers do more harm than good.

At the 2008 PASCH[5] Conference, held in Washington, D.C., Nancy organized a panel to discuss some of the challenges and opportunities related to referral practices between pastors and counselors in secular community-based agencies. Dialogue focused on how to build bridges. Everyone agreed mistrust abounds. Everyone agreed this must—and can—be overcome. Yet building bridges takes time. It involves establishing relationships, a common purpose and a will to collaborate.

Violence is a multifaceted community problem with social, psychological, spiritual, legal and economic aspects. It cannot be eradicated by any one segment of society, however well intentioned, working in isolation from the broader community. Churches and clergy have a unique role to play in responding to the needs of abuse victims and their families. Faith communities can raise awareness of abuse and support violence-free family living by offering educational programs for men, women and children during the weekly routine of church life. Holding abusers accountable while offering hope for those desiring to change their violent behavior is another avenue of intervention by congregations.

Spiritual leaders have a valuable, distinct role in the fight to end violence in the family, but their practical and emotional assistance is far more effective when offered alongside the resources of other professionals and agencies. Working together, combining expertise and mission, augments the healing journey of victims and has the potential to transform the neighborhoods that churches serve. Sometimes clergy and police may cooperate. Sometimes it may be the transition house and a church women's group. Other times it may be workers at the mental-health clinic and pastors. Or collaboration between schoolteachers and youth leaders in the church. Or initiatives involving a community center and a mission-oriented social-action group of a congregation.

Given that funding for public services is shrinking while many evangelical congregations are expanding their community mission statements, the message of the childhood song rings truer than ever: "The more we work together, together, together, the more we work together, the happier we'll be." Pooling our strengths and talents to respond compassionately to victims and to work toward a less violent society benefits everyone.

The rewards of cooperation notwithstanding, some very real challenges face religious and secular organizations thinking about *how* to begin to collaborate on the issue of woman abuse. The road to partnership does not necessarily involve endorsing all the interventions of another agency or group of professionals. But it does involve accepting and understanding the specific value and contribution of workers trained in different disciplines. Ultimately it comes down to developing trust and respect among ministers and secular community workers, paving the way for a pathway between the steeple and the shelter.[6]

One of the most effective ways faith communities are reaching out to women who have been abused involves the informal support network that operates within most congregations, where one woman meets another woman at her point of need. Women who meet to celebrate their faith and to be challenged to live it out reach out to women in their family, women who are neighbors, women they work with or sisters in the faith, doing acts of kindness that say much louder than words, "I care about you and I want to help ease your pain." By providing childcare, a bed for the night, a referral suggestion, some groceries, transportation to a medical or legal appointment, or a listening ear, they form a circle of support around the battered woman who feels as if her world is caving in all around her. Such acts of mercy build a violated woman's sense of self and empower her to face the challenges ahead. They build the credibility of the caregiver and reinforce the significance of the mission of her faith community.

Ultimately, as one woman ministers to another woman, both caregiver and care receiver are empowered. This woman-centered spiritual empowerment helps meet the individual needs of hurting women even as it reinforces a sense of community connectedness within the church family. As women help each other, they do not demand that a battered wife sever all ties to her abusive husband forever, nor do they encourage her to return to a home where her physical or emotional health was in jeopardy. Rather, the circle of support offered by church women provides an abused and vulnerable woman with choices, therapeutic and practical options destined to augment her journey toward healing and wholeness of body and spirit.

THE HEALING JOURNEY

First and foremost, churches need to be safe places to disclose abuse.[7] Are they? While some women see their local congregation as a "safe haven," others report that "it's not a safe place to come . . . because nobody knows what to do with you."[8]

The first step on the road to recovery for women suffering abuse is to disclose the pain and humiliation they have endured to someone who is willing to listen in an environment that is safe and supportive. But before a woman can disclose her suffering, she has to interpret her past or present experiences as abusive. In other words, she has to name the pain and conflict as abuse. For the average Christian woman, this is very difficult to do.

In 2004, InterVarsity Press published *Refuge from Abuse: Healing and Hope for Abused Christian Women,* our book written directly for women who are suffering. It is our attempt to offer hope in the midst of crisis. In that book, we outline some of the struggles victims experience: the shame, the betrayal, the sense of hopelessness. And we attempt to answer some of the questions that surface: What did I do to deserve this? What does God expect of me? Must I continue to love until death do us part?

Many Christian women who have been victimized turn to their pastors for help. Yet, again, most clergy are reluctant to name the behavior of a violent man toward his wife for what it is; they would rather interpret the conflict as relational and the partners as equally responsible to seek help and resolution. Pastors prefer to see persistent verbal abuse as a couple's problem with communication and to downplay the economic and social dependency that a married woman often experiences. Ministers are slow to recognize unrestrained male power in a relationship, though they are usually decisive in their condemnation of violent physical outbursts.

Women believers, on the other hand, are far more likely than their leaders to understand the nature and severity of violence and to grasp the long-term consequences in the lives of victims. In part this is because Christian women have learned about the frequency and im-

pact of wife abuse through the lives of their daughters, mothers and friends. Consequently, evangelical women are more likely to criticize the failure of the church and its leaders to respond compassionately to the problem than to condemn a woman's failure to leave an abusive relationship or to blame women for choosing their husbands poorly.

When abuse is addressed from the pulpit, in the pastoral study, in women's Bible-study classes, in Sunday school or in premarital workshops, those who have experienced its pain receive encouragement to come forward. The implicit message rings out: this church, or this pastoral study, is a safe place to recount your experience of being hurt. Giving violence a name and condemning it publicly is one tangible way that congregations and their leaders can respond directly to violence that occurs among women and men in their church family. The Sunday-morning sermon gives the average pastor a valuable opportunity to speak to victims, their families and the perpetrators in an environment where they are not singled out but can choose to respond. Research in various countries has indicated that large numbers of victims, approximately one in five, never disclose their experience of wife abuse until they are asked by an anonymous telephone interviewer to do so; they wait until they are asked.[9]

Once a disclosure of current abuse has been made, it is imperative to take immediate steps to ensure the physical and emotional safety of the victim and her children.[10] Does she have somewhere to go? Does she need transportation? The number-one priority must be to safeguard a woman's life, taking account of the possibility that the abusive man will seek retaliation.[11]

Once her safety is ensured, a plethora of practical needs surfaces: the provision of emergency financial assistance, lodging,[12] child care, legal counsel, transportation, help for ongoing emotional needs, medical attention, spiritual counseling. Battered women who are Christian often feel that their spirit has been broken, that God does not care about their life, that they are worthless in every way. Among the unique challenges facing conservative Christian women are the enthusiasm among evangelicals for the intact nuclear family[13] and theological doctrines such as forgiveness, separation from the world, glorification of suffering and instantaneous conversion.[14]

One of the real challenges for evangelical pastors counseling abusive men is to be able to differentiate between inauthentic pleas for the victim's forgiveness (or God's) and genuine repentance that makes them accountable for the hurt they have caused and its consequences, as well as accountable for changed behavior. A victim who has heard an abuser say he is sorry many times before will need time and will need to see altered actions to believe that he is serious about living differently. No helping professional, however well intentioned, can set a time frame for the process of forgiveness and reconciliation.

Because evangelical men who are violent often want their pastor to encourage their victim to "forgive and forget," it is imperative that ministers understand the delicate terrain of a manipulative man's ways and a wounded woman's heart. This is not to suggest that evangelical clergy discount the power and potential of change in an abuser's life. But they must understand that many men who abuse their wives, whether they claim the name of Christ or not, say they want to stop their violence but never do.

The healing journey for victims is long and arduous; many caregivers are required and ongoing emotional support is needed for the transition from victim to survivor. Many Christian women who are battered would like assistance from both community agencies and their faith fellowship. Healing requires both the language of the spirit and the language of contemporary culture. Help that negates the support of others often thwarts the recovery process and augments pain and despair. The struggle to stop violence and to bring wholeness into the lives of its victims requires that the ideological fences between Christian and secular caregivers have many gates, enabling hurting men and women to take advantage of the expertise of the physician, the pastor, the lawyer, the shelter worker and the psychologist. It is shortsighted to expect that one profession alone can respond to what years of neglect and misuse have created.

ENSURING CARE AND COMPASSION IN THE
CONGREGATIONAL SETTING

Hurting men, women and children present the local church with an opportunity to put into practice what is preached from its pulpit, taught in its Sunday school classes and studied in its home groups: that God cares about all human life and that congregations exist to bring that love to every person. Together God and Christian people are in the heart-mending business. But individuals must want the healing balm of Gilead to be applied to their wounds, and congregations must be prepared to offer it.

What does it mean to apply the healing balm of Gilead to our individual and collective hurts?

> "The harvest is past, the summer is ended,
>> and we are not saved."
> For the wound of the daughter of my people is my heart
>> wounded, I mourn, and dismay has taken
>>> hold of me.
> Is there no balm in Gilead?
>> Is there no physician there? (Jer 8:20-22 ESV)

> The Spirit of the Lord GOD is upon me,
>> because the LORD has anointed me;
> he has sent me to bring good news to the oppressed,
>> to bind up the brokenhearted . . .
>> to comfort all who mourn . . .
>> to give them a garland instead of ashes,
> the oil of gladness instead of mourning,
>> the mantle of praise instead of a faint spirit. . . .
> Because their shame was double,
>> and dishonor was proclaimed as their lot,
>> therefore they shall possess a double portion;
>> everlasting joy shall be theirs. (Is 61:1-3, 7)

> Go up to Gilead, and take balm. (Jer 46:11)

Applying the healing balm of Gilead involves proclaiming good news to the poor, for whom news is often bad; binding hearts that have been ripped apart by loneliness, disappointment and pain; comforting those who mourn; placing on the downcast a garment of praise; and offering everlasting joy to those who feel shame. Men and women bring to God and their church their brokenness, disappointment, shame, grief and despair, and in turn they are offered strength to fight, hope to endure, a sense of belonging—in essence, *love*. That is the biblical model. We bring to Christ our worn-down self and it is replaced, rejuvenated and renewed.

The church, motivated and empowered by God's Spirit, is like a spiritual recycling center. Christianity is not a solo sport: it is togetherness, relationship, bonding under the umbrella of God's love, power and forgiveness. We offer our humanness and its associated frailty; God offers us the Comforter, peace and promise. We will never be alone. When congregations catch a glimpse of what they have to offer to hurting men and women—practical acts of kindness, lifelong compassion, hope that extends human capacity—they will never be the same.

How caring is your congregation? How caring are our denominations? How caring is each of us? There are scores of men, women and children who need God's touch, mediated by people of faith.

HOW CARING IS MY CONGREGATION?

Are safety mechanisms in place?

- Have abuse victims been counseled to ensure that they have made some preparations in case they need to leave their home quickly? Is there a safety plan?

- Who can be called on short notice if there is an emergency facing a family in your congregation?

- Are there people in the congregation who are aware of the important safety issues for women and children in your area?

- Are there any members who are trained to provide emergency medical or social services?

- Does the church have a support group for victims of violence?

Do you know a transition worker by name?

- Does the pastor know the contact information and location of the nearest community shelter for battered women?
- Has the church established some contact with at least one worker at the shelter?
- If there are no community-based housing resources, has the congregation itself made some provision for emergency shelter?

Is information available in safe locations?

- Where is the safest location in your building to place information that abuse victims can look at in privacy (such as restrooms)?
- What information can be offered to women in immediate crisis or those in relationships that are sometimes abusive?
- Is a contact name and phone number provided on the literature?

Have you asked the shelter about its needs?

- Has a contact been made between your church and the nearest shelter for battered women?
- Has the pastor ever called the shelter to inquire how the church might assist in its work (for example, painting a room, moving a woman and her children, childcare, food treats at Christmas, spiritual counseling)?

Is dating violence discussed in youth group?

- Has the youth pastor been informed about the prevalence and severity of dating violence, even among church teens?
- Has information on dating violence been provided in a place where a teen can see it in privacy?
- Has the issue been raised from time to time in youth meetings,

together with suggestions on how to respond to violence and how to help friends who have been abused?

- Is there ongoing discussion about healthy and unhealthy interpersonal relationships?

Is abuse discussed in premarital counseling programs?

- Is printed information on abuse (such as a brochure) given to all couples who undergo premarital counseling prior to their wedding?

- Are couples asked whether there has ever been an incidence of violence in their relationship?

- Are couples admonished to live violence-free lives and offered suggestions for dealing with anger and disappointment?

Have sermons condemned abuse in the home?

- Has the pastor ever preached a full message on abuse or family violence?

- Is the congregation reminded periodically that family living needs to be violence-free?

- When families are discussed, does the pastor mention that many families do not fit standard cultural and church ideals for family life?

NO PLACE FOR ABUSE

In many corners of the world, the Christian family is considered sacred. It may be sacred—but is it safe?

Wounding and betrayal by someone who is (or has been) loved and trusted is a central feature of most forms of abuse. Like Jesus in the garden of Gethsemane, who was seeking relief from the heat, shelter from the crowds and privacy to pray when Judas led the soldiers to his place of refuge, victims of battery are often assaulted in the very place where they have been taught to expect rest and renewal, the family home.

We have tried to draw attention to the inconsistency between the high priority evangelicals place on the family and the relative paucity of programs and resources for women and men experiencing family crisis. We believe that there is both a biblical mandate and sociological evidence to support violence-free family living so that women, men and children can live without fear. There is sound biblical—as well as social science—justification for listening to the voices of those who have been silenced and offering practical and emotional support in their search for wholeness. Offering hope and modeling compassion are the twin pillars on which Christians must respond to victims of violence within and beyond the walls of the faith community.

Our churches are no place for abuse. They ought to be well equipped with men and women of vision who are able and willing to apply the healing balm of Gilead to the wounds created by distress and suffering. Our homes are no place for abuse. They ought to contain believers, male or female, young or old, who resist physical force as a means of resolving disagreements and disappointments. The programs our congregations support and the ministries in which we are engaged ought to serve our constituencies and communities alike. Compassion is everyone's business. It needs to start at home. It needs to be encouraged in our congregations, the places where we seek guidance and strength.

May God grant us eyes to see the suffering of women and men around the world, ears to hear their sometimes silent cries for help, hearts that are moved to respond to their pain and feet that are willing to accompany victims on their healing journey.

5

Searching the Scriptures

We are told that batterers abuse those in their family because in this manner they achieve the results they are seeking. Frequently the abuser convinces his family members that his treatment of them is in response to their own misdeeds. Victims are humiliated, degraded, shamed, reproached, made to feel inadequate and guilt-ridden.

Thus they are coerced into compliance with the perpetrator's wishes. Whether by physical, sexual or emotional abuse, abusers are able to exercise control over the household. The harm done to individual members is ignored or justified. Frequently the reproach falls on the victims rather than on the offender. If they had only been more prayerful, more submissive, more careful not to arouse anger, the problem would not have arisen. But this is not where the Bible puts the responsibility. The Bible says that the offender is at fault: "In your hearts you devise wrongs; your hands deal out violence on earth" (Ps 58:2). We fail to understand that abuse hurts the abuser. "The trouble he causes recoils on himself; his violence comes down on his own head" (Ps 7:16 NIV). His own spiritual life is drastically imperiled (Prov 2:6-15; Is 58:4; 1 Pet 3:7).

THE SCRIPTURAL WITNESS

The power of the Spirit works not only to restrain evildoers but also to empower those who would obey the biblical command to deliver the helpless from the hand of the violent, to correct those of the family of faith who fall into sin, to set free those who are oppressed, to rebuke, admonish and instruct. Let us, the people of God, be instructed by the Scriptures.

Both the Old and the New Testaments vigorously condemn violence of many sorts. A major theme is God's abhorrence and denunciation of violence. Such behavior is a characteristic of sinful people and brings the judgment of God (Ps 11:5-6; Ezek 7:11; Joel 3:19; Amos 3:10; Obad 10; Hab 2:17; Zeph 1:9). Because of violence, the earth was destroyed:

> Now the earth was corrupt in God's sight, and the earth was filled with violence. . . . And God said to Noah, "I have determined to make an end of all flesh, for the earth is filled with violence because of them." (Gen 6:11, 13)

Violence is associated with Satan (Ezek 28:16). It is accompanied by many sorts of wrong attitudes and conduct (Is 59:6-8; Jer 6:7; 22:17; Jon 3:8). The wicked drink "the wine of violence" (Prov 4:17), and the unfaithful "have a craving for violence" (Prov 13:2 NIV). Offenders develop a way of life sustained by their violence (Ps 73:4-8). Hebrew law made special provision to prevent violence within the home. Even a household slave was not to be treated abusively.

> If a man hits a manservant or maidservant in the eye and destroys it, he must let the servant go free to compensate for the eye. And if he knocks out the tooth of a manservant or maidservant, he must let the servant go free to compensate for the tooth. (Ex 21:26-27 NIV)

Proverbs also addresses violence in the home.

> Those who trouble their households will inherit wind. . . .
> The fruit of the righteous is a tree of life,

but violence takes lives away. (Prov 11:29-30)

Do not lie in wait like an outlaw against the home of the
    righteous;
  do no violence to the place where the righteous live.
(Prov 24:15)

The New International Version offers an interesting alternative
translation for a famous passage on divorce: "'I hate a man's covering
his wife with violence as well as with his garment,' says the LORD Almighty" (Mal 2:16 NIV marg.). According to the New Testament, violent persons are not eligible for church leadership (1 Tim 3:3; Tit 1:7).

PATTERNS ACCOMPANYING ABUSE

With great frequency, verbal abuse accompanies physical or sexual
abuse. It is one of the most common forms employed to exercise control over another. Such abuse, of course, is not more appropriate if the
perpetrator is a woman. As James remarked, the tongue can bless God
or abuse one made in the image of God (Jas 3:9). Jesus spoke most
poignantly of the damage that wrongful speech can inflict on another:
"If you insult a brother or sister, you will be liable to the council; and
if you say, 'You fool,' you will be liable to the hell of fire" (Mt 5:22).
Why is it so hurtful to call another person stupid or a fool? Because it
leaves that individual feeling less than human, unable to think things
through or to see issues clearly. A proverb sums this up well: "The
tongue has the power of life and death, and those who love it will eat
its fruit" (Prov 18:21 NIV). And the psalmist prayed, "Let the heads of
those who surround me be covered with the trouble their lips have
caused" (Ps 140:9 NIV).

Word twisting is another "crazy-making" technique of the abuser.
Victims can be confused and overwhelmed by the adroit manner in
which offenders distort what they have said to turn their own words
against them. "All day long they twist my words; they are always plot-
ting to harm me," cried the psalmist (Ps 56:5 NIV).

A similar technique is to declare that what was said was only in jest. "What's the matter? Can't you take a joke?" In this way, the victim becomes even more bewildered as to what is really happening. She doubts her own sanity. Malachi 2:17 decries those who call right wrong and wrong right.

A further tool in an offender's arsenal is that of threats. The psalmist says, "In their arrogance they threaten oppression" (Ps 73:8 NIV). The mouth of the wicked "is full of curses and lies and threats; trouble and evil are under his tongue" (Ps 10:7 NIV). Threats can leave a victim constantly fearful, unable to develop a secure and confident attitude. The New Testament speaks of threats as being the work of the wicked (Acts 4:17, 21, 29; 9:1) and commands believers not to threaten those in their own household (Eph 6:9).

More distressing yet is the use of scriptural distortions to oppress women and justify abuse. J. Lee Grady, editor of *Charisma* magazine, wrote,

> There is an epidemic of domestic abuse spreading through the church, and most Christian leaders are not addressing this problem. It is usually swept under the rug because pastors feel helplessly untrained in how to counsel abusers (or, in some tragic cases, because the pastors themselves are abusing their wives). And sadly, in some instances, pastors actually use Bible verses about wifely submission to fuel this epidemic of abuse.[1]

In 1966 the General Conference of the Wesleyan Church went even further:

> While we understand there are differing interpretations among us on the role of the husband and wife in the home, we totally reject any exercise of abuse by one spouse . . . by twisting these scriptures out of context. Such abuse is sin, and the sinner should be called to repent and to cease all such behavior.[2]

When faced with an abusive situation, Paul wrote, "We have renounced secret and shameful ways; we do not use deception, nor do we distort the word of God" (2 Cor 4:2 NIV).

QUOTING PAUL

There are certain doctrines being propounded nowadays that lend themselves to abuse. Even the writings of the apostle Paul are distorted to provide justification for abuse. The apostle Peter was already aware that there was a problem and gave a specific warning:

> Consider the patience of our Lord as providing an opportunity for salvation, just as our beloved brother Paul wrote to you according to the wisdom given to him, speaking in all his letters concerning these things. In the letters are some things that are difficult to understand which those who are ignorant and unstable distort, as they do the other writings, thereby leading to destructive ends. And you, O beloved, watch out now that you have been forewarned, lest you also become led astray by the deception of mistaken legalism and fall away from your own firm footing. (2 Pet 3:15-17, my translation)

Actually, the Bible contains a number of warnings that those who prophesy in the Lord's name don't necessarily have things straight. Jesus declared, "You will know them by their fruits" (Mt 7:16).

In the world of contemporary Christianity, the issue of authority in the home is hotly contended. We can do no better than to follow the example of the noble Bereans who "examined the scriptures every day to see whether these things were so" (Acts 17:11). The Scriptures emphasize the power of moral influence, loving support, kindly guidance and responsible conduct toward members of the family. When we turn to dynamics in the family, the issues of power and control are essential to address. We must begin, of course, with what Jesus had to say. Always he calls us to consider our guiding principles carefully. He warns that some "have let go of the commands of God and are holding on to the traditions of men" (Mk 7:8 NIV). He maintained that the wielding of power imperiled intimacy (Jn 15:15).

THE PROTECTION OF CHILDREN

The protection of children is a theme sounded frequently in the Bible (for example, Deut 14:29; Job 31:17; Mt 18:2-6; Jas 1:27), but it is often forgotten when the church is informed of an abusive situation. One-third of all abused women are battered during their pregnancy, with the majority of blows being delivered to the abdomen and breasts. The March of Dimes identifies prenatal abuse as one of the leading causes of birth defects. Other results of such abuse include premature birth, miscarriage, learning difficulties and emotional problems. Although the Bible speaks of prenatal influence, this is usually disregarded when there is a situation of abuse within a local congregation. Churches will do much to protect the unborn from the hands of an abortionist but little to protect the unborn from batterers. Of all mothers who die in the United States during pregnancy, childbirth or the first year following delivery, 27 percent are murdered by their intimate partners.[3]

The U.S. Department of Justice concludes that "between 50-70 percent of men who abuse their partners also abuse their children."[4] Even children who are not themselves abused suffer serious trauma as they sense that their mother is being hurt. The list of emotional, psychological and spiritual problems that can develop in those who witness the abuse of their mothers is even more appalling. All too often we fail to recognize the harm that is done to children who are in the home while the abuse is occurring. Parents can assume that they are upstairs or asleep or otherwise occupied, but recent research suggests that as many as 90 percent of children from violent homes are aware that their father is battering their mother.[5] Some observe the actual event, others hear and hide, while still others observe the wounds and bruises.

The Presidential Task Force on Violence and the Family of the American Psychological Association found that "a child's exposure to his father abusing his mother is the strongest risk factor for transmitting violent behavior from one generation to the next."[6] Michele Penta of the Family Safety Project of Caritas Holy Family Hospital in Methuen, Massachusetts, reports that by age three, children can identify stress and that by age four they may try to intervene to protect their mother.[7] Furthermore, stress causes a child's brain to develop differently from that of an unstressed child. The damage is irreversible.[8]

According to the Massachusetts Department of Youth Services, children who witness violence in their home are

- six times more likely to commit suicide;
- twenty-four times more likely to commit sexual assault;
- 50 percent more likely to abuse drugs and alcohol;
- 74 percent more likely to commit crimes against others.[9]

Over 60 percent of murderers between the ages of fifteen and twenty-one are incarcerated for having killed their mother's abuser.[10]

Where is the church's concern for those of the household of faith? Do we not have a responsibility to intervene before sons are driven to such desperate acts?

> Thus says the Lord:
> Execute justice in the morning,
>   and deliver from the hand of the oppressor
>   anyone who has been robbed,
> or else my wrath will go forth like fire. (Jer 21:12)

THE STRANGERS WITHIN OUR GATES

The Scriptures repeatedly speak of the imperative of caring for the alien and the stranger. The people of Israel were reminded that they themselves had once been oppressed in an alien land: "You shall not oppress a resident alien; you know the heart of an alien, for you were aliens in the land of Egypt" (Ex 23:9).

In this present time, many strangers appear at our gate—refugees and immigrants who often have little command of the language or understanding of our laws and resources. Such people are exceedingly vulnerable and have few resources to protect themselves from domestic abuse. The rural communities in which some have been relocated are hard pressed to provide adequate services, especially when there are language and cultural challenges. It is here that a missions-minded church may serve afflicted aliens who have no-where else to turn. Churches are often able to locate food, clothing, emergency funding, child care and lodging far more expeditiously than a public agency. Here is an opportunity to demonstrate the love of Christ to those who come from beyond our borders, to reach beyond cultural differences to a universal language of compassion and grace.

THE BIBLICAL CALL FOR INTERVENTION

The Bible issues a strong moral mandate to come to the aid of those who are in distress.

> Again I saw all the oppressions that are practiced under the sun. Look, the tears of the oppressed—with no one to comfort them! On the side of their oppressors there was power—with no one to comfort them. (Eccl 4:1; see also Jer 21:12; 22:3)

Indeed Jeremiah equated defending the cause of the poor and needy as an essential ingredient of knowing the Lord (Jer 22:15-16). Tragically, there has often been a failure to address volatile situations that arise within our own families of faith. We need to reexamine our reluctance.

Often, well-meaning Christians assume that what happens within the household is a matter between God and the family. They may refuse to become involved in situations of domestic abuse because they "don't know whose story to believe." Assigning guilt is not our prerogative (see Mt 7:1; Rom 14:4). In many instances, there is some contribution to the malaise on both sides, but that does not justify abuse. The issue is not to "take sides" but to stand against abuse, regardless of who may be the perpetrator. It is best to take the side of safety, to adopt measures that will restore calm to a troubled situation.

It is important to understand that sometimes we are not the best qualified to intervene; law enforcement officials are trained and equipped for those tasks. It may be our duty to intervene, however, and to call for outside help in an appropriate manner. It is not lack of

faith to initiate such measures. Rather, it is honoring God to "pursue
what makes for peace" (Rom 14:19).

The Bible does not represent faith communities as being perfect.
The churches of the New Testament era were beset with perfectly awful problems, and the apostles, as they wrote, made no secret of their
concern or of their efforts to remedy bad situations. Forthrightness
can lead to healing, but expending efforts on concealment only causes
the problem to fester.

THE CALL FOR RELIGIOUS LEADERS

Those in positions of religious leadership are particularly called to assume responsibility in cases of abuse. The charge is spelled out in
great detail in the thirty-fourth chapter of Ezekiel:

> You have not taken care of the weak. You have not tended the
> sick or bound up the injured. You have not gone looking for
> those who have wandered away and are lost. Instead, you have
> ruled them with force and cruelty. . . . As surely as I live, says
> the Sovereign LORD, you abandoned my flock and left them to
> be attacked by every wild animal. And though you were my
> shepherds, you didn't search for my sheep when they were lost.
> . . . I now consider these shepherds my enemies, and I will hold
> them responsible for what has happened to my flock. I will take
> away their right to feed the flock, and I will stop them from
> feeding themselves. (Ezek 34:4, 8, 10 NLT)

Have we understood the demand that God places on the leaders of
our faith communities? Since the shepherds have failed, God himself
will become the pastor of the flock. He has not been blind to the mistreatment of the sheep, to the exploitation of the weak by the strong.
There must be a reckoning.

> As for you, my flock, thus says the Lord GOD: I shall judge be-
> tween sheep and sheep, between rams and goats: Is it not enough
> for you to feed on the good pasture, but you must tread down

with your feet the rest of your pasture? When you drink of clear water, must you foul the rest with your feet? And must my sheep eat what you have trodden with your feet, and drink what you have fouled with your feet?

Therefore, thus says the Lord GOD to them: I myself will judge between the fat sheep and the lean sheep. Because you pushed with flank and shoulder, and butted at all the weak animals with your horns until you scattered them far and wide, I will save my flock, and they shall no longer be ravaged; and I will judge between sheep and sheep. (Ezek 34:17-22)

Faithful shepherding consists partly of the obligation to defend the sheep who have been victimized by others in the flock. We have indeed allowed the stronger to victimize the weaker. All too often, the church has found it acceptable to hang back when it comes to issues of domestic abuse. But "remember, it is sin to know what you ought to do and then not to do it" (Jas 4:17 NLT). How very often we have failed to respond to God's call! "Those who oppress the poor insult their Maker, but helping the poor honors him" (Prov 14:31 NLT).

6

Man and Woman

Dimensions of Their Union

THE VIEW FROM THE GARDEN AND WOMAN

To gain deeper understanding of the relationship between men and women, we must begin with the book of Genesis, since the Bible is our only infallible rule of faith and practice. In a marvelously poetic story, we are told of a wise God who made all things and saw that they were good—that is, until it comes to the creation of humankind. Then God saw that it was "not good" that the man should be alone. Humanity, made in God's image, must be relational as God is relational, sharing mutual love and joy and wholeness.

In the creation story, male and female are made equally in the image of God, as woman is drawn from the very substance of man, to share his dreams, his intellect, his emotions, his spirituality. Greek tradition held that woman was made of an inferior substance, a cruel trick of the gods to despoil the potential of man. Hebrew tradition tells of a helper who is of a shared essence, a blessed gift from the true and living God. Woman was bestowed to save man from loneliness.

The creation of the family is celebrated with Adam's song: "This at last is bone of my bones and flesh of my flesh" (Gen 2:23). The two became one flesh, naked and unashamed, joyful in their togetherness, tender and caring in a newfound relationship.

This garden relationship is still possible for those who seek it according to God's guidelines, as husbands and wives are able to share themselves freely. The Song of Solomon contains a recurring image of a garden as a place of lovemaking and delight (Song 4:12, 15-16; 5:1; 6:2). This walled garden accommodates two people deeply committed to each other. There they may walk together as did the first pair (Amos 3:3). The deeply satisfying and exclusive bond is intended to last throughout life, a renewable resource. The Bible speaks of marital love as a world of wonder.

> Three things are too wonderful for me;
> four I do not understand:
> the way of an eagle in the sky,
> the way of a snake on a rock,
> the way of a ship on the high seas,
> and the way of a man with a girl. (Prov 30:18-19)

We are given a sublime picture of the pinnacles of married love in the Song of Solomon. Each of the two partners seeks and cherishes a communion of mind, soul and body. They perceive the beauty of one another's body, the joy of being made one. Like Adam and Eve, they are naked and unashamed, ready to share their inmost souls. Affirmed as a person by her husband ("his speech is most sweet," Song 5:16), the bride is free to communicate her thoughts, experiences and emotions, as is the bridegroom. Their world is marked by a shared intimacy that is possible only because each is confident in the other. There can be no hint of abuse, control, humiliation, betrayal, belittling or manipulation.

Such union grows only in the garden of mutual respect and sharing. A wife who is considered of less worth than her husband cannot bring her full self to the marital union, nor can the husband know the

joy of full communion. God's plan involves the two participants' total
beings. They have a new awareness of all the beauty around them,
and they burst into rapturous poetic expression:

> Your rounded thighs are like jewels,
>> the work of a master hand.
> Your navel is a rounded bowl
>> that never lacks mixed wine.
> Your belly is a heap of wheat,
>> encircled with lilies.
> Your two breasts are like two fawns,
>> twins of a gazelle. (Song 7:1-3)

How is it that this remarkable description of marital love is so often read devotionally? Why do people use it to guide them to an ado-
ration and love of Christ as the heavenly bridegroom? Hymns and
Christian devotional literature throughout the centuries have been
heavily dependent on the language and concepts of the Song of Solomon, and this is no mistake. The spiritual in our nature lies very
close to the sexual. The union depicted in the Song is exalted to the
highest pinnacle of human lovemaking. What better way to meditate
on our seeking of God than in the sublime language with which Solomon's song vests human love?

FROM GARDEN TO DEGRADATION

The Bible makes a strong differentiation between sex that enriches the
human spirit and that which degrades it. Scripture speaks candidly of
the sordid uses to which sex can be put: manipulation and exploitation, violence and aggression. It can debase the relationship, demean
the person and violate the soul. Victims can be left with wounds that
will last the rest of their life. And abusers, if they take responsibility
for their deeds, are left with intolerable guilt. If sex is so powerful that
it can bind two people into one flesh, then it must be used reverently
and with great caution.

"Let marriage be held in honor by all, and let the marriage bed be kept undefiled," urges the writer of the epistle to the Hebrews (13:4). Though sometimes wrongfully used, this Bible passage was not given to justify sexual abuse within marriage but to affirm the goodness of matrimonial union. *Timios*, the Greek adjective used here to describe marriage, means not only "esteemed" or "honored" but also *conferring* honor, esteem or respect. We might alternatively translate the passage, "Marriage confers honor on all, and the marriage bed should be untainted."

Tragically, there is much that can spoil a blessed union. As the passage goes on to point out, fornication and adultery destroy the bond and create a terrible breach of trust. But there are many other kinds of betrayal that can rupture the bond. To dishonor the body, mind or sensibilities of one's mate cannot fail to flaw the union. The apostle Paul understood this:

> For this is the will of God, your sanctification: that you abstain from fornication; that each one of you know how to control your own body in holiness and honor, not with lustful passion, like the Gentiles who do not know God; that no one wrong or exploit a brother or sister in this matter, because the Lord is an avenger in all these things, just as we have already told you beforehand and solemnly warned you. For God did not call us to impurity but in holiness. Therefore whoever rejects this rejects not human authority but God, who also gives his Holy Spirit to you. (1 Thess 4:3-8).

Women are frequently demeaned, even in Christian circles, by sexual harassment. Yet the church is called to repudiate all obscenity (Eph 5:4; Col 3:8). Dirty jokes are not funny; indeed they can inflict far more harm than we might imagine.

Abuse of any kind—whether verbal, emotional, physical or sexual—destroys true intimacy. Within the marriage bed, honor and holiness are essential. First Thessalonians 4:4 may alternatively be translated "that each of you know how to hold a spouse in holiness and honor," since *skeuos* (literally "vessel") means both one's own body and one's spouse's. Demanding sexual acts that are demeaning, offensive or repugnant does not respect the other. It is to defraud one's partner of her or his dignity.

There are many kinds of sexual abuse. Perhaps the most common form of abuse in Christian homes is coercion. Taking Paul's dictate that neither party should defraud the other of sexual fulfillment (1 Cor 7:5), husbands too often demand sexual submission of unwilling wives. Many women are defrauded by the sexual treatment that they receive—whether rape, coercion or manipulation. They are not allowed free choice in the relationship and may end up as toys, sex objects or slaves. Paul is clear that each partner holds power over the body of the other, and each is to show consideration for the other (1 Cor 7:3-4). Withholding of conjugal rights clearly constitutes cruelty, while persons caught in the coils of sexual addiction frequently inflict untold misery on their spouses.

Rape, even in marriage, is reprehensible and receives condemnation in the stories of the Old Testament. In 1 Corinthians, rapists are singled out as being unworthy of the kingdom of God. Though usually concealed by translation, the word *harpax* is used for one who commits rape (1 Cor 5:10-11; 6:9). *The Greek-English Lexicon of the New Testament and Other Early Christian Literature* gives as its first rendering of the word *harpax* as the word "rapacious."[1] In the context of the epistle, this word occurs in conjunction with perpetrators of other sorts of sexual sin. Their conduct is not acceptable in the household of God.

THE ABUSE OF WHICH NO ONE SPEAKS

A therapist told of a client who went to the board of elders in her church to report that she was being abused. "The sex part is really bad," she said, but there was no elaboration. The elders insisted that it was her duty to comply with her husband's demands, although they did not inquire into the horrifying nature of those demands.[2]

Persons trying to help victims are sometimes mystified by the willingness of a victim to reveal that they have been abused yet remain vague about what happened. This may be indicative of sexual abuse that the victim does not dare to reveal. She fears that she will be viewed as insensitive herself if she were to name the outrage to which she has been subjected; the more ugly it has been, the greater reticence on the part of the victim. The shame and humiliation in which she has been engaged render it well nigh impossible to speak.

The abuse may involve being forced into performing sex acts that she does not wish. This may include demands to sleep with the husband's friends, to view pornographic material or to engage in group sex, intercourse with an animal or participation in "key clubs," where sexual partners are exchanged. Violent sex creates its own aftermath of injury. One victim suffering from such a trauma told of how her husband sat beside her in the emergency room, inventing a story to offer as an explanation to the gynecological surgeon.[3]

Remember that the story of abuse is not told all at once. Often a victim will tell one part to one individual and another part at another time to someone else. The story is painful to tell, and it takes patience to gain an understanding of the whole scope. Indeed, compassionate listening does not require that everything be divulged.

BETRAYAL OF TRUST

Many a child in a Christian household has known the agony of betrayal by those they trusted. Aunts, uncles, grandparents, siblings and parents have all been guilty of manipulating naive children for their own sexual gratification. All too often Christian sentiments and twisted Scriptures are utilized to serve the offender's purpose. However,

> If any of you put a stumbling block [cause to sin, shock, fill with disgust] before one of these little ones who believe in me, it would be better for you if a great millstone were fastened around your neck and you were drowned in the depth of the sea. (Mt 18:6)

When the perpetrator is a Christian or uses religious arguments, the child becomes even more confused and often carries scars that remain through his or her life.

Any kind of abuse destroys the joyous spontaneity that should characterize marital union. Some women's shelters have pointed their clients to a psalm that expresses well the feelings of a victim:

> It is not enemies who taunt me—
> > I could bear that;
> it is not adversaries who deal insolently with me—
> > I could hide from them.
> But it is you, my equal,
> > my companion, my familiar friend,
> with whom I kept pleasant company;
> > we walked in the house of God with the throng. (Ps 55:12-14)

Gone are the delight and the trust that must be basic components of sexual intimacy at its most profound level.

1

Does the Suffering of an Abused Woman Bring Salvation to Her Husband?

1 PETER REVISITED

Recently a woman went to confession and poured out to the priest a story of the abuse she was enduring. He encouraged her to go home and demonstrate a more loving attitude toward her husband in order to win him to Christ, according to the instructions in 1 Peter 3:1-6. The priest concluded, "You really have nothing to fear. If he kills you, you'll be a martyr in heaven."[1]

Another woman was wakened at two in the morning by furious blows wielded by her husband with a child's metal tricycle.[2] In terror she consulted a popular women's speaker and was told to return to her husband in order that her gentleness might lead him to conversion. Again, the text was 1 Peter 3:1-6. Underlying the advice was the assumption that her suffering would result in his salvation.

First Peter 3:1-6 is often used to argue that women should endure domestic abuse heroically in order to convert their husbands. In point of fact, the passage addresses spousal abuse only to insist that husbands honor their wives as equals and that failure to do so will obstruct the abuser's prayer life. It is significant that New Testament calls for wifely submission are always constructed within a framework of mutuality (1 Cor 7:3-5; Eph 5:18-33; Col 3:13-19; 1 Pet 2:16-3:8) and always accompanied by specific directives to prevent abuse on the part of the husband (Eph 5:28-29; Col 3:19; 1 Pet 3:7).

A LETTER TO THE PERSECUTED

First Peter is essentially a letter addressed to those whom others viewed with hostility simply because they were Christians (1 Pet 4:13-16). The treatise deals with those who "are reviled for the name" and who suffer as Christians (4:14, 16). There is a threefold call to submission in 1 Peter: (1) by citizens to properly appointed authorities (2:13-16); (2) by slaves to masters (2:18); and (3) by wives to husbands (3:1-2).

Proper definition is important, as some faith groups insist that the Bible demands wifely obedience regardless of the husband's behavior. The word for submission is *hypotassō*, over against a somewhat related term, *hypakouō*. The latter denotes obedience and in 1 Peter is applied to a believer's obedience to Christ (1:2, 14, 22). But *hypotassō*, rather than *hypakouō,* is applied to wives in 1 Peter 3:1, 5, as well as in Ephesians 5:22, Colossians 3:18 and Titus 2:5. *Hypotassō* is rendered "accept" (NRSV) or "submit yourselves" (NIV, KJV, 1 Pet 2:13) but has a wide semantic range. We find implied synonyms in 2:17 ("honor," "love," "fear"). The literal meaning "to place oneself under," or in military parlance, "to draw up behind," developed other meanings: to serve as an ally, to attach to, identify or associate with, adhere to or relate in such a way as to make meaning.[3] The term also had the sense of loyalty and of orderly and accountable behavior.

In view of Peter's resolute insistence that obedience must be yielded to God rather than human beings (Acts 4:19; 5:29), one can hardly construe a believer's submission to civil authorities as absolute obedience. In no way can duty to state be placed higher than the dictates of God or of individual conscience. Rather, there is a call to

Christians to comply within the structures necessary for the peaceful functioning of society and to discharge all rightful obligations of citizenship. Since Christians met for worship in private houses, the household was particularly open to the inspection of those curious about the new faith. This occasioned special instruction to members of the family, especially women and slaves.

THE SUFFERING OF CHRIST

The passion of Christ is a recurring theme throughout the epistle (1 Pet 1:18-20; 2:21-25; 3:18–4:1; 4:13; 5:1), with assurance to believers that his sacrificial death had procured their salvation and that he would keep their souls safe if it became necessary for them to suffer "for the sake of the name." Sometimes those engaged in addressing domestic violence charge that the Father was abusive to the Son in sending him to Calvary. But this was the action of sinful human beings, not of God.

Christ came into the world to take on human flesh, to partake of our common experiences "tempted in every way, just as we are" (Heb 4:15 TNIV). He knew the joys and glories of human existence as well as its miseries and injustices. He entered the world knowing all too well the extent of abuse and atrocity that human beings are capable of heaping on one another. God enfleshed in human form was not to escape that terrible scourge. If he was to walk in a sinful world, he must be prepared for the consequences. It was his choice to identified with the lowly, the poor and the disenfranchised—those most vulnerable to abuse.

The Son came willingly at the Father's direction, yet both understood the mystic combination of free will and providence that are active in human affairs. The false trial, brutalization and ultimate crucifixion were engineered by power-hungry and corrupt individuals for their own purposes. As is so often the case, God does not rescind the option of free will, even when the choices are unspeakably evil.

Jesus himself fully understood the extent of the abuse as he stopped along the way to the cross and identified with the mistreatment of women. He too was experiencing what it was to be stripped naked, beaten, humiliated, mocked and ultimately murdered. He spoke of the increased vulnerability of pregnant women and those who are nursing, with small children in their arms. He asked, "If they do this when the wood is green, what will happen when it is dry?" (Lk 23:31).

FACING THE PARADOX

In Christ's suffering and death, we find a paradox, one of many to be found in Christian doctrine. How can we worship one God who is yet three distinct persons? How can Christ be both human and divine? How can the Scriptures be both the work of earthly mortals and breathed by the Holy Spirit? How can we explain the biblical affirmations of both free will and divine providence?

The Father did not stop the exercise of free will among those who had conspired against the Son, but he did bring meaning and redemptive grace to the event. Jesus pointed out that the Father could easily have sent legions of angels to deliver him (Mt 26:53), but that would have destroyed the very meaning that he sought. Greco-Roman dramas featured semi-divine beings in dire danger who were delivered at the last moment by *deus ex machina* (a god swung onto the stage by a mechanical device). For Jesus to have been so rescued would have been a denial of his full humanity. There was to be no superhuman fire escape. In his death, he was one with all who are oppressed, denigrated, deprived of justice.

The malefactors meant to do away with Jesus, to trash his person and trivialize his message and mission. But God transformed the atrocity and anguish and ignominy into a glorious instrument for the redemption of the human race.

Sometimes victims are encouraged to endure abuse as Jesus did. Yet we need to make a differentiation between his voluntary suffering to procure our redemption and his ability in other situations to defend himself against verbal abuse (Mk 3:22-30; Jn 8:48-59) and the threat of violence (Lk 4:28-30; Jn 8:59; 10:31-39). Being a doormat in an abusive situation is *not* following the example of Jesus. In some situations women submit to abuse because they feel they are being punished for some misdeed. This is to deny the power and efficacy of Christ's sacrifice. He bore our sins so that we might be free from them (1 Pet 2:24). Women can accept the deliverance that is so freely offered as they contemplate different purposes of suffering:

The suffering of Christ

- was the result of his free choice;
- permitted sin in order to do away with sin at a far deeper level;
- was undertaken to fulfill a grand purpose in redeeming humanity.

The suffering of victims of domestic abuse

- is not their free choice—it is inflicted upon them;
- allows the perpetrator to continue the sinful conduct;
- stems from a crime against humanity.

The results are destructive for offender, victim, children and the wider society.

PETER'S WORDS TO SLAVES

First in Peter's letter comes advice and consolation for slaves who are mistreated (2:18-20), followed by the observation that Christ too was abused and mistreated (2:21-25) and then the directive to wives (3:1-6). The juxtaposition has led many to conclude that it is the will of God for both slaves and women to suffer as Christ suffered. First Peter makes a careful differentiation between the constructive behavior that should be expected from a Christian slave and the abuse he or she might suffer as a consequence of professing faith in Christ. To be beaten for unruly conduct brought no reward from God, but suffering for the sake of one's faith was another matter (2:20).

PETER'S WORDS TO WIVES

During a persecution, it was not unknown for a husband to deliver his Christian wife to the authorities.[4] A wife in such circumstances might do well to reveal her spiritual convictions only after her husband had been won over by her grace-filled lifestyle. According to 1 Peter 3:1-4, "submissive" wives should demonstrate exemplary conduct, and their style of dress should avoid characteristics commonly thought to be most aggravating to husbands. Braided hair was considered enormously seductive, and gold, the mark of a harlot.

The call for slaves to submit can be seen as a challenge to render responsible and constructive behavior even in unjust circumstances, but not to surrender their faith or the dictates of their conscience. The call for wifely submission is significant because in the most critical area the wife is encouraged to stand her ground.

Classical literature abounds in expressions of the aggravation men felt at the free practice of women's religion. They found the cults of women noisy, depraved, debauched, abandoned, ridiculous and disgusting. By contrast, the Christian wife is to demonstrate her convictions with silence instead of clamor, decorum instead of depravity, faithfulness instead of promiscuity. Instead of worshiping the gods of her husband's family, as was expected of a dutiful member of a household, she aims instead to win him over to her faith.

Her submission is not a renunciation of her own spiritual capacity or conscience, any more than is the decree to be subject to governmental authorities. "Submission" here involves scrupulous fulfillment of all legitimate obligations of marriage while upholding freedom to serve Christ. The aim is not subordination but conversion, not by enabling what is wrong but by persisting in what is right.

The women addressed have made a radical decision about their personal faith. As daughters they were expected to worship the household gods of their fathers' families. The text presupposes that these women will make their own decisions about religious matters. A *sine manu* marriage, literally "without hand," would make them still members of their father's household, still bound to the familial religion.

A *cum manu* marriage transferred a woman's guardianship to her husband and thereby transferred her allegiance to the gods of his hearth. While the text seems to favor a woman's alignment with her husband rather than with her birth family, personal faith lies quite outside. The directive is issued to women whose husbands disapprove of their spiritual convictions, and to these a wife should hold fast (1 Pet 5:9). Her conduct should be irreproachable, but her faith is her own; and she should be fearless in maintaining it.

ASSESSING HUSBAND-WIFE RELATIONSHIPS

The relationship of Sarah and Abraham was held up as a model of marriage (1 Pet 3:6). In fact, it was more mutual than a cursory reading of the preceding text might envisage. Certainly in the biblical account, Sarah accompanied Abraham as a faithful companion on his journey of faith. The observation that Sarah "obeyed" her husband must be contrasted with God's command to Abraham to heed and obey his wife (Gen 21:12).

First Peter 3:6 tells us that Christian women as daughters of Sarah should be fearless in doing what is right. Perhaps as a deterrent to possible abusive behavior by believing husbands, Peter gave a set of instructions outlining the norms for Christian family living. The section begins with "in the same way" (3:7), connecting the man's submission to that of the wife (3:1-6), to counsel for household slaves (2:18-25) and to the more general earlier commands (2:13, 17).

However, the text calls for husbands to honor their spouses as joint heirs. An heir is one who receives an inheritance and manages it. The concept of a woman as joint heir with her husband would have been radical in both Jewish and Roman society. Here women are presented as coheirs of the "gracious gift of life" (1 Pet 3:7), equal in the sight of God and of the believing community. The allusion to the wife as a weaker vessel seems to be an acknowledgment that men possess greater physical strength and should therefore refrain from using it abusively. The husband who lived "according to knowledge," affirming his wife in honor and equality, would find power in his prayers. Abuse or denigration would bring an obstruction to his prayers (3:7), a deterrent to the husband's spiritual life and growth. Here we find an echo of Isaiah's warning that God will not hear the prayers of the violent (Is 58:4).

CAN ENDURING ABUSE
BRING ABOUT A SPOUSE'S SALVATION?

Enabling human beings to perpetuate their sin certainly does not open the doors of salvation to them. A woman may suffer for her faith, but brutality at the hands of her husband is another matter. The mandates of 1 Peter 2:18–3:8 are not a blanket call for slaves and women to endure abuse. Suffering that allows a perpetrator to continue abusive conduct can never be redemptive. Rather it brings an enablement of sin that is damaging to the soul of both perpetrator and victim. In many of today's societies, there are legitimate avenues of recourse for a laborer or a wife to gain relief from abusive treatment. Where there is legal redress for abuse, patient endurance is more likely to be seen as codependence than as exemplary conduct.

DAUGHTERS OF SARAH

How may these passages, written to ancient believers caught in persecution for their faith, be applied to present-day situations that involve no oppression for one's faith? First, believers must demonstrate a lifestyle that can withstand criticism. Second, many biblical passages condemn violence, and verbal and sexual abuse. Christian women can profitably be directed toward passages that call on communities of faith as well as victims to take positive steps to stop the wrongdoing.

Third, God calls husband and wife, as coheirs, to live joyfully with respect and love for each other. A distortion of this balance brings obstruction not only of effective prayer but also of true communion in marriage. Jesus specifically condemned one person's exercising dominance over another (Mt 20:25-28; Mk 10:42-45) and declared that it hinders intimacy (Jn 15:15). All believers are called to unity of spirit, sympathy, love for one another, a tender heart and a humble mind. Christianity is based on mutuality, interdependence and equality. Shared decision making is the pattern sanctified by Scripture and proven effective in human experience.

8

A Concern for
the Christian Family?

The Dangers of Idolization and Idealization

After an abusive incident, a missionary child asked, "Are we going to go downstairs and pretend to be a happy Christian family again?"[1] The pretense of being a happy Christian family only confuses and compounds the tragedy of abuse against women and children. To deny, minimize or ignore the problem obstructs the work of the Holy Spirit. The Scriptures offer the hope of healing for troubled families, but it requires honesty, faith, hard work and the support of the believing community.

As people of faith, we hate to admit that the problem exists in our midst. As a result, we offer few resources to people in our own churches, whether the problem is incest, rape, battering, intimidation or verbal, sexual or emotional abuse. We hesitate to believe the victim who summons up enough courage to seek help in the church. Often our biggest priority is making sure that no one knows, that the behavior of a supposedly model church member is not revealed, that the status quo is not shaken.

Abuse is almost always covered with secrecy. Often persons caught in oppression do not even recognize their own abuse, much less name it. Few, especially in times past, have dared to reveal a secret that would disgrace both themselves and their family. Central to the issue is that of a theology that emphasizes male dominance and female subservience within the home. Twisted theology wreaks incalculable harm. All too often this rationale has lent itself to abuse. Various research studies have demonstrated a higher incidence of problems in authoritarian households: The long tentacles of oppression may furtively reach to all members of the family and create a need for escape.

BIBLICAL PATTERNS

The Bible is devastatingly honest. The sacred texts make no effort to deny or conceal sad realities. Many of the families described in the Bible are perfectly awful, not to mention incredibly dysfunctional. Cain kills Abel; Joseph's brothers sell him into slavery; Jacob practices deceitful stratagems on his father, brother and father-in-law and barely escapes with his life. Abraham and Isaac both allow their wives to be inducted into other men's harems and even deny their marital relationship. Adultery, incest, murder and jealousy punctuate other accounts of family life.

The good news is that God still works in families, even rotten ones. God is still the God of Abraham and Isaac and Jacob. Again and again the Bible promises grace to the children and children's children of those who love and trust God. And repeatedly special mercy is shown to families, whether those of Noah or Rahab or the Philippian jailer. The "begats" represent believing folk who struggled to impart their faith to their children as they ate simple meals and walked along the roads with them or told them bedtime stories. The faith of parents still ignites the faith of children. It is not automatic or without struggle, but homegrown faith is still contagious. The promise of salvation is still there for those who will believe, and also for their children (Acts 2:39).

SAVING A LIFE VERSUS SAVING A MARRIAGE

It is critically important to think biblically about the family. While the family has great importance in Scripture, it is not accorded ultimate status. Jesus indicated that there were other priorities, higher than those of family. His followers must love him far more than they do their own father, mother, spouse, children, brothers or sisters—even more than their own life (Lk 14:26).

His disciples had left their families to follow the Master's call (Mt 4:21-22; Lk 5:11; 18:28). These separations were temporary but nevertheless real. Like the brothers of Jesus, Peter was later to engage in missionary travels with his wife (1 Cor 9:5), but his remark that "we have left all" (Lk 18:28 NIV) indicates that husbands and wives were not always together during our Lord's earthly ministry. Jesus acknowledged that the sacrifice had been made, and he pointed to a necessity higher than family togetherness.

Jesus also declared that his mission might drive families apart rather than bringing them together (Mt 10:35-37; Lk 12:51-53) and that loyalty to him must supersede family loyalty (Mt 8:21-22; Lk 9:59-62). He himself was homeless (Mt 8:20; Lk 9:58), and relationships with his family were sometimes strained. Some of the interchanges between Jesus and his mother are not altogether harmonious, and he recognized a kinship deeper than the biological one with those who heard the word of God and did it (Mt 12:46-50; Mk 3:31-35; Lk 8:19-21). His family understood him so little that at one point they came to take him away, having concluded that he was "out of his mind" (Mk 3:21).

Later his earthly siblings would become committed leaders in the church who shared important insights with their brothers and sisters in Christ, as the epistles of James and Jude attest. James, the brother of our Lord, was a pillar in the church at Jerusalem and a major influence in decision making at critical junctures in the process of world evangelization (Acts 15:13-21; 21:18-25; Gal 1:18-19; 2:9). Even in the holy family, solidarity did not come easily or without pain. It is not lack of faith to admit that there are difficulties within our families.

IDEALISM VERSUS REALITY

Is it possible that promoting an unrealistic view of family life can actually compound the problem? Glorifying marriage and prescribing rigid roles do not lead to healthy relationships. David Hempton writes of the disenchantment experienced by many children raised in evangelical homes:

> It is not surprising that a religious tradition which attracted the loyalty of millions of people world wide should have failed to sustain the faith of some of its own converts or capture the imagination of some of its own children. Many of its most famous leaders have experienced the shock and grief caused by the alienation from the tradition of their own children. . . . The list of casualties is too impressive to be merely accidental.[2]

Why is there so disproportionately large a group of disaffected among those who have been raised in evangelical homes? Was there within the family a dynamic that was inconsistent with the love and grace of Christ?

Hempton mentions elements that draw persons to the evangelical faith: love, forgiveness, grace and especially the person of Jesus Christ. Elements that repel include disillusionment with the conduct of significant Christian leaders and insensitive legalism as well as "doctrines and dogmas, and precepts and propositions." A young man struggling to undo the abusive patterns of his father remarked, "The churches sure get people confused when they teach about hard and fast roles in the family."[3] Consider how a well-known Christian psychologist characterized an attitude displayed by some of his clients: "We're *going* to have a perfect Christian marriage even if I have to *beat* you to get it!"[4]

A survey by George Barna's organization reveals that born-again Christians divorce at a higher rate (27 percent) than those who are not born again (24 percent). Among Christian denominations, Baptists had the highest rate (29 percent), while those belonging to non-denominational Protestant churches were even more likely to have experienced a divorce (34 percent). Likewise the Jewish faith community, which puts great emphasis on marriage and family, has a high divorce rate (30 percent). Among Christian groups, Catholics and Lutherans, with their emphasis on pastoral counseling, had the lowest rates.[5]

A concern for hurting families is more likely to lead to marriages that can be made whole. Within our churches, there must be freedom to acknowledge problems and to seek the support of fellow Christians. When the silence is broken, God's people can address the problem. Energies can be directed to healing instead of hiding. The biblical pattern is not to conceal abuse but to bring it to light and seek solutions. Let us confess that we are the imperfect and sinful people of God. We cannot be a forgiven people until we have confessed our failures and sought restitution and healing. It's messy and costly and embarrassing. But God can work when there is honesty. Separation is not necessarily failure. It may be the path to something far better. God's purposes for the family are higher than ours.

BIBLICAL METAPHORS OF MARRIAGE

We are fond of saying that marriage is a beautiful metaphor of God's love for his people. We must understand that a metaphor is a word picture that helps us comprehend what a speaker is trying to convey. If a young woman is told that her cheeks are roses, we understand that her cheeks do not actually have all the qualities of roses. They do not have thorns, are not rooted in dirt and will not attract bees or produce rosehips. And certainly we would not want to imply that a lovely young woman's cheeks were like roses in having a propensity to wither rapidly, to be subject to rot and to thrive on manure. It is important to know where the likeness begins and ends. In fact, there is only one quality that cheeks and roses share: a beautiful color. Even the fragrance is not the same, unless it is achieved with the help of a perfume bottle.

When the Bible speaks of God's marriage to Israel or of the church as the bride of Christ, the concept is a metaphor to help us understand the covenant relationship. What should be the closest and most meaningful human bond is selected to portray divine love. This does not mean that earthly marriage necessarily partakes of heavenly aspects but rather that what is potentially best in human experience is being used to give some understanding of a far more profound reality. The metaphor is intended to convey the tenderness and enduring fidelity of God, the lengths to which God will go to ensure the safety of his beloved.

Marriage as the most intimate of human ties is indeed used as a metaphor, but it is surely not an exemplar. We cannot possibly say that an abusive marriage is a picture of Christ's love for the church. Rather, Christ's love is an exemplar for what earthly marriage should be. The wedding of Christ to his bride, the church, lies in the future. In the meantime the heavenly bridegroom is assisting the bride to be fully developed spiritually, socially and morally. Both parties look forward to a joyous union.

A PICTURE OF A FAILED MARRIAGE

The biblical image of God's marriage to Israel is developed not at Sinai, where the covenant is made—I will be your God and you shall be my people (Ex 19:1-8)—but after Israel has broken faith with God. When there is no longer faithfulness to the one true God, we find the metaphor of the betrayed husband. He has given all, and the faithless wife has betrayed him. Actually, the concept is first introduced as a metaphor for an extremely bad marriage. Israel is the flagrantly unfaithful wife and God the heartbroken husband. Isaiah, Jeremiah, Ezekiel and Hosea all represent the covenant relationship of God and his people in terms of a destroyed marriage.

The theme is introduced by Hosea, who lived in the northern kingdom and prophesied in the last days before it fell to Assyria. His was the task of revealing the apostasy of Israel and calling the nation to repentance. God commanded Hosea to act out a parable symbolically. He was to take Gomer, a prostitute, as his wife. After she bore three children, her conduct was so wanton that Hosea divorced her.

She was set free to pursue her many lovers and suffer the consequences of her behavior. As the marriage had been broken, so had Israel's covenant with God: "You are not my people and I am not your God" (Hos 1:9). God declared, "She is not my wife, and I am not her husband" (2:2). How poignant is the anguish that Hosea expresses on behalf both of God and of himself.

Israel too had been adulterous, going after other gods, even though she had promised to be true to the Lord. Gone was the covenant that bound the Israelite people and the abundance and fertility with which God had blessed them. The separation was bitter for both parties. God mourned for his people, and Israel would at last realize that God's kindness and mercy are far better than the treachery of her paramours (2:7). Ultimately there would be reconciliation, but not until Israel had known the bitterness of alienation and divorce from the source of all true good.

Isaiah, Hosea's contemporary, took up the theme as he addressed the sins of the southern kingdom. Judah too had been an unfaithful wife (Is 54:4-6) who had been cast out and would not repent. God had divorced her because the marriage had been rendered meaningless, devoid of trust or commitment (50:1). Both the anger and anguish of God are apparent; even the heart of God can be broken.

Yahweh is pictured here not only as husband but also as Creator of a moral universe. In that world God has given human beings freedom of will. They have liberty to choose their actions but cannot control the consequences of their choices. Decisions opposed to the will of God lead to disaster. God is patient and forgiving, but ultimately there is a price that must be paid for violation of spiritual, ethical and moral codes.

The picture painted by Jeremiah is even bleaker. Both Judah and Israel had given themselves to others and had to pay the price of their adultery. Israel had gone into exile with a decree of divorce, yet Judah continued to play the harlot (Jer 3:1-3, 6-10). It is hard for us to imagine the degree of apostasy that had been reached. Both the biblical account and archaeological evidence demonstrate explicitly that the Israelites had adopted the cult and culture of the neighboring peoples. They practiced every abomination that had been forbidden them.

GOD AS WRONGED HUSBAND

Such a travesty of marriage could not be preserved. Yahweh, the wronged husband, ultimately severed the covenant that Israel had breached and instituted a divorce, saying, "What right has my beloved in my house, when she has done vile deeds?" (Jer 11:15).

> I had sent her away with a decree of divorce. . . . As a faithless wife leaves her husband, so you have been faithless to me, O house of Israel. (Jer 3:8, 20)

The most shocking metaphors of broken marriage are found in the prophecies of Ezekiel (chapters sixteen and twenty-three). In some ways his rendering is the most tender. God found Jerusalem as an abandoned newborn girl. He took her up, cleaned off the blood of childbirth and tenderly nurtured her. In time she grew up to be a beautiful young woman whom God adorned and cherished. But Jerusalem turned wanton, forgetting all the kindness that her husband had shown, all the blessings he had heaped on her. She turned instead to heathen lovers, preoccupied with luxury and fertility. She was enamored of their opulent lifestyle, their gaudy trappings, their phallic art (23:14, 20). Her lewd behavior is spelled out in detail. At last God declared, "When she carried on her whorings so openly and flaunted her nakedness, I turned in disgust from her, as I had turned from her sister" (23:18).

Yahweh spelled out in detail the behavior and infidelity of the one to whom he swore constant love. That love had been rejected and denigrated. Despite his longsuffering, God had not been blind. His patience had ultimately encouraged Judah in her misconduct. The righteousness of his character demanded a severance of this farcical relationship.

Whom did you dread and fear
   so that you lied,
and did not remember me
   or give me a thought?

Have I not kept silent and closed my eyes,
   and so you do not fear me? (Is 57:11)

God would not be an enabler. The covenant had been flagrantly broken, and his continued provision for Israel only perpetuated her infidelity. There were limits to what should be endured in a marriage, whether from infidelity or from other forms of abuse. The heavenly husband was justifiably angry, and he vehemently expressed his anger, insisting on a separation. In the end, the time apart would be curative, but not until considerable pain had been endured and well-needed lessons had been learned. During the period of separation, the errant wife would discover that her lovers were abusive and destructive. Those by whom she had expected to be enhanced had demeaned and despoiled her.

ISRAEL'S CHOICE RESPECTED

An aspect often disregarded is Yahweh's respect for Israel and for her own choices, though they were bad ones. The texts reflect God's anger but also a sorrowful acceptance of Israel's rejection of him. Divine action does not force God on anyone. In the moral universe God has created, people must face the consequences of their wrong choices. Although he does not actively bring about the evil, the heavenly husband will no longer shield the errant wife from the bitter products of her own folly.

The forces that swung into effect against Israel were those of her own choosing. Former lovers proved treacherous when they were no longer restrained. God is not a vengeful husband inflicting malicious abuse on a wayward wife but rather a righteous judge who long ago established righteous decrees.

Your tormentors . . . have said to you,
   "Bow down, that we may walk on you";
and you have made your back like the ground
   and like the street for them to walk on. (Is 51:23)

She had made herself a doormat. Those by whom she had expected
to be enhanced had instead demeaned and despoiled her. They, not
Yahweh, had abused her. The chastisement she received was what she
herself had sought.

Some women scholars perceive Yahweh as an abusive husband,
but it may be more accurate to say that God withdraws the privileges
of a wife. Israel had been brought to birth, raised and adorned by her
loving bridegroom, but now her ornaments are no longer hers to
wear. Marital status is no longer hers, nor protection from the depre-
dations of other cultures and nations. In a world of free choices, evil
lurks where one might not expect it.

Your ways and your doings
   have brought this upon you.
This is your doom; how bitter it is!
   It has reached your very heart. (Jer 4:18; compare 2:17)

THE DAUGHTER OF ZION ABUSED

In this context, Jeremiah depicted God's estranged people as a woman
at the mercy of her former lovers. Although she had been enamored of
them, now they batter her unmercifully. The lovers whom she had
chosen are false. Here we find a remarkable perception of the plight of
the abused woman:

What are you doing, O devastated one?
   Why dress yourself in scarlet
   and put on jewels of gold?
Why shade your eyes with paint?
   You adorn yourself in vain.
Your lovers despise you;

they seek your life.
I hear a cry as of a woman in labor,
    a groan as of one bearing her first child—
the cry of the Daughter of Zion gasping for breath,
    stretching out her hands and saying,
"Alas! I am fainting;
    my life is given over to murderers." (Jer 4:30-31 NIV)

Men who abuse women will find themselves likened in the Bible not to God the tender lover but to the heathen nations that despoil Israel. But where is there help for the abused woman? Jeremiah expressed enormous compassion as he raised troubling questions:

Hark, the cry of the daughter of my people
    from the length and breadth of the land:
"Is the LORD not in Zion?
    "Is her King not in her?". . .
For the wound of the daughter of my people is my heart
        wounded,
    I mourn, and dismay has taken hold on me.
Is there no balm in Gilead?
    Is there no physician there?
Why then has the health of the daughter of my people
    not been restored?
O that my head were waters,
and my eyes a fountain of tears,
that I might weep day and night
for the slain of the daughter of my people!
    (Jer 8:19, 21–9:1 RSV)

Jeremiah's poignant description leaves us with no doubt that God empathizes with those who have suffered abuse, even if their judgment has not always been good. At last the erring wife says to herself that it was better when she was with her true husband (Hos 2:7).

She decides to flee her abusive lovers, to seek forgiveness and the reestablishment of the marriage.

GOD AS RECONCILING HUSBAND

There must of necessity be a separation, but amid the tragedy of a dissolved marriage, God gives promise of renewal and reconciliation. Isaiah in particular spells out the tender reconciling love of the heavenly husband:

> For the Lord has called you
>   like a wife forsaken and grieved in spirit,
> like the wife of a man's youth when she is cast off,
>   says your God.
> For a brief moment I abandoned you,
>   but with great compassion I will gather you. (Is 54:6-7)

The wife who was bruised and abused by her lovers is now promised a future in which she shall have a home free of violence.

VIABLE CONCLUSIONS FROM THE BIBLICAL METAPHOR

What conclusions may we draw from this tragic metaphor that still promises a happy ending? How can we apply this material to the current problem of domestic abuse? In the biblical parable, the wife is clearly the abuser of the marriage, although she suffers cruelly herself.

If we seek to draw a paradigm from the metaphor of God's marriage to Israel, we must be mindful of its implications. First we must note that God is not portrayed as vindictive abuser but as righteous spouse who refuses to allow his wife's flagrantly wanton conduct to continue indefinitely. Even in this picture of marriage, where one spouse is our loving God, there are limits. There must be a time of separation.

And even after repentance, the reconciliation is not instantaneous. Like Gomer, Judah must be given the opportunity to prove herself. This can come, however, only after repentance and a period of proving that it is genuine (Hos 3:3). In the case of Israel, the period of waiting is a long one (vv. 4-5).

If God can institute a protracted time of waiting for Israel's change of heart (Is 54:6-7), should not victims of abuse wait for evidence of a truly changed heart on the part of the abuser? Even God does not shield the offender from the consequences of her own mistakes. We must be careful not to deprive perpetrators of the opportunity to grow through reaping the harvest of what they have sown. We may learn most, however, from the wonderful promises of domestic tranquility and safety as God envisions a joyous reunion: "My people will abide in a peaceful habitation, in secure dwellings, and in quiet resting places" (Is 32:18). If we are to use God's love for Israel as a paradigm for the marriage of believers, we must include this fundamental objective of peace and safety for all within the household.

Indeed, the prophetic promises of a wonderful reconciliation are put in the future. Israel has been the offender, but God takes the lead in fashioning a renewed marriage covenant. The picture of reconciliation is a beautiful one that can well be a model of Christian family life (Is 54:6-7). The wife who was bruised and abused by her lovers is now promised a home free of violence: "I have sworn that I will not be angry with you and will not rebuke you" (v. 9).

A feature of many abusive marriages is the deliberate humiliation of one's spouse. Self-image is destroyed as the individual is made to feel inadequate. But God's pattern is one of empowerment and affirmation, not disgrace and defamation: "Do not fear, for you will not be ashamed; do not be discouraged, for you will not suffer disgrace" (v. 4). Recrimination is not part of God's reconciliation package; there will be no inducement of guilt or shame, no slurs on her past, no innuendo or unkind allusions.

> For the mountains may depart and the hills be removed,
>   but my steadfast love shall not depart from you,
>   and my covenant of peace shall not be removed,
>   says the LORD, who has compassion on you. (v. 10)

In volatile marriages, there often is a cycle of abuse. An incidence of violence or intense mistreatment is followed by a period of contrition, with promises that the behavior will not be repeated. Gradually the tension builds to another eruption of destructive behavior. Extravagant promises are made, only to be broken. With God it is not so. His promises are eternal, his love unfailing. There is no volatility with God, only the steadfastness of kind treatment.

In many instances children who see violence in the home later perpetuate violence in their own families. But God's promises include peace and instruction in righteousness for children (v. 13). They will learn new patterns of family life, of holiness, faith and love.

So Zion will find a new basis for her existence. Her life will be ruled not by fear and oppression but by righteousness and peace (v. 14). She is promised growth and stability, a rediscovery of her own integrity within the forgiveness and acceptance of her heavenly husband. Home life will be characterized by peace rather than strife; the wife will be secure against all violence:

> If anyone stirs up strife,
>   it is not from me;
> whoever stirs up strife with you
>   shall fall because of you. . . .
>   No weapon that is fashioned against you shall prosper,
>   and you shall confute every tongue that rises against you in
>   judgment. (vv. 15, 17)

Verbal abuse will be prohibited, as will word twisting, ridicule and insult. More than this, the wife is promised empowerment to rise to her own defense—to become a full person in her own right. She has been delivered from physical, mental and sexual abuse, and brought to a place of safety and assurance.

9

Repentance and Forgiveness

"He broke my arm, and then I had to get right back into bed with him," grieved a woman whose faith community had forced her into a premature reconciliation with her husband.[1] Too often Christians demand that others forgive immediately, before it is appropriate or advisable, before there can be adequate contrition, reflection or amelioration.

FORGIVENESS: A LONG ROAD

Although the Bible does exhort us to forgive, it does not insist on our returning to the circumstances that occasioned an offense in the first place. Forgiveness does not necessarily imply reconciliation. In the case of domestic violence, to continue on as before may throw open the door to continued abuse. The perpetrator may see that the consequences of his misbehavior were relatively light. A period in which to prove himself is likely to be more curative of both soul and emotions. A time of separation from his family is more likely to be conducive of willingness to change and take whatever steps are necessary to bring about that change. The abuser may become willing to accept counseling, to put himself under the care of an accountability group, to join a batterers' group. Such a process does not bring the automatic resolution that many Christians would like to see, but we are instructed to "let endurance have its full effect" (Jas 1:4).

All of us have wronged others and been wronged ourselves, and all of us understand the need for healing in such situations. But the healing must be done in a careful and prayerful process as the Holy Spirit gives enablement. The first step is simply to acknowledge to oneself that there has indeed been a hurt. If we are the offender, we must repent and seek to make matters right with the one whom we have harmed. If we ourselves have been hurt, we must first admit that the offense did indeed occur. If we deny the reality of what has happened, the wound will only fester.

In the healing process, we need to be clear-sighted enough to understand the responsibility of the person who wronged us. If we are partially at fault, that must be acknowledged; but ultimately we must also understand what is *not* our fault and *not* our responsibility. If we are confused about responsibility, we will probably continue to harbor vengeful feelings. St. Paul records that Alexander the coppersmith did him much harm (2 Tim 4:14). It was helpful to Paul to be clear about Alexander's role in what had happened to him. He appears to write without rancor, simply to be stating a fact that might enable someone else to steer clear of dangerous waters.

He does not end with the statement of the wrong done him but with the conviction that "the Lord will pay him back for his deeds" (2 Tim. 4:14). The Bible discourages us from "getting even" by numerous promises that God will take care of the vengeance (Lev 19:18; Deut 32:35; Prov 24:12; Rom 12:17-21; 1 Thess 5:15; Heb 10:30). Here we may experience a real struggle of faith, but we may safely leave the matter in God's hands. Perhaps this explains why many of the psalms are so angry, and why hostilities toward enemies are so fully expressed. We need to let God know just how we feel. Then it is God's job to bring justice and transformation to the troubled situation.

THE NEED FOR SEPARATION

Although we can by God's grace ultimately give up deep grudges against an abusive spouse, there may well need to be a time of moving apart. When Jacob and Esau were at last reconciled, they still found it best to live apart (Gen 33:1-17). Paul separated from Barnabas after they quarreled over Mark's defection (Acts 15:36-39; see also Gal 2:13). There was later reconciliation, though they no longer traveled together (Col 4:10; 2 Tim 4:11). Peter and Paul had a sharp disagreement (Gal 2:11-14) that was later resolved with the help of the Jerusalem Council as the boundaries of their individual ministries were defined (Gal 2:1-10). Though they maintained subsequent distance from each other, the writings of both apostles show evidence of profound respect and mutual cooperation (1 Cor 1:12; 3:22; Gal 2:7-8; 2 Pet 3:15-16).

The victim of domestic abuse will be better able to come to a point of true forgiveness if she does not immediately return to the situation that triggered the abuse in the first place. Forgiveness does not mean going on as though nothing ever happened. Human beings cannot forgive in a vacuum.

Repentance calls for a transformed attitude and lifestyle. Before reconciling with his brothers, Joseph engaged in an elaborate stratagem to test the genuineness of their repentance (Gen 42–44). Jesus and his followers called for a repentance that goes far beyond a mere expression of contrition (Mt 3:8; Lk 3:8; 19:8-9; Acts 26:20; Eph 4:28; see also Is 1:16-17). Whether or not a woman decides to be reunited with her husband, the offender needs enough time to take the steps required for true recovery.

For a reconciliation to occur, the groundwork should be laid carefully. If there is too hasty a reunion, the abuser may conclude that the offense was not actually a serious one because the consequences were so light. The victim needs time to pray and think through many aspects and implications of a reunion. Both parties must carefully consider how to prevent a recurrence of the abuse and victimization. In effecting a reunion, the faith community may be very helpful, though members must be very careful not to rush or force the process. After reconciliation, the church should continue to lend support and step in to help whenever the need arises.

GETTING OVER THE BITTERNESS AND ANGER

Aphiēmi, the Greek word for "forgive," means to put something away, to set it free, to put one thing aside in order to move on to something else. Forgiveness is essentially a putting away of our anger toward another, putting it aside so that it no longer controls our life. Only by doing so can we be free to move on to something better. *Apolyō*, another Greek word for forgiving, includes as well the idea of loosing or freeing ourselves from anger and resentment toward another.

Instead of holding something against another, we will be able to release it and thereby to be free of the grip that hatred, resentment and vindictiveness have had on us. Breaking free can be a long and difficult process. We cannot go ahead as though nothing has happened. We need the freedom to acknowledge the harm that has been done and to assess the damage wreaked in our own life and the lives of those we love.

An Exodus narrative tells a story of bitterness turned sweet at Marah (the name means "bitter"; Ex 15:22-25). The children of Israel have been traveling for three days without coming to a source of water. In those days water was carried in animal skins—and after three days any water that was left must surely have been unappetizing. At last they reach a pool, only to discover that its taste is so nasty that they cannot drink it. There are many such brackish pools and wells in the desert.

The newly delivered people now face a sobering disappointment. The hope of quenching their thirst is dashed by the cruel reality. Why had Moses led them to such a wretched place? How were they to survive?

How many victims have come in their journey to just such a spot of disillusionment and despair! Love and trust have been betrayed, that which seemed most precious has become most hurtful. As one survivor told me, so many places evoked dreadful memories of how her abuser had mistreated her or her children at that particular site. Another pointed out that so many of the major events of her life were marred by the cruelty that she had endured at the death of a relative, the birth of a child, the request to be taken to the hospital during a miscarriage. So many things can trigger the memories—an old photo or a song or even a scent. How can the waters ever turn sweet?

In our Bible story, God showed Moses a piece of wood (or branch with leaves) that he cast into the water, and it became sweet. To this day, Bedouins throw certain shrubs into the brackish water that act as a catalyst so that the salts sink to the bottom and remain there. Above them lies excellent drinking water.

Some have allegorized the branch of Moses as being the cross of Christ, who can bring sweetness into our lives. Surely his redeeming grace is the great transformer. It was there at Marah that "the LORD made for them a statute and an ordinance and there he put them to the test" (Ex 15:25). God first gave his people a promise of guidance and protection if they would walk with him in obedience and then declared, "I am the LORD who heals you" (Ex 15:26). The place of transformed bitterness became a place where the Israelites grew in their understanding of God.

But just as God showed Moses a particular piece of vegetation, there can be other means of sweetening. To these we too may be led by God in many different ways.

Recently a therapist remarked to me that a victim can begin to let go of her resentment and anger when she sees that there has been repentance on the part of the abuser. She told of a husband who, while he was seeking to change his ways, missed a flight connection. He was forced to sit for several hours in an airport far from home, and suddenly the enormity of what he had done to his family began to surface. As the hours passed, the realization grew. He was able to return to his family and to express his shame and remorse. Both his confession and his altered conduct delivered his wife from her bitterness.[2] Another woman told of how her ex-husband sought her out after many years, and said, "I never would have deserted you if I had known that I would wake up every morning of my life, realizing that I had abandoned you with a two-year-old child and no real way to support yourself."[3]

Genuine repentance on the part of the offender is a great sweetener that facilitates forgiveness (Lk 17:3), but there are other healing shrubs that God may lead the abused to find: prayer, spiritual fellowship, the solace and affirmation of the Scriptures, the confidence that a better part of the journey lies ahead.

PASSING THE PROBLEM ON TO GOD

Forgiveness involves letting go of the right to "get even." That is God's job, not ours (Prov 20:22; Rom 12:19; Deut 32:35). We would suggest the following techniques:

1. *Praying the 3-G prayer.* Ask God to give the person who has wronged you grace and guidance and good. How the Lord intends to dispense these blessings may safely be entrusted to the heavenly Friend who "has done everything well" (Mk 7:37). As you ask for God's grace and good and guidance on the life of a person who has wronged you, anger can begin to dissipate. Remembering the person before the Lord lessens the bitter memories. Prayer for blessing on another's life can bring a blessed attitude in our own.

2. *Praying innovatively.* Despite surgical intervention, one survivor's gynecological wounds continued to bleed periodically for many years.[4] At last the woman said, "God, I'm trying so hard to forgive, and then the bleeding brings the abuse all back again. Won't you please stop it so that I can do better at forgiving?" From that time on, there was no more bleeding, and she found a new path to forgiveness.

3. *Praying the "imprecatory" psalms.* These can be exceedingly useful in our spiritual lives. The psalmist pours out his pain, rage and sense of injury. The negative feelings that we would be ashamed to air in God's presence are exposed in full detail. We cannot rid ourselves of anger until we have examined the cause. Like the

psalmist, we need the opportunity to spread out the shame, hurt, distress and bewilderment that we have experienced. Within the psalms, an abused woman will find many expressions of her own feelings and circumstances. The psalms were both the hymn book and the prayer book of ancient Israel, and they have been so used by God's people ever since. If they can express our sentiments in times of trouble, they can also guide us to look at the King of Glory, who leads us to new confidence and joy.

4. *Contemplating Psalm 94.* Psalm 94 reviews the harm done by evildoers and directs the soul back to a trust in God.

Marie Fortune lists the following guidelines for forgiveness:[5]

WHAT FORGIVENESS IS NOT

- *Forgiveness is not condoning or pardoning harmful behavior, which is a sin.*

- *Forgiveness is not healing the wound lightly, saying "peace, peace" when there is no peace.*

- *Forgiveness is not always possible.*

- *Forgiveness is not an expectation of any degree of future relationship with the person who caused the harm.*

WHAT FORGIVENESS IS

- *Forgiveness is letting go so that the immediacy of the painful memories can be put into perspective.*

- *Forgiveness is possible in a context of justice-making and the healing presence of the Holy Spirit.*

- *Forgiveness is God's gift, for the purpose of healing, to those who have been harmed.*

- *Accountability is God's gift to those who have harmed another for the purpose of repentance (read "fundamental change").*

5. *Trying a bit of whimsy.* Another survivor[6] resorted to a bit of whimsy when she felt overwhelmed with the garbage that still littered her soul. She explained that she simply telephoned the Heavenly Rubbish Removal Service for a pickup. She never got a busy signal or a recorded message. The service provided was prompt, reliable and efficacious. Then she enjoyed a chuckle as she envisioned Jesus rumbling away with the dump truck.

We are delivered from a lot of anger and stress if we simply shift the problem onto God. This may also help us to view the offender more positively. It is not to minimize the harm done—just to recognize that you are waiting for a divine outworking.

10

Issues of Abuse and Authority

The breaking down, forcing people to do behaviors that are denigrating. The language, the control of behavior, that if you're not doing what the group wants, you're violating God's will. It's certainly abusive personality control.[1]

Intimate terrorism begins with the male asserting control, demeaning the female partner constantly; it progresses to more pervasive control of the female's life, later punctuated by threats of violence. It often climaxes with severe physical battering and, all too often, with death of the female.[2]

When we turn to dynamics in the family, it is essential to address the issues of power and control. We must begin, of course, with what Jesus had to say. Always he calls us to consider our guiding principles carefully. He warned that some "have let go of the commands of God and are holding on to the traditions of men" (Mk 7:8 NIV). He maintained that the wielding of power imperils intimacy (Jn 15:15).

Furthermore, Jesus expressed an abhorrence of "lording it over" others.

> You know that among the Gentiles those whom they recognize
> as their rulers lord it over them, and their great ones are tyrants
> over them. But it is not so among you; but whoever wishes to
> become great among you must be your servant, and whoever
> wishes to be first among you must be slave of all. (Mk 10:42-44;
> see also Mt 20:25-28; Lk 22:24-27)

Such a heathen attitude was not to be adopted by his followers. Rather
Jesus advocated an "upside-downing" of power in which the strong
yielded to the weak, the older to the younger, the greatest to the least
(Mk 9:33-37; Lk 9:46-48). He said, "The least among all of you is the
greatest" (Lk 9:48).

In the great hymn known as the Magnificat, Jesus' mother, Mary,
had sung of this reversal of power structure in the coming kingdom
(Lk 1:52-53), as had Hannah long before her (1 Sam 2:4-8). The reversal of dynamic between male and female is a recurring theme in the
earlier portions of the Bible, one promised by Jeremiah as he intro-
duces the new covenant (Jer 31:22). The "biblical mandate" that
"every man should be master in his own house" is found only in the
narrative of an enormous drinking party, made by a king with notori-
ously poor judgment. His wife, Queen Esther, managed to reverse the
decrees of the despotic Ahasuerus, in regard to both marital dynamics and genocide of the Jewish race (Esther 1:22; 3:13). Thereafter it is
said that she "gave full written authority" (9:29).[3]

Throughout the Bible, it is difficult to find a godly person who
exercised a dominant control over others. For centuries the people
of Israel had no king until there was an inexorable demand from
the people. Despite the warning of what a repressive rule would
bring, Israel persisted; and all that had been foretold fell upon her
(1 Sam 8:10-18). In the New Testament realm as well, there is a
council rather than a single leader that makes shared decisions after earnest prayer and deliberation. The initial leadership of Peter
was soon replaced by that of James, the brother of the Lord, as he
guided the deliberations of the Jerusalem Council. We are given

the names of the five major leaders of the executive committee in Antioch (Acts 13:1-3).

Like Jesus, both Peter and Paul deplored "lording it over" others. Paul wrote, "I do not mean to imply that we *lord it over your faith*; rather, we are *workers with you for your joy*, because you stand firm in the faith" (2 Cor 1:24, emphasis added; see also 1 Pet 5:3).

Ezekiel wrote, "You have ruled them harshly and brutally" (34:4 NIV). The writers of Scripture were well aware that an imbalance of power could bring abuse. It is spelled out clearly by the apostle Paul in his second letter to Corinth: "You put up with it when someone enslaves you, takes everything you have, takes advantage of you, takes control of everything, and slaps you in the face" (2 Cor 11:20 NLT).

Here we have a classic definition of multiple sorts of abuse. Paul specifically mentioned physical, verbal, financial and psychological aspects. He also details that his own tactics had contained no vestige of abuse: "We have wronged no one, we have corrupted no one, we have taken advantage of no one" (2 Cor 7:2). He wrote these words to the Corinthian congregation when he was encouraging them to face some very difficult issues.

There had been a falling out between Paul and the beloved folk at Corinth, and some new people had moved in to assume leadership. Judging from Paul's description, they were a suave bunch. Like other abusers, they had impressive platform manners, boasted of their super-spirituality and did their best to alienate the credulous flock from the one who had led them to Christ in the first place. In typical style, they had isolated the victims from their old friends.

As is so often the case, it was very difficult for Paul's readers to make the admission that abuse was occurring. The offenders were so very plausible, appearing as angels of light. In his response, Paul dealt with them honestly, saying, "Don't worry; we wouldn't dare say that we are as wonderful as these other men who tell you how important they are!" (10:12 NLT).

Nor would he use their dishonest methods—especially that of twisting the Scripture—to gain control over another.

We reject all shameful and underhanded methods. We don't try
to trick anyone or *distort the word of God*. We tell the truth before God, and all who are honest know that" (2 Cor 4:2 NLT,
emphasis added).

His objective is not control but collaboration, being careful to respect
the integrity of others.

We will not boast about things done outside our area of authority. We will boast only about what has happened within the
boundaries of the work God has given us, which includes *our
working with you*. We are not reaching beyond these boundaries
when we claim authority over you. . . . For we were the first to
travel all the way to Corinth with the Good News of Christ.
(2 Cor 10:13-14 NLT, emphasis added)

Paul then gave a definition of the authority that he considered legitimate in his relationship with the Corinthians, using a text from
Jeremiah 24:6: "I will build them up and not tear them down. I will
plant them, and not uproot them" (NLT).

I may seem to be boasting too much about the authority given
to us by the Lord. But *our authority builds you up; it doesn't tear
you down*. (2 Cor 10:8 NLT, emphasis added)

As he finished the letter, he wrote,

I write these things while I am away from you, so that when I
come, I may not have to be severe in using *the authority that the
Lord has given me for building up and not tearing down*. (2 Cor
13:10, emphasis added)

This lies very close to Paul's two definitions of the relationship of the
head to the body:

From the head the entire body *grows* with the *growth* of God as
it is supplied by the head and held together by every ligament
and sinew. (Col 2:19, my translation, emphasis added)

Let us *grow* up in all things unto Him who is Christ, the
Head. He causes the body to build itself up in love as the head
provides *empowerment* according to the proportion appropriate
for each member as they are bound and supported by every
sinew. (Eph 4:15-16, my translation)

If we are to follow Paul's view of headship, the question within family relationships should not be "Who's going to be the boss?" but "Who
is going to help others to grow, give others an opportunity, support
and empower them, stay in close connection with each member?"

In the world of contemporary Christianity, the issue of authority
in the home is hotly contended. We can do no better than to follow
the example of the noble Bereans who "examined the scriptures every day to see whether these things were so" (Acts 17:11). The Scriptures emphasize the power of moral influence, loving support, kindly
guidance and responsible conduct toward members of the family.

Paul's essential analysis of power and authority is that it is given
to build up and not to tear down; its purpose is not self-aggrandize-
ment or to have one's own way; it is to be used in sharing rather than
in dominating; it stems from service developed within a context of
humility and voluntary restriction of power. May God grant us an
understanding of authority that will build such attitudes in our own
homes.

11

Good News for
and About Abusers

THE STORY OF A MAN WHO ACTED ABUSIVELY

Chris Holland[1] has just switched careers and recently changed marriage partners. He is almost forty, teaches science to junior-high students and lives under the same roof as his seven children in a blended family situation. In the aftermath of a violent incident, Chris sought help in a faith-based batterer intervention program because his wife was unwilling to allow him to return home unless he agreed to go to classes. His wife, a physiotherapist, learned of the agency through her Christian friends.

Desperate, Chris is willing to do anything that will get him back in the house. From his perspective, he is better than other men in the program, many of whom have been mandated by the courts to attend. No judge ordered him, he is swift to add. He is "wife mandated." Often in conversation Chris uses religious language and scriptural references. He wants to intimidate, but since the facilitators at the program know this language too, this dismantles his power.

Chris talks about being unequally yoked with his wife, a reference to the biblical notion that they do not share the same worldview or theological beliefs. But this is not exactly how Chris is using the term. Rather, he is referring to the fact that his wife called 911, involved the police and the courts, and is now considering divorce, something that he believes Christians should never do. He does not deny that she is a Christian, but he firmly believes that she is not living the way he feels a Christian should live—why else would she involve non-Christians in their disputes? And in Chris's world, everything is either right or it is wrong.

Before he began attending classes at the intervention program, the Hollands sought help at their church. But Chris was not happy with the pastoral counsel they received. He wanted their minister to invoke church discipline against his wife and make public their marital woes. When the pastor would not collaborate with this plan, Chris left the church.

Coming from a very conservative Protestant tradition, Chris feels fully empowered as a layperson to interpret the Scriptures without any guidance from the ordained leadership. With his father serving as a pastor, Chris grew up in a household that he claims was very strict and orderly. He laments that this is not the case in his own household. As he speaks about family life, it appears that there is excessive rigidity and very little fun.

When we return to interview Chris six months later as part of our ongoing research, he has left the program without completing its requirements for graduation.

✳ ✳ ✳

For several years, Nancy has been attempting to understand the lives of religious men who act abusively. She and colleague Barbara Fisher-Townsend have conducted studies of faith-based batterer intervention programs, examined the closed case files of more than one thousand men who have attended the classes, and for a four-year period followed the lives of fifty men who were mandated, or otherwise encouraged, to join a batterer intervention group. The results of this work will form the basis of their upcoming book, *Acting Abusively: Faith,*

Hope and Charity in the Lives of Abusive Religious Men.

When the violent men began the program, most were unwilling—and some were unable—to interpret their acts as abusive. "I am not violent" was a common phrase they used in their early days of program attendance.[2] Some interwove spiritual overtones in a direct way, like Chris. They talked about submission or authority or hierarchy in the family. But most talked only indirectly about these issues, choosing instead references to how "she pushed my buttons."

As others have observed, there is great reluctance among batterers to assume responsibility for their actions.[3] Abusers tend to both justify what they have meted out to their partner and blame her for the abuse. Essentially, most of the men believed, at least in the early days of coming to the agency, that they were entitled to certain things in a relationship and angry when their expectations were not met.

As the men we interviewed reflected back to their childhood, teen years, trouble with the law, altercations with adults, relationships at school, friendships and the early days of intimacy, there was a sense that for many—but not all—life had occurred at the margins of the broader society. There was a shared experience of feeling "left out," or at least not being able to be well integrated at school, at home and within the communities where they lived. Sometimes their faith background and church attendance helped to ease these strains; sometimes not. For some men we interviewed, there was a point when, during or after the group, they realized they had become just like their own father. This realization offered both a reminder of their abusive past—together with all its ugliness and personal pain—and a resignation about the future.

There was a small group of men whose stories involved overcoming enormous obstacles on their journey toward healing and accountability. They reported how it was very hard work coming to group each week, engaging in sustained talk about their failures and learning about—and deciding to use—tools that might help them to change how they think and how they act.

There were stories of hope among the men, but these were muted by ample evidence of failures, tragic choices and despair. When religious leaders are able to walk alongside abusive men and their families, the possibilities of ongoing accountability are enhanced. It is very powerful for a man who has acted abusively to see his faith community as supportive of his decision to change and pursue wholeness. In this way, pastors and other religious leaders are uniquely positioned to augment the process of recovery.

BUT WOMEN ABUSE TOO

In a small percentage of cases of domestic abuse, the offender is a woman. Sometimes both parties in a marriage engage in violent or abusive behavior. The abuse inflicted by women is usually verbal or emotional and can cause cruel suffering. Literary descriptions of termagant wives occur repeatedly—all the way from Socrates to Rip Van Winkle and Ethan Frome; but in real life, such spouses can pose an insurmountable problem for committed Christian men. Some points to remember:

- Abuse can be perpetrated by persons of either gender.

- Abuse is an effort to exercise power and control over another person, whether by physical, sexual, emotional, verbal, financial or spiritual means.

- No one deserves to be abused. All forms of abuse are wrong and are strongly condemned in Scripture.

- It is important to recognize that persistent demeaning, embarrassing, insulting, taunting, humiliating, withholding of sex or refusing to speak are all abuse. Often the victim thinks only that there is unhappiness in the marriage. Things can move in a better direction only when there is recognition that abuse is present.

- A basic first step is for abused persons to stop believing the lies that have been told about them. They are made in the image of God and are people of worth and dignity. The negative things spoken by the abuser do not represent a truthful picture of the individual, but rather are hurtful instruments to bring the abused person under control.

- The Scriptures can help a person to understand that he is not the wretch being portrayed by the abuser. King David was often vilified by his detractors, but he was able to affirm his basic integrity. (See Ps 26:1-11; 41:12; 101:2.)

- Another basic step lies in finding another Christian to whom one can disclose the situation. Often it takes great courage to reveal that a man has been reduced to such a humiliating status.

- A man may be fearful of taking any steps to remedy the situation, for fear of losing his reputation, job, ministry, respect of friends or witness in the church. Like other victims, he may find that few are willing to believe him and that he may be reprimanded rather than helped. (This, of course, is true for women too.) Nevertheless, there are some Christians who will understand and can offer assistance and support.

- Community resources frequently offer counseling for victims of domestic abuse, whether male or female. An important and appropriate avenue for assistance is using a seasoned counselor with experience in cases of this sort. Remember that the problem has long been recognized and addressed in general society; the church is having a hard time catching up.

- Couples' counseling is not a good option when abuse is involved. Often it has been found to make matters worse. Frequently the best therapy is in an abusers' intervention group that meets weekly for an extended period.

- Remember that perpetrating the abuse is the abuser's problem, and it is his responsibility to change his conduct. There may well be features of the victim's behavior that also need work, but the fundamental responsibility for stopping the abuse lies with the offender.

- Prayer works wonders. A small prayer and support group can be very helpful when seeking to bring healing to a troubled situation.

• Don't forget the healing power of worship.

Abuse is no respecter of persons. Perpetrators and their victims are found in all classes, all genders, all races and all societies. Abusers are often frightened, insecure people who need the grace of God in their lives. Surprisingly, many have a great fear that their spouse will leave them, and they seek to prevent this abandonment through the various kinds of control they exert. And so the cycle of misery is perpetuated.

Often "tough love" is the best way to bring abusers to transformed attitudes. An evangelical woman who ran several court-mandated batterers' groups for a sheriff's office found that born-again Christians were the ones who most often asked to be excused from a group.[4] Somehow they felt that they were above associating with ordinary sinners. Sometimes a pastor will try to convince a judge that he can counsel a perpetrator on a one-on-one basis. But group intervention is powerful.

It is important to understand that abuse involves sinful conduct and that offenders should receive no special leniency. The Bible speaks of appropriate judgment. Christians should not try to help the perpetrator escape the consequences of the behavior. That is no kindness to anyone.

All parties should understand that it is exceedingly difficult for abusers to alter their patterns of behavior. The victim should not entertain false hopes; the church should not assume that change is forthcoming. In fact most abusers do not change, even though they may profess repentance and promise never to repeat their behavior. We knew of one man who deceived two different accountability groups to which he was supposedly answering.[5]

BIBLICAL PRECEDENTS

But God's power is still adequate to bring about radically altered con-

duct. The fanatic Saul, who murdered Christians, became the apostle
Paul, the bearer of the gospel of life. While "breathing out threats and
slaughter," he was stopped short by a direct intervention of the risen
Christ, and from that time forth he was never the same. Other biblical
characters also made successful interventions. The Scripture quite directly calls for intervention.

> Whoever winks the eye causes trouble, but the one who re-
> bukes boldly makes peace. The mouth of the righteous is a
> fountain of life, but the mouth of the wicked conceals violence.
> (Prov 10:10-11 NRSV, following Septuagint text)

David, livid with anger, was deflected from murderous intentions
against an entire family by a wise and gracious intervention. He had
gathered a band of followers and started off with the explicit purpose
of slaughtering every male in the churlish Nabal's household in order
to avenge an insult. Abigail, the churl's wise and judicious wife,
learned of the incident and realized that reparations must be made in
haste. The wise woman bowed to David and offered her apologies,
but more important, she reminded him of God's purpose. He had
been anointed king of Israel, and the murders he intended would always be a blot on one who was to be raised up by God as defender of
the Israelite people. It behooved him not only to care for sheep but
also to care for people, even recalcitrant ones. David responded grate-
fully to Abigail:

> Blessed be the LORD, the God of Israel, who sent you to meet me
> today! Blessed be your good sense, and blessed be you, who have
> kept me today from bloodguilt and from avenging myself by my
> own hand! For as surely as the LORD the God of Israel lives, who
> has restrained me from hurting you, unless you had hurried and
> come to meet me, truly by morning there would not have been
> left to Nabal so much as one male. (1 Sam 25:32-34)

Yes, by God's power and the faithful witness of godly people, the violent can become peaceful.

Consistent with this pattern is the story of David's general Joab, who laid siege to a city without following the biblical command that first there must be communication and a definition of the issues (Deut 20:10). A wise woman saw the dire straits to which her city had been reduced, and she had the moral courage to mount the city wall and demand a hearing with Joab. She reminded him that she was obeying the dictates of God and inquired why he was threatening the city and its people with extermination. The loss, she pointed out, would be great to the entire nation. This little city of Abel of Beth-maacah was famed for the wise counsel its citizens dispensed to people who came from all over Israel, seeking advice.

Realizing the moral implications, Joab quickly retrenched his position. The woman effected a wise resolution: the city would deal with the offender itself. This they did with directness and dispatch. Joab lifted the siege and went home in peace (2 Sam 20:1-22).

The valiant Queen Esther risked her very life to intervene for the endangered Jewish people. Only then did her husband realize the vicious plan for their extermination to which he had unwittingly given his consent.

Let us not forget that confronting people on moral grounds can make a difference. We can be faithful witnesses of what the Scriptures have to tell us. While every effort must be made to keep victims safe, we must never underestimate the power of the Holy Spirit in the lives of sinful people.

Sometimes we (the authors) are asked whether we know of actual offenders who have been changed. We do indeed know such people, some of whom are exceedingly anxious to make amends to those whom they have wronged. In most cases the family is very anxious to conceal the fact that there has ever been abuse.

THE COMMAND FOR ZERO TOLERANCE

"Put away violence and oppression, and do what is just and right," commanded Ezekiel (45:9). God's people are expected to repudiate the ways and companionship of the violent. The righteous avoid "the ways of the violent" (Ps 17:4). The writer of Proverbs cautioned, "Do not envy the wicked, nor desire to be with them; for their minds devise violence, and their lips talk of mischief" (24:1-2). The same thought is repeated in Proverbs 3:31: "Do not envy the violent and do not choose any of their ways."[6] The New Testament as well calls for denunciation and intervention in such cases: "Take note of those who do not obey what we say in this letter; have nothing to do with them, so that they may be ashamed. Do not regard them as enemies, but warn them as believers" (2 Thess 3:14-15; see also Mt 18:15-17; 1 Cor 5:1-6; 1 Thess 5:14; 1 Tim 5:20; Tit 3:2-11; Jas 5:19-20).

Furthermore, the Pastoral Epistles twice warn not to put a violent person into a position of church leadership (1 Tim 3:3; Tit 1:7). The Greek noun *plēktēs* means literally "one who beats or batters." Though translated "violent" in many of our modern translations, the King James Version very accurately renders the term *striker*. Abusing one's family is an automatic disqualification for appointive leadership in the church.

CORRECTIVE MEASURES

The Scriptures repeatedly tell us that if a brother or sister is overtaken in a fault, it is the duty of the church to lead the offender back into paths of righteousness. Frequently church leaders are terribly embarrassed and uncomfortable at the thought of having to address an offender. More often than not, no direct dialogue ever takes place, and the perpetrator assumes that the problem is not serious after all. To pastoral counselors who feel embarrassed, inept or uncomfortable about broaching the subject with the abuser, Carol Adams suggests speaking along these lines:

> I am on your side as you become a person who does not batter. I am against your battering behavior. I do not believe you should treat your wife as an object that can be battered. But I am in total support of you as you seek to change. I am calling you to repent and to change. You will probably suffer in the process of

change. You cannot rely on old coping mechanisms that include battering. New life is possible, but it requires work.[7]

At a later stage, the batterer—when he is willing to acknowledge his behavior—can be helped to repentance and reconciliation with God.

EMPOWERING THE VICTIM

Sometimes the victim can be led to an understanding of herself as a person of worth with a right to respect and kindly treatment. Created by the Father, redeemed by the Son and empowered by the Holy Spirit, she can become more respectful of herself. She can realize that it is wrong for anyone to call her names, to humiliate her or to treat her disrespectfully. A victim can perceive that she did not cause the abuse or "make him do it." While direct confrontation of the abuser may be very unsafe, she can understand that mistreatment is condemned by the Word of God and that she need not be a helpless mass of jelly nor accept cruel injustice. Sometimes such quiet conviction starts to bring about altered conduct from the offender, but by no means can this be assumed.

At times there has been a supposition that the wife can extricate herself if the situation becomes too difficult. Many people assume that the woman is able to leave an abusive situation of her own volition, that it is actually her own responsibility. But many women are too traumatized to take that step. A director of a battered women's project recently noted, "Victims of domestic violence are in an altered state. Up seems down. . . . It's also important to understand that if [someone] was a victim all these years, it's sort of like she's been brainwashed. You are in essence a prisoner." A woman at the shelter added,

> They break you down. You feel less than human. They isolate you. They say, "No one cares about you. Only I love you." And you start to believe it. Then it builds to the physical. It's worse for people with higher social status. Society puts more pressure on them. It's more embarrassing.[8]

In such circumstances it is very difficult for the victim to take initiative. Recently an attorney for the Greater Boston Legal Services wrote a letter to the *Boston Globe*. In part she said,

> Too often the victim is expected to leave the situation, so victims of domestic violence are essentially blamed for staying. We should never be asking why victims stay. The real question is why, as a society, do we continue to portray intimate victim violence as anything other than it is: a crime. If the parties to an assault were not in a relationship, no one would ever suggest that the victim was to blame for permitting the assault to occur.
>
> My experience working with victims of domestic abuse has shown me that society treats these crimes differently. Why else would the media persistently refer to an assault on one's partner as a "domestic dispute"? It's a crime, and it needs to be treated as such. To do less is to perpetuate prejudice against victims, permit perpetrators to continue to deny responsibility, and allow the judiciary to impose sentences that send a message to perpetrators that it is not really a crime to beat up your spouse.[9]

The church is called to free the oppressed from violence, but we prefer to shift the responsibility. Many a victim has told us that things would have been different if only they had offered serious objection when the abusive treatment first started. Rather, thinking it was God's will, they meekly accepted the misconduct as it escalated to dismaying proportions. Then resistance becomes much more dangerous.

FIRMNESS ON THE ROAD TO RESTORATION

Firmness is more likely to bring transformation than ignoring the problem. Indeed, failing to address the situation may convey to the offender that the sin is not really so bad. The New Testament speaks of the work that may be done in the hearts of errant believers while they are being disciplined by the church "so that his spirit may be saved in the day of the Lord" (1 Cor 5:5; see also 1 Tim 1:8-11). The church may mentor, monitor and minister, but there can be no pretending that everything is all right.

Neither can the church accept an abuser's excuses. If the spouse's behavior has been less than perfect, that is still not justification for striking her. There are other ways to resolve differences. Anger is frequently used as justification for battering, but the Scriptures warn us not to sin when we are angry (Eph 4:26).

Mere rebuke is not enough. The community of faith is called to action rather than indifference. It is tempting to say that what goes on in somebody else's home is none of our business, but that is not true in the household of faith. Steps must be taken to ensure that the abuse is stopped. This will require time, effort and endurance from the church.

It is good if the abuser asks forgiveness and promises never to repeat the offense, and even his tears may be of value. Yet even confession in front of the church body may not produce altered behavior. The perpetrator needs to be helped to hold himself accountable. It is necessary that there be fruits "worthy of repentance" (Mt 3:8; see also Jer 35:15; Lk 3:8; Acts 26:20). This means taking whatever steps are necessary so that the abuse is not repeated.

CHANGING LONG-HELD ATTITUDES

Batterer intervention programs seek to educate abusers both about their own personal attitudes and about those that are deeply entrenched in society. A director of a Massachusetts state certified program explained:

> The course includes eighty hours of group intervention, group methodology that focuses on the batterer taking responsibility for his abuse. . . . Domestic violence is not viewed as just an individual problem, but rather as a societal and human rights issue. The entire community needs to respond to help the victim and hold the batterer accountable. The good news is that these programs believe that the abuser can change![10]

Those who work in batterer intervention projects repeatedly hear protests from attendees that the male should be in charge, that men are of a higher order of creation, that their needs must be placed first. All too often, offenders cite theological positions to defend their actions. Lundy Bancroft, the author of *Why Does He Do That?* has treated thousands of offenders and has declared that what all perpetrators have in common is their mindset: their conviction that they own their intimate partner. From that sense of possession sprouts a feeling of entitlement—the right to control the actions, speech and attitudes of their wife or girlfriend. Religious conviction is not the only predisposing factor, but it is a very important one that impacts far wider social attitudes. Doug Gaudette, director of the Family Safety Project at Caritas Holy Family Hospital, states flatly, "Patriarchy is the breeding ground of abuse."

In their weekly group meetings, abusers are required to speak of their intimate partners with respect. They are not permitted to refer to their wives as "the old lady" or "the ball and chain." Derogatory statements about women are swiftly corrected. Male supremacy is challenged.

Sad to say, there has been age-old acceptance of discrimination against women. This is evident in many aspects of our everyday life, but takes its ugliest form in violence against women. The old English "rule of thumb" came from the legislation that a man might not beat his wife with a rod thicker than his thumb. And consider this old rhyme:

A woman, a dog and a walnut tree
The more you beat them, the better they be.

While the verse was intended to be humorous, all too often a grim reality lay behind it. In some societies, there is a saying that a man should beat his wife once a week. "He may not know why she should be beaten, but she will know." We could enumerate endlessly the instances of a societal acceptance of injustice against women. All of us need to work on bringing about changes in attitudes such as these.

But we must especially address ourselves to those attitudes that have been generated by the church. All too often, faulty theology has produced faulty conduct. Thus it is that offenders need to unlearn such warped sentiments.

When abuse happens in church families, everyone should understand that there cannot be an instantaneous solution. Situations that developed over years cannot be addressed in a day. It is always easier to look the other way than to demand redress for evil, but to this God has summoned us, and we must shoulder the responsibility for problems that we in part have helped to create. If we have tolerated a shocking situation in our midst, we must pray, study and act to right the wrong.

12

The Biblical
Option of Divorce

Often an abuser feels no real need to change, because he is convinced that divorce is not an option. He assumes that a good Christian wife is required to remain with him regardless of his treatment of her. Divorce is viewed as simply not an option. At times, this attitude can cause pastors and congregations to ignore a major instrument that can be used to correct inappropriate behavior: divorce. Divorce is clearly the least desirable option, but sometimes it is a necessary option—and it is indeed a biblical option. The possibility of divorce reinforces the serious nature of the offense and serves as an incentive for changing abusive conduct. An evangelical therapist who operates several groups for batterers reports that men participate not because of a court order but because of their wife's mandate: failure to attend group meetings will result in divorce.[1]

WHEN GOD DIVORCES

When we announce that the Lord hates divorce, we do not add that the same verse declares that God hates violence. Indeed, the Malachi 2:16 passage is translated alternatively in New International Version this way: "'I hate divorce,' says the LORD God of Israel, 'and I hate a man's covering himself with violence as well as with his garment,' says the LORD Almighty. So guard yourself in your spirit, and do not break faith."

Why do we not tell victims and abusers that Proverbs 6:17-19 lists seven things that the Lord hates: "haughty eyes, a lying tongue, and hands that shed innocent blood, a heart that devises wicked plans, feet that hurry to run to evil, a lying witness who testifies falsely, and one who sows discord in a family"? Why do we compel a victim to remain in a marriage characterized by these seven evils that the Lord hates? All too often, the preservation of marriage has been exalted as the highest good, even when human life is at stake. This is not what the Bible says.

Marriage was given to bind together a man and woman as one flesh in enduring union (Gen 2:24; Eph 5:31). Much in the Bible is said to safeguard the bonds of matrimony (Ex 20:14; Lev 20:10; Deut 5:18; 22:22) and to affirm the strength of permanent marriage (Prov 2:16-17; 5:15-20; 12:4; 18:22). It was the duty of a husband to "bring happiness to [his] wife" (Deut 24:5 NIV). Individual marriages involved private covenants within the larger context of the covenant with Israel. At Mount Sinai, the people had agreed to a covenant by which God would set Israel apart from all the nations of the earth. They were to demonstrate to the rest of humanity what it meant to serve the true and living God. In return, God promised to bless them and to be their God, as they were a people dedicated to Yahweh.

According to the covenant between God and Israel, the believing community promised not to give their daughters in marriage to those of alien faith nor to take for their sons wives who did not worship the Lord (Ex 34:16). This was a promise not only to God but to the entire faith community. To embrace those who adored false gods was to vitiate a covenant intended to extend from one generation to another. Those within the covenant community were required to marry a believing spouse and to instruct their children in the ways of the Lord. This knowledge of the true and living God was at the very core of the

cohesion and perpetuity of Israel. Faith was passed from one generation to another; the genealogies that seem so boring are, in fact, a
dynamic account of that transmission.

With the giving of the law, however, provision was made for human sin. As there was sacrifice for those who trespassed, so there was
also provision for divorce in case of untenable situations (Deut 24:1).
A formal document gave termination and clarification to what otherwise might be a confused situation (Judg 15:1-3). God's covenant with
Israel was likened to a marriage union that was betrayed by an adulterous and idolatrous wife. At three points in Scripture, we are told
that Yahweh has divorced his people (Is 50:1; 54:6-7; Jer 3:8). Divorce
was given not as a desirable option but as the least undesirable one in
certain cases. The evangelical church cannot wholly condemn an action adopted by the Lord of heaven and earth in response to willful
and persistent human sin.

DIVORCE AND COVENANT RESTORATION

A passage in the Old Testament recounts the writing of a decree of
divorce for those who would reestablish a covenant relationship with
God. Judah as well as Israel had lapsed into idolatry, but in Babylon
there had been a renewed study of the Scriptures and a commitment
to the ways of the Word. The dispossessed and chastened people had
returned to Palestine to build anew a nation committed to God, but
the return had brought for some a transgression of the covenant between God and the people. They had set aside their believing wives to
forge more advantageous matches with local landowners' daughters. It
was this practice that Malachi condemned (Mal 2:11-14).

Forbidden intermarriage had brought acculturation with the heathen rather than perseverance in God's call to holiness (Ezra 9:1-2;
compare Ex 34:15-16; Deut 7:3-4). Just such intermarriage and acculturation had destroyed the identity of the ten northern tribes; now
those who remained were exposed to the possibility of the same fate.
Ezra exhorted unfaithful Israelites to divorce their mates if they
wished to continue as part of the covenant community (Ezra 9:10–

10:11). Unlike Ruth and Rahab, who embraced the faith of Israel, these Gentile wives had rejected the patterns and culture of Judaic lifestyle. The husbands had invested so little in their home life that half of the children could not even understand the Hebrew language (Neh 13:23-25). Thereby the offspring were denied an understanding of the Scriptures and of God's purposes for their lives, both individually and collectively. These marriages were a violation of the covenant itself (Ezra 9:10-15) and constituted a threat to the continuing faith of Israel.

Even the priests and Levites had forgotten their sacred duty, not only to conduct the worship of Israel's God but also to train their children for the holy office (Ezra 10:18-44; Num 1:53; 3:5–4:49; 8:19). Nehemiah prayed, "Remember them, O my God, because they have defiled the priesthood, the covenant of the priests and the Levites" (Neh 13:29; compare Ezra 9:1). The priests and Levites had a spiritual obligation to the whole of Israel. Only descendants of Aaron might offer incense and conduct the services of worship (Num 16:40; 18:1-7; 2 Chron 26:18). The priesthood was for them a gift (Num 18:7) and a responsibility. A concomitant obligation was instruction in the ways of God (Lev 10:8-11; 2 Chron 15:3; 17:7-9; Ezra 7:25; Neh 8:7-8; Mal 2:7). Theirs as well was the duty of judging disputes and maintaining public health standards to ensure the well-being of the community (Lev 13:2–14:57; Deut 17:8-13; 19:17; 21:5; 24:8; 1 Chron 23:3-4; 26:29; 2 Chron 19:8-11; Ezek 44:24). For others to attempt this ministry was considered heinous sacrilege (Num 16:1-40; 2 Chron 26:16-21).

Descendants of Aaron were required to marry women of other priestly families and to train their children from infancy in the traditions of Israel (Lev 21:7, 13-14; Ezek 44:22). Early childhood impressions and instruction reach most deeply into a person's consciousness and personality. Here the influence of the mother is often paramount, and so special provision was made for the selection of a suitable mate. Clearly the men had proven unfaithful in setting aside Israelite wives who could have reared another generation of priests (Mal 2:11, 15) and in failing to teach their children even the language in which worship must be conducted. In short, they had forfeited all the things that gave them a distinctive identity and mission (Ezek 44:10-16).

Ezra called them to rethink marriages that had deprived their lives of meaning and purpose, and denied them a sense of spiritual worth and rectitude. The marriages had drawn religious leaders away from the covenant community and concomitantly had produced children who had no knowledge of God's ways or of Israel's distinctive role among the nations. Levites and priests alike had forgotten their sacred trust to preserve the worship of the true and living God. Theirs was a hereditary office, passed from parents to children, to render to God praise and service and to regulate the cult of Yahweh. In their dual role as priests and public-health officers, they had a responsibility to the entire community (Num 1:53; 3:7; 8:19).

If the men were to maintain their membership in the covenant community, they must end the marriages that had caused them to rupture their ties with the people and purposes of God. Thus, under the direction of Ezra, those who had broken faith committed themselves to a new covenant that required them to put away their heathen families and to give their sons and daughters in marriage only to those in the community of faith (Ezra 10:1-14). Careful provision was made for the women and their children who were being returned to their own society (10:12-17), and the husbands were restored to a place among God's people.

CONSIDERING THE COMMUNITY

The account suggests that divorce must also be considered in relationship to the wider community, the couple's children and others beyond the family. If a marriage endangers the physical, emotional, social or spiritual welfare of others, there must be sober reflection on the consequences of continuing the union. If all of one's energy must be expended on maintaining a relationship that is a violation of God's purposes and provision, one must think through what it is that gives meaning to life.

Seldom do we mention Israel's covenant that was based on divorce. It was far from an optimal arrangement, but this harsh step was the least undesirable solution to a terrible problem. One of the purposes of the covenant is the perpetuation of a "godly offspring" (Mal 2:15). In considering an action of divorce, the welfare of the children must be given a high priority. The purposes of the biblical covenants again and again involve the entire people and their progeny. Consigning children to lives of terror and abuse is a violation of the biblical intent for marriage and the home.

We need to look carefully at what Jesus says about divorce. He was confronted by legalistic Pharisees who wished to embroil him in an ongoing argument (Mt 19:3-9; Mk 10:2-12). The issue was a source of lively debate among the rabbinic scholars of the day. The school of Shammai maintained that only for adultery could a woman be divorced, while the school of Hillel had derived a whole battery of reasons justifying putting away one's wife, including finding another woman who was more attractive. Other bases for divorce included burning a man's dinner, spinning in the street, having untidy hair, even having a dog bite that did not heal. A major objective was to find a pretext for a man to send away his wife but retain her dowry.

In this context Jesus vehemently condemned the practice. His sayings in the Sermon on the Mount likewise contain responses to the religious establishment's decrees: "You have heard that it was said . . . but I say to you" (Mt 5:21-22, 27-28, 31-34, 38-39, 43-44). The system itself created patterns of adultery, divorce and remarriage that wreaked havoc in souls. Divorce was carried out at the man's discretion, and there were few options for a woman but to be given to another, in either marriage or prostitution. This was not God's purpose in the creation of male and female given to one another to reflect the glory of God in lives of loving commitment.

Christ's purpose was not to create a legalism that would lock people into life-threatening situations. Indeed it was his repudiation of legalism that caused the Pharisees to hate him. He maintained that the Sabbath was made for people rather than people for the Sabbath, that it was legitimate for the near-starving David to eat the holy showbread. We need to look beyond legalism to the purposes of God's life-bringing law. As Jesus quoted Isaiah 29:13—"In vain do they worship me, teaching human precepts as doctrines"—he added, "You abandon the commandment of God and hold to human tradition" (Mk 7:7-8).

Can meaningful marriages be built on violence, bloodshed and wickedness? The New Testament gives two exceptions in which divorce is approved. The first is given by Jesus: the case of *porneia* (Mt 5:32; 19:9). *Porneia* can mean any sort of inappropriate sexual attitude or action, whether fornication, adultery, prostitution or sexual abuse. A second exception is given by Paul in 1 Corinthians 7:10-16. He addresses those who have come to Christ and find themselves married to an unbeliever. He declares that those who do divorce should not remarry another (v. 11)—a clear indication that some divorces are taking place. The apostle instructs the Christian not to leave the marriage but not to compel the non-Christian to remain (vv. 12-16).

The consideration is in part the matter of relationship to the whole community of faith. If union with a believer causes a prostitute to have a relationship with the body of Christ (1 Cor 6:15), how much more a legitimately married spouse? We are told the partner is sanctified and the children holy (1 Cor 7:14). Here it is assumed that the children are being raised with an understanding of the gospel and its claims on their lives. Adherence to the community standards may well have aggravated an unsympathetic spouse: patterns of worship, acts of charity, hospitality to strangers and gifts to the poor. Paul's implication is not that the spouse should desist from the requirements of Christian discipleship but that their fulfillment might be repugnant to a nonbeliever.

CALLED TO PEACE

The Ezra-Nehemiah episode requires divorce in order to preserve the integrity of the covenant community. First Corinthians 7 attempts to bring a peaceful resolution to a conflict involving matters of faith and practice. This passage is well worth considering, especially in situations where all the covenantal aspects of marriage have been lost, whether through infidelity, desertion or abuse. A marriage of abuse cannot be a marriage reflecting Christ's love for the church. Paul comments that "in such a case the brother or sister is not bound" (1 Cor 7:15). *Douleuō*, the word translated as "bound," literally means to serve in bondage as a slave. We might translate "a sister or brother is not held captive in such circumstances, for God has called you to peace." It is with this apostolic call to peace that Paul ends his discussion of divorce.

All of us earnestly desire that troubled marriages be healed, but the option of divorce should be recognized. Often indeed the contemplation of divorce has a very curative effect on one or both partners in a painful marriage. To declare that divorce is not an option is to deprive believers of an avenue that the Bible holds open.[2]

PICKING UP THE PIECES

Often, survivors tell us, the bitterest parts of abuse happen after the marriage has ended. Of domestic murders, 75 percent occur before, during or after the victim has attempted to leave. As the couple separates, every sort of bitterness is sometimes unleashed. Child custody can become a battleground in which each partner attempts to inflict vicious wounds on the other. All too often the children themselves become the weapons of warfare against the former spouse. Matters of custody, visitation and child support can all serve as points of virulent conflict. There are, however, programs that the church might undertake to bring peace and stability.

Supervised visitation. In many instances, an abuser is allowed unsupervised visits with the children because there are few good alternatives. A recent case that profoundly affected the Christian community involved a former missionary and dedicated pediatrician who had petitioned the court to stop her children's unsupervised visits with their father. Amy Castillo was a member of East Cooper Baptist

Church in Mount Pleasant, South Carolina, where she played in the orchestra, led Bible study and worked with the singles ministry. To quote a local news report:

> Dr. Amy Castillo sought a protective order in Montgomery County District Court on Dec. 25, 2006, and asked that her husband, Mark Anthony Castillo, receive psychiatric counseling because he threatened to kill the children. Circuit Judge Joseph Dugan granted a temporary protective order but rejected a permanent order on Jan. 10, 2007. In explaining his decision, Dugan wrote there was "no clear or convincing evidence that the alleged acts of abuse occurred." The parents divorced in February. Their battle over child visitation rights came to a horrific conclusion Saturday when police say Mark Castillo drowned the children in a Baltimore hotel bathtub.[3]

Other survivors tell us of children engaged in seriously unsafe practices adopted by the abuser simply to upset the former spouse. Here faith communities could offer better protection.

A few churches are now setting up supervised visitation programs, where the children can visit with the abusive parent in safe, pleasant surroundings. Sometimes the custodial parent drops off the children, and the other parent arrives for the visit fifteen minutes later. At the end of the visit, the process is reversed. The endeavor might well require that several churches band together to provide the staffing and supervision on a weekly basis. A judge might be more willing to order such a visitation process if the option were available.

The Duluth Model[4] offers the following tips on its program of supervised visitation:

- We work individually with families to develop transition goals and plans that keep the spotlight on safety for the time they are using the visitation center and when they leave.

- Each parent is asked at orientation to define what the ideal situation would look like for visitation and communication.

- A written agreement of plans is created that can start while the parents are using the center, to ensure that the plans can be practiced under supervision.

- If there are orders for protection violations or other safety concerns, the plan will be stopped and more time given in the visitation center.

- The plans are provided to the decision makers—judges, guardian *ad litems* and attorneys who may not have the time or information to develop plans that fit the individual situation, therefore increasing safety for battered women and their children.

Damage control before the trouble starts. Many Christian communities are so resolutely opposed to divorce that little is given except disapproval at the time of the rupture. While it is true that God hates divorce, the Bible also says that God hates a lying tongue, hands that shed blood and stirring up trouble in the family (Prov 6:16-18).

Sad to say, some surveys report a higher rate of divorce among Christians than among the general population. The Barna website notes:

- Born-again adults are more likely to experience a divorce than are non-born-again adults (27 percent and 24 percent, respectively).

- Multiple divorces are also unexpectedly common among born-again Christians. Barna's figures show that nearly one-quarter of the married born-agains (23 percent) get divorced two or more times.

- The survey showed that divorce varied somewhat by a person's denominational affiliation. Catholics were substantially less likely than Protestants to get divorced (25 percent and 39 percent, respectively). Among the largest Protestant groups, those most likely to get divorced were Pentecostals (44 percent), while Presbyterians had the fewest divorces (28 percent).

The ugly truth is that in significant numbers, members of our faith communities are experiencing divorce. As little as we like it, this is a reality. Often we shun those whose marriages are breaking up, some-

how supposing that our disapproval will drive the couple back together again.

Usually the reverse is true. Alienation from the church serves to
deepen the embitterment both are feeling. We might better ask what
we can do to lessen this bitterness and to prevent an ugly feud that
can only damage all concerned. Before it is allowed to fester, the
wound could be addressed constructively. The church can be there to
intervene before tensions rise impossibly high. Mediation services
are provided by the courts, but usually not until there have been
some very ugly developments. Pastoral care can begin much sooner.
Hostility is best deflected early on.

When a child is presented for dedication or baptism, the congregation stands to indicate its support of his or her nurture and Christian
instruction. But is our protective concern present for them when they
need us most?

Instead of trying to fix the marriage, we might do better to work at
fixing the relationship. Even if a couple separates, there are still many
matters on which they need to work together, the most important being humane treatment of their children. Can they be assisted to figure this out in a reasonable fashion?

Here kindly guidance may help to focus on the need of the children rather than the need to "get even." Some children are shuttled
back and forth unmercifully and may have no stability in their lives.
We knew of a child who was required to alternate every single night
between her parents, never able to sleep in the same bed two nights
in a row.

As they develop their plans, parents can be encouraged to seek out
guidelines that will be the least traumatic for their children. To have
the support rather than the opprobrium of the faith community can
be a stabilizing influence in the midst of the upheaval.

Providing an environment of caring concern. Shaming and blaming
do little to help, however much we may deplore the dissolution of a
marriage. Most Christians already carry a tremendous sense of shame
that their marriage has ended in divorce, and many cannot even face

their old friends at church—just when they need them most.

This juncture can provide a significant opportunity for spiritual growth and fellowship. The church might sponsor a divorce recovery group or a program for single parents and their children. The congregation can be encouraged to adopt a hospitable attitude; there is no sense in "divorcing the divorced."

Church members need to be cautioned not to intrude and start giving advice for which they were never asked. One survivor declared, "I suffered more from the unaccepting attitude of the church than I did from the actual abuse." Everybody wanted to play the role of marriage counselor, even though they certainly did not have all the facts nor did she feel any necessity to divulge them.[5]

If both parties to a divorce attend the same church, care needs to be taken so that there is appropriate space between them and that there is no stalking. Some victims quake with terror in the back of the sanctuary while the abuser sits prominently at the front. Churches need to be places where there is zero tolerance for stalking in any form.

A safe, welcoming faith community can help bring stability back into the life of a child. Familiar, smiling faces are a great comfort. In view of our Savior's repeated concern for children and their safety, it behooves us to place our priorities where Jesus placed his.

13

What Can Church Folk Do?

Many conscientious Christians are uncertain as to what they might do to help those who find themselves in an abusive relationship or marriage. Many have never heard the subject of abuse discussed at church. Surely a problem affecting so many inside and outside our church family deserves honest study and reflection.

The first step is a willingness to listen and to believe the victim. All too often, those who screw up their courage to tell their story meet only disbelief. The stories that they tell are often hard to accept—how could such a nice Christian man treat his family so? How could this bright Christian woman have gotten herself into such a problem?

It is at this point that we must be willing to listen. Often the first reaction is one of shock: such a lovely family, absolute pillars of the church! Remember, it can happen to anybody, and it is important that the victim be believed, especially if safety issues are involved. Some church members hold back because they "don't want to take sides." To make adequate provision for such an abused person's needs does not imply "taking sides" but rather a responsible way of handling a ticklish problem. It is always appropriate to act in the interests of safety.

Those in need should be able to count on the rest of us to work toward their safety rather than to assail them with expressions of our disbelief. There is a saying that a family that looks too good to be true probably is too good to be true. God's people need to be ready to respond even in scenarios that defy belief.

Sometimes church folk are baffled because the victim will tell different parts of her story to different people. This makes people wonder whether she is being truthful. Usually victims will not tell the whole story to a single individual unless they know that person very well. Seldom do they lie, but seldom will they disclose everything at once. Church members also need to understand that the stories told by the two different members in a relationship may be widely divergent.

"Why in the world does she stay? I'd be out of there in ten minutes!" There are said to be some fifty-two reasons people remain in bitterly adverse circumstances. One of them most certainly is the pressure applied by the church to make sure that the family stays together under any and all events. Many fear the social alienation that would take place; others fear losing their church home. Some consider the potential change in their immigration status. Some cling to the vows they made at the altar, even after the covenant has been broken. The financial challenges are enough to give anyone pause, and then there is the effect on the children. Many mothers will endure almost anything if their staying guarantees a good education for their children. Some stay because they fear that it will be more dangerous to leave. Statistically, they are right. Seventy-five percent of domestic murders occur before, during or after a victim tries to leave. Any arrangements to leave an abusive situation should be made, if at all possible, with great care and great secrecy.

A source of intense exasperation is the return of a victim to an unsafe situation from which Christian folk have made enormous efforts to rescue her. She was given a ready ear, food, clothing for herself and children, a place to stay, transportation and a quick transfusion from the deacon's fund. And now she has gone back to her abuser, and all the effort appears wasted. On average the woman who will

eventually leave returns seven times as she wrestles with the circumstances, the pleas and pressures for her to return, her own discomfort
and her fear of a future alone.[1]

We can remember the story of Hagar, the abused slave who ran
away, and how the angel commanded her to return (Gen 16:9). In that
way her needs for food, shelter, protection and assistance for her upcoming delivery could be ensured. As we retell the story, we like to
imagine that she received more kindly treatment from Abraham and
Sarah after she returned, but the text does not tell us that. It says that
she went back with a promise that sustained her spirit. According to
ancient Near Eastern law, a slave woman could be impregnated and
then delivered of her child across the lap of her mistress, who was
then considered the legal mother of the child. That had been Sarah's
strategy to gain a son.

But the child was to be Hagar's own, rather than Sarah's, and she
was destined to become the mother of a mighty nation. She was to
name her son "God Shall Hear" (Ishmael), for she had entered into a
personal relationship with the loving God who had been revealed to
her. She could understand herself not as a slave who had been used as
breeding property but as a full person made in the divine image with
a divine purpose. These were the factors that could keep her soul
afloat until at last Abraham was commanded by God to send her and
her son forth as free persons (Gen 21:10-13).

Others also need to have their spirits sustained. Even if those who
persist in returning to a dangerous place may disappoint us, they are
still in need of our ongoing prayer and care. It is important that we
respect their integrity and their choices. Even if we judge them to be
unwise, we need to let victims know that we are there for them if they
choose to come back to us.

ASPECTS OF HIGH RISK

Regardless of the reason, many individuals, both female and male, opt
to stay in tragically difficult circumstances. It is here that the church
must be ready to minister, to be aware of some of the very high risks

that require our watchfulness. According to a report published in the October 12, 2009, issue of *Archives of Internal Medicine,* the Group Health Research Institute and the University of Washington in Seattle discovered that abused women suffered "an almost six-fold increase in clinically identified substance abuse, a more than three-fold increase in receiving a depression diagnosis, a three-fold increase in sexually transmitted diseases and a two-fold increase in lacerations."

Pregnant women are especially vulnerable, with blows frequently directly toward the abdomen and the breasts. The March of Dimes lists domestic abuse as one of the major contributory factors in birth defects.

Another danger to which victims of abuse are peculiarly suscep-tible is that of suicide. Thirty-five to 40 percent of abused women at-tempt suicide. Wife abuse accounts for 25 percent of suicides by all U.S. women and 50 percent of suicides by African American women. It is here that particular sensitivity can save lives. Both men and women can feel themselves trapped by circumstances for which they see no biblically sanctioned means of escape. In many instances, ver-bal and mental abuse have left them with so low a self-image that they do not consider their lives worth saving.

We can present God's purpose of freedom from oppression, of re-spect for the individual. Prayer partnership and friendship are invalu-able. We can supply Bible studies and inspirational materials to keep the soul afloat. More than once we have been told of how literature placed in the women's restroom of the church prevented suicide.

ENCOURAGING PREPAREDNESS

One of the surprising factors in working with domestic abuse is the unexpectedness with which ugly situations confront us. Church folk need to do some careful thinking ahead of time. Our ability to minister begins when we take the trouble to inform ourselves about the issue. Many tell us that they have never heard domestic abuse discussed in a church setting. Awareness raising is one of the first steps in readiness to help: "As shoes for your feet put on whatever will make you ready to proclaim the gospel of peace" (Eph 6:15).

While it is imperative to respect the victim's right to make an adult decision, it is also important to strongly encourage safety planning. Is she ready to move quickly if the situation becomes too dangerous? Has she been warned to heed the danger signals?

A woman whose boyfriend's gun had left her blind (along with other physical and emotional wounds) realized that she had failed to recognize the early signs. She wrote,

> I believe that domestic violence is an issue that is where breast cancer was 15 years ago. It's an issue that most people know little about. And it's an issue where much of the impact can be dealt with if you learn the signs and intervene early.[2]

Victims can be helped to understand that leaving when things grow too dangerous does not prevent them from returning at a later point when the scene is stabilized. Sometimes victims can also be helped to understand that leaving is the most responsible course of action. It protects the offender from rash action that might lead to years in prison, and it protects the victim and children from a terrible tragedy. Some devoted women would rather die than do anything that might dishonor Christ, yet what could dishonor him more than a domestic murder?

WHEN THE PROBLEM IS IN YOUR OWN CHURCH

Ordinarily a church, even when it wishes to respond, cannot supply all the services that might be required in a complex situation within the congregation. Usually the victim needs to be helped to connect with appropriate community services. Others can give specialized help better than well-meaning amateurs in most areas, but nobody can pray more effectively than we. The church excels in its ability to give concern, to demonstrate strong respect during a time of crisis, to give moral support, prayer, simple friendship, acts of kindness and practical assistance. We are marvelous at rounding up food and toys and clothing and transportation and help from the emergency deacons' fund.

Often victims' self-image has been so utterly demolished that they dare not make any effort to help themselves. But let us begin by teaching them that they are of infinite worth to themselves, to others and to God.

If the perpetrator is a member of the congregation, there also needs to be caring and concern for him. It is difficult to sit next to the wrongdoer in church, to participate in the same prayer or small Bible-study group. If we have been told of an abusive situation in confidence, we must retain that confidentiality. We can treat all persons with respect and take constructive steps to share our position. We can mentor and monitor and minister but not condone the conduct. We can find ways to bring into our discussions the scores upon scores of Bible passages that condemn physical, emotional, sexual, verbal and financial abuse.

As we come upon such a passage during a group Bible study, let us note that God is not silent and that all of us need to grow in our understanding on these points. Our prayer life also can reflect our concern for individuals caught in the web of abuse, for children living in abusive families, for those who do not understand that it is wrong to oppress and terrorize another. Our prayer circles can include a request for God to bless the families of our congregation with homes that are safe, with kindness and mutual respect for each of their members, and for their growth in peace and joy and fruitfulness in Christ. Thus we not only remind the Lord of our concerns, but also plant them in the hearts of those who share our prayers.

If there is an arrest, the church needs to make sure that someone will be present in the courtroom for the hearing. The church needs to make it plain that, while an offender will be affirmed as a human being, there is zero tolerance for abusive behavior. If the victim is afraid of an encounter with the perpetrator at the church, arrangement should be made to avoid an incident. Often the perpetrator is very anxious to make amends and very anxious to see the victim return to the home again. Apparent remorse does not always translate into altered behavior, and learning new behavior patterns is a time-consuming and difficult process. Remember that we are not usually qualified to be referees; that is best done by a qualified counselor. We're highly qualified in the prayer department.

IMAGES OF HEALING

When we approach those in the depths of despair, we can bring new visions of healing from the Scriptures, sacred song and devotional literature. We do best to bring what speaks most to our own soul. Here the thoughts of yesteryear may prove very important. *Streams in the Desert* is one such work, using the image of abundant water meeting our needs in the midst of a dry and barren desert. The author, Mrs. Charles Cowman, produced several other books with daily readings that also focus on sustaining the soul in times of adversity.

Still older and still widely read is the *Interior Castle*, written by Teresa of Avila as a guidebook for her nuns.

> I thought of the soul as resembling a castle, formed of a single diamond or a very transparent crystal, and containing many rooms, just as in heaven there are many mansions. If we reflect, sisters, we shall see that the soul of the just person is but a paradise, in which, God tells us, He takes His delight. What, do you imagine, must that dwelling be in which a King so mighty, so wise, and so pure, containing in Himself all good, can delight to rest? Nothing can be compared to the great beauty and capabilities of a soul; however keen our intellects may be, they are as unable to comprehend them as to comprehend God, for, as He has told us, He created us in His own image and likeness.

What good news for a victim who thinks she hardly has a soul at all! The image of building within oneself a castle can be a very helpful one for victims of abuse. The walls of a soul's interior castle must be built on a foundation strong enough to resist such onslaught.

A castle is designed to provide safety for others in need of protection. The soul that has found security for itself can offer a shelter to other souls. A castle is positioned on high ground to provide a wide view of the surrounding landscape and the movements of hostile forces. Within the castle, a soul can look down on things from a higher perspective and gain a more comprehensive view. So often the self-perception of a victim rests on the demeaning treatment that she has received from her oppressor. She believes the lies that she has been told about being stupid and incompetent and the fault of all the problems in the relationship. The view at the top brings better understanding of the lay of the land, enabling the soul, created and redeemed by Jesus Christ, to recognize its own self-worth.

HAVE ALL OUR PRAYERS BEEN WASTED?

How often we are discouraged in our prayer efforts, especially when things don't go at all the way we had hoped. Why did the perpetrator not change the abusive pattern of conduct? Did we "ask wrongly" as James puts it, that is, from selfish motives (4:3)? When there is divorce or death or destitution, did God not hear our prayers—or were they of no avail?

The biblical record suggests that God reserves our prayers for response on a divine time schedule. Cornelius the centurion was told that his prayers and alms had "come up as a memorial offering before God" (Acts 10:4 NIV). The archangel Michael told Daniel, "From the first day that you set your mind to gain understanding and to humble yourself before your God, your words have been heard, and I have come because of your words" (Dan 10:12).

During a time of terrible persecution when believers cried out to God, John had a vision of the throne of God. Before it were four living creatures and twenty-four elders, each of whom held a harp and a golden bowl. Within each bowl was stored the prayers of the saints (Rev 5:8). With their harps, they sang a new song of praise; and from the golden bowls the prayers of the saints rose as incense. The prayers had not been wasted or ignored but preserved to rise at the appropriate time, before God's presence.

Another angel, who had a golden censer, came and stood at the altar. He was given much incense to offer, with the prayers of all the saints, on the golden altar before the throne. The smoke of the incense, together with the prayers of the saints, went up before God from the angel's hand. (Rev 8:3-4 NIV)

While many things of earth have passed away, the permanence of earnest prayer remains always before the throne of God. The psalmist prayer, "Let my prayer be counted as incense before you, and the lifting up of my hands as an evening sacrifice" (Ps 141:2). Just as prayer ascends, mingled with incense, so prayer, our most important resource, must be mingled with the actions of concern and compassion Christ enjoins upon us.

14

Taking Action

Web-Based and Print Resources
to Assist Pastors and Congregations

$\mathcal{S}$peaking out against violence in the family context or responding compassionately to those who have been impacted by it requires knowledge as well as practical resources. Educational resources are paramount to taking appropriate action on the issue of abuse. Certainly this is true for the pastor or religious leader who is called on to offer counsel or assistance. But it is also true for congregations, family members and friends who find themselves caught between the reality of domestic violence and the dream of peace and safety in homes across the nation. The prophetic voice paired with contemporary resources of both a practical and spiritual nature is powerful both within and beyond the walls of congregational life. It challenges those in the pew even as it applies the healing balm of Gilead to the wounds of those who suffer. Offering a cup of cold water to someone who is thirsty has always been central to the call of God on every believer.

In this chapter, the reader will be introduced to a wide range of resources that have been—and are continuing to be—developed and expanded as part of Nancy Nason-Clark's RAVE [Religion and Violence e-Learning] Project.[1] In our first edition of *No Place for Abuse*, we offered a variety of practical and religious resources as part of an expanded series of six appendixes placed at the end of the book. In this revised edition, we build on these resources by employing the web-based training, best practices and worldwide links of the RAVE Project.

Integrating the book with the RAVE initiative enables us to provide you with the most recent statistics, shelter contact information, referral guidelines and downloadable resources. All of these can be printed out or viewed on a laptop, and some can be downloaded as a podcast so you can listen while on the move. All the web-based resources are updated regularly and expanded frequently, so that when you access the RAVE website (www.theraveproject.org), it is possible to view the most recent material created by our team. There are resources specifically designed for pastors, small-group and youth leaders, victims of and survivors of violence, those who act abusively and youth.

The RAVE Project attempts to build bridges between religious leaders and other community-based professionals by providing up-to-date, relevant and spiritually enriched resources on the issue of domestic violence. It offers pastors knowledge and guidance as they negotiate their place among other community agencies when responding to the issue of domestic violence and to the enormous pain and consequences created as a result of its prevalence and severity. The RAVE Project also offers knowledge and guidance to community-based workers as they negotiate their place in responding to violence within families of faith. All of this involves delicate terrain and uncharted waters.

Building bridges of collaborative action among churches and community agencies on the issue of domestic violence involves finding a language and a will to alter the status quo. It involves issues of trust. It involves issues of safety. It sometimes involves issues of comfort—

that of the pastor or the police officer or the social worker.

We began this initiative with the belief that pastors need training on how best to respond to women, men, teens and children whose lives have been impacted by domestic violence. The data was unequivocal: in studies we conducted over the past twenty years, less than one in ten clergy (8 percent to be exact) believed they were personally well equipped to assist abuse victims who sought their help. Yet most clergy cannot avail themselves of training opportunities that would equip them to help those who face the fear, the pain and the despair of domestic violence currently or in their past.

There are many reasons for this chasm between pastoral preparedness on issues of abuse and the call of ministry to the abused. First, most training takes place on weekends, a time when the average pastor is not able to be away from the parish. Second, training costs money, and many church budgets offer little in the way of continuing-education dollars for their leaders. Third, many workshops and other educational events—on subjects such as innovations in worship, dealing with aging buildings, activities to keep youth involved, developing a leadership style—compete for limited training dollars.

We have learned from our research, speaking engagements and informal conversations with religious leaders over the years that there are several other reasons pastors do not attend training. First, most pastors are not willing to attend a public training event where they understand little about the subject matter. The fear of saying the wrong thing or asking a "stupid" question simply keeps them away. Second, many pastors are not willing to go alone to a workshop where they do not know others nor are they known by them. The fear of standing alone at coffee break or eating alone at lunch is a major deterrent. Given that pastors are frequently surrounded by a crowd of parishioners after a worship service, many vying for their attention, handshake or "word of encouragement," the expected discomfort with strangers tips the balance against attendance. Third, training priorities are often identified by clergy on a "crisis" basis—when the crisis is averted, the "need for training" subsides. And fourth, many pastors want a "quick fix" to their need for information—data available at their fingertips at the moment it is needed—but are reluctant to engage in sustained reflection on issues regarded as peripheral to their ministry priorities.

Sometimes there are other factors too. In some community contexts or secular training modules, religious leaders are not really welcome. They are not regarded as part of the coordinated community response to domestic violence, and there may be reluctance by members of the therapeutic community, by advocates or by the criminal justice system to be inclusive of religious leaders. In situations such as these, pastors and others informed by religious perspectives may feel uncomfortable. When the minister is able to see this reluctance of secular professionals as a challenge or as an opportunity to "build a bridge," an unfamiliar training venue holds enormous potential for both networking and knowledge acquisition.

Religious leaders, like other professionals in the community, are caught in a delicate balance between being proactive and being reactive in their day-to-day work lives. Most pastors say they spend more time counseling parishioners than they expected when they first answered the call to ministry. It is not uncommon to hear ministers lament that they spend large portions of their week engaged in activities outside the domain of what they personally consider most central to ministry—for example, preparation for and preaching of the Word. Pastors do respond to family crises, whether or not they are trained or equipped for the task. What happens next depends on the pastor's experience, wisdom and maturity.

"Taking Action"—the title of this chapter—suggests that, though most pastors are ill equipped to offer immediate, compassionate and helpful practical and spiritual assistance to families impacted by abuse, this dire situation can change.

The RAVE Project was first created to respond to the unique training needs of religious leaders. We knew it needed to be available free of charge and accessible in the privacy of the church or home office. It also needed to offer, in an expeditious manner, exactly the information required to enable pastors and other religious leaders to engage in sustained study and reflection as time, need and interest allowed. And it appears that the RAVE Project has begun to meet that need.

The RAVE website has been "live" since 2008, and each week a thousand new users have visited the site and accessed a variety of resources and information we have to offer. In fact, the average user looks at six to seven pages per visit and stays an average of twelve minutes. More than 60 percent come back to the website within the next month to access more of the resources.

What is available on the RAVE website? There is *information* packaged in unique ways. There are *guidelines* involving best practices to imitate and pitfalls to avoid. There are *voices* of real people who have walked alongside survivors—including clergy, therapists, police, advocates, judges, social workers and prosecutors—and of survivors themselves. There are *illustrations* based on the lives of real people who have been part of our extensive research program over the past twenty years. There are *referral sources* to shelters across North America and contact information for faith-based initiatives responding to violence. There are *curricula* for youth events, including the innovative Dating Game—an educational tool to help young people identify healthy and unhealthy dating experiences. There are *resources*, such as sample sermons, prayers, Bible passages and Bible studies. There are *blogs,* for those who would like to communicate with other learners, and *podcasts* for those who would like to listen to the training as they drive or exercise. There is even a section on the site specifically for seminary students.

In short, the RAVE website is a comprehensive e-learning initiative directed toward pastors and others who are called on to respond to the issue of abuse. Many of the resources speak directly to victims and survivors of domestic violence—those currently in a situation involving abuse or coping with the long-term consequences of abuse in their past.

Below are three directed "tours" of the website to help the reader become aware of the range of these e-resources. If you have access to the Internet right now, access the RAVE website at <www.therave project.org>. If not, place a bookmark here, and access the website later, using the information below in the same way that a traveler might consult a travel guide before embarking on a trip.

Before you begin browsing the RAVE website, make sure that (1) your computer will temporarily allow "pop-ups"; (2) your sound is on; and (3) you bookmark our site so you can find it easily later. You may later wish to incorporate some of the RAVE resources into a team meeting for your staff, a board meeting of your church leaders, a small-group study or a sermon. Using a data projector and a laptop, you can show any of the materials provided on a large screen in the sanctuary of your church in much the same way you would project the words of a worship song or a trailer for a DVD series.

TOUR 1: SEEKING BASIC INFORMATION
ON DOMESTIC VIOLENCE

The RAVE website is designed to help anyone interested in understanding the prevalence or severity of abuse in families of faith or within the broader culture. We offer data on abuse, words from those who have suffered, answers to some basic questions about violence in the family and an overview of violence against women around the world.

If you are interested in general awareness about abuse, we suggest that you start by orienting yourself to our home page (the page that opens first when you enter our website). The home page sets the tone for the website. Our logo, featuring a white dove whose wings are outstretched, represents the centrality of compassion, spiritual strength, renewal and new beginnings for those whose lives have been impacted by domestic violence.

Our use of stained glass is a reminder that beauty can be birthed from brokenness. When violence strikes, chaos is created. What once was intact is shattered into many pieces. Yet jagged pieces of glass, rough to the touch and piercing to the skin, can become something new. Stained glass, long a symbol of the Christian church, reminds us that connection and diversity is part of family life too. The language of the Spirit brings hope: a new day awaits. There is spiritual strength to overcome even the greatest of challenges.

The ugly reality of violence and the hope of our Christian faith are intertwined on the RAVE website as we seek to document the nature, prevalence and severity of abuse both within and beyond the walls of our churches. As you listen to the "Words of Hope" (found at the upper left-hand corner of the home page) from a variety of men and women, some of whom have personal experience with violence and others who have sought to provide assistance to those who have suffered, you will find that the challenge to take this issue seriously cannot be avoided. In case you momentarily forget that abusers also need the support of churches and clergy, click on the stained glass and hear them speak.

There are plenty of opportunities on our website to become oriented to our RAVE Team, the men and women who have helped to create our resources, their credentials and past experiences. You can find out about the goals of our work and the variety of research projects on which it has been built. We offer information for the pastor who has had little exposure to the issue of domestic violence and for those who have participated in training opportunities. The information and resources you receive depends on the places you visit as you navigate the site.

If you wish to begin with the "basics" of domestic violence, we suggest that you spend some time on the frequently asked questions (click on the "FAQ" tab near the top of the page). This section of the website has been organized around a series of questions, each of which is addressed by a variety of people representing different professions and perspectives. For example, when you first click on "What is abuse?" there will be a general response to it. Then, on the right-hand side of the screen, you will find a list of other people you can consult, for example, "Ask a Survivor," "Ask a Therapist" and so on. As you read various responses to the same question, it will become clear that there is more than one way to think about how domestic violence impacts families across the nation. One of the things we have tried to do on the site is to ensure that there is a good mix between basic information and advanced, in-depth knowledge for those who require it.

After you have considered some of the answers to the FAQs, you might be wondering about the frequency of woman abuse—in the United States or somewhere else in the world. Many people find the statistics on woman abuse or other forms of domestic violence hard to comprehend. There are so many things to know about statistics, including the actual questions that were asked, who asked them, how the data were gathered and analyzed, the size of the sample, the year of the study and where it was published. Obviously, it is not possible to consider all of that here. Interested readers can consult our online lessons for a brief discussion of research considerations or our "Useful Fast Facts" on various types of information related to domestic violence.

The statistics on woman abuse presented on our RAVE map (found under "Violence Against Women Around the World" on the home page) are organized by the country about which they have been collected. Using data assembled mainly by large organizations, like the World Health Organization, UNICEF or national governmental agencies, such as Statistics Canada and the U.S. Department of Justice, we have sought to provide a snapshot of what is known about violence against women around the world.

In chapter one, we highlighted in point form some "data bytes" related to woman abuse and domestic violence from various countries. More information—and greater detail, often including links to the original sources—can be found by clicking on the red circle of your country of interest. Each time you wish to consider a different country, click on the small-scale world map on the right of the screen, and then return to the larger map to click on your next country of interest.

In some parts of the world, there has been a virtual explosion of information on domestic violence and other forms of family abuse affecting women, men and children. In other places, there is very little information available. Another place on the website where we provide statistics related to violence in the family is within the "Useful Fast Facts" section. To access this, click first on the "Online Training" tab.

If you have followed through on some of the suggestions above on the RAVE website, here are a few questions you might ask yourself:

- What are some of the key features of the "Words of Hope" offered on the home page of the RAVE website? Do the words of these men and women offer me a challenge, or are they comforting? Why?

- Do I find it hard to believe that domestic violence is so prevalent both in my own country and elsewhere? Why, or why not, might that be?

- Which piece of new information from the website haunts me the most? Why?

- Do I need to do something about what I have learned, for myself or for someone else?

TOUR 2: SEEKING HELP FOR PREPARING
A SERMON ON DOMESTIC VIOLENCE

Some religious leaders decide that it is a good idea to preach a sermon on abuse, especially during Domestic Violence Awareness Month, which in the United States is October. To help religious leaders to do this, the RAVE website offers a very basic understanding of the dynamics of abuse in families of faith through the creative use of data collected from our research studies. There is an opportunity to listen to the voices of those who have been impacted by abuse, to view video clips and to consider some of the key points in identifying whether (and how) to get serious about the issue of domestic violence in your local church setting.

We have attempted to provide a variety of mechanisms on the website to enable pastors and others to become acquainted with how the story of abuse unfolds. Using stained-glass art, we show the story of abuse through the presentation of a series of six windows, each one depicting part of the story of what happens when abuse strikes the home of a Christian. (Click on "Stained Glass Story of DV" on the home page.) We have worked with stained-glass artists to share the stories of Christian women, told to us so many times through our fieldwork. The stained-glass windows tell the story of despair, and eventually of hope:

Window 1: *In the beginning . . . there is peace;*
Window 2: *The chaos . . . life will never be the same again;*
Window 3: *The aftermath . . . the impact is felt by young and old alike;*
Window 4: *Rebuilding . . . new portraits of family living are created;*
Window 5: *Renewal . . . beauty from brokenness;*
Window 6: *New beginnings . . . the Spirit brings hope.*

Visuals, such as the "Stained Glass Story of DV," help to convey a very important message: life after abuse does not "return to normal," as if the abuse never happened. Pastoral intervention normally involves helping the family pick up the pieces—the fragments of glass—and journey toward safety, healing and a new start.

As important as visuals are, there is nothing quite as powerful as listening to a survivor's firsthand account. In many places on the website, survivors of domestic violence speak of their own story. In the "Words of Hope" section on the home page, you can listen to Michael Phillips or Marilyn Young or Debra Wideman tell part of their own story, each revealing that there are so many women and men whose lives have been impacted by domestic violence. Phillips's wife was murdered as they attempted to help a couple next door who were fighting. Young is a grieving mother: her daughter was murdered in her early twenties shortly after she was married. And Wideman knows firsthand about a husband's violent ways.

These are all examples of people who have chosen to tell their stories on our website, as a result of contact with our work in one of the RAVE project's three locations outside Canada: Charlotte, North Carolina; Columbia, Missouri; and Eugene, Oregon. But there are others—many others—who have been part of our research program, which has extended over almost twenty years. As you navigate the website, we expect that you will be surprised at the variety of ways you encounter the words of those who have been personally impacted by the reality of abuse.

You can hear segments of stories, told anonymously, through a speaking circle. Sometimes you will find the voices of victims, survivors or their families. Other times it will be the voices of pastors and others who have walked alongside those whose lives have come in contact with domestic violence. It is important to remind you, at this point, that all of these resources can be used as a teaching tool for a small-group study or within a sermon, as long as you have access to a laptop and an Internet connection. As you can probably attest by now, a picture or a voice helps you to catch a fuller understanding of the pain and despair.

At this point, you may be thinking, Domestic violence impacts far more people than I ever imagined. In every country, in every neighborhood and in every church, there are those who suffer the devastating consequences of violence in the family context. For most people, it comes as a shock to learn of its frequency and severity. Once aware, however, many people want more information. That's why selected clips from the *When Love Hurts* series,[2] which tells the story of one family, are offered on the RAVE website.

We also provide sample sermons, Scripture verses that bring comfort or challenge, and sample prayers for those who are suffering the devastating consequences of abuse. After you have read two or three sermons, perhaps it is time to search the Scriptures yourself. The Bible has quite a lot to say about anger and abuse. A number of Scripture passages also call Christians to accountability for their behavior, and others speak directly about God's care for the brokenhearted. We offer a sampling of these passages and also provide an overview of biblical references throughout the Old and New Testaments that can be used to assist those who live face-to-face with domestic violence.

We have learned from many victims and survivors in our research that when they approach a religious leader for help, rarely does that person pray with them. So we asked many pastors to help us to understand why such might be the case. And we learned something alarming: they were not sure how to pray for someone in the midst of domestic violence. Yet prayer is an important resource for a religious leader to bring to a hurting man or woman. Prayer followed by action offers spiritual strength to enact practical support.

You may have lots of ideas about what might be possible in your church or within your own ministry. If you want to get serious about the issue of abuse, what are some things to consider? We have provided a "Top Ten" list of how to assess whether a church or its leader is serious about the issue of abuse. (Click on "Clergy Resources" on the home page.) Then we can help you put into action some of these suggestions. Take the idea of a brochure in your church restroom as an example. We have prepared a variety of pamphlets and placed them on our website. Once you have accessed these, you can either customize them for your church or print and copy them as they are. Or perhaps you like the idea of placing a poster concerning abuse in your office or prayer room, which also can be downloaded and printed. (Click on the "Resources" tab, and then on "Would you like to . . . download resources?")

Here are a few questions for you to consider at this point:

- What message from the Scripture might I convey to people in my congregation who are suffering the pain and humiliation of abuse?

- What are some of the creative ways for me as a pastor or a small-group leader to encourage violent-free family living?

- What new insights have I gained by reading the prayers and the sermons prepared by others for the RAVE website? Are some ways of approaching this topic more appealing to me than others? Why?

TOUR 3: RESOURCES FOR THE PASTORAL COUNSELOR

When a woman goes to a pastor for advice in the aftermath of domestic violence, information and referral sources are required immediately. Safety is a top priority for the woman and any dependent children she may have. The RAVE website can help to identify the most critical pieces of information that a pastor can convey to a family in crisis.

It might be useful to see some of the ways abuse impacts a family and how the church can help. Beginning in the "Words of Hope" section on the home page, listen to Joyce Holt, a survivor; Gabrielle Macon, a prosecutor; or Mark Koch, a domestic violence advocate. Each offers practical suggestions for religious leaders. Consider too the imagery on the home page: the dove and the stained glass. When the various windows come into focus, think about the role of the pastoral counselor at each step in the journey.

- What does it mean to be a pastoral counselor when someone's life is falling apart, like the shattered glass in the second window pane?

- How can one be the most effective pastoral counselor at the point where a woman is assembling what is left in the aftermath of devastation, or reconfiguring her life, like the third or fourth panes of glass reveal?

- In essence, how can pastoral counselors bring the healing balm of Gilead to the wounds of the afflicted?

Now might be a good time to watch the forty-five-second demonstration of a shattered life provided on our website. This might be appropriate to share with a survivor in your office or to employ as a visual illustration during a sermon.

We have learned from many survivors of domestic violence that the "Stained Glass Story of DV" and the short clip on the "shattered glass" are both descriptive and therapeutic. These visuals describe an important part of the journey from pain to healing, but they also offer hope and celebration. As such, they are useful tools in responding to those who come for help.

Having offered a general perspective, we move to the story of one woman, Julie Owens, told to Jeff Baxter of the Day of Discovery team at RBC Ministries and offered on their DVD series. A video resource may be useful not only in your own training, but also to a victim of violence. She might wish to view it in the privacy of a church office, or somewhere else where she is safe and where her access to the RAVE website will not be detected by her abuser. A pastoral counselor might watch the video with her, responding to her questions and fears afterward. As we noted in earlier chapters, often women do not consider that they have been abused, even though they may have been hurt, threatened or living in fear.

Our "Stained Glass Advice" (under "Women's Resources" on the home page) allows you to see the faces of several religious leaders and to have access to their words of advice to an abused woman who might be coming to the website in search of spiritual support. Each of the pastors has something unique to say to a survivor on the road to healing and wholeness. She may still be very afraid. She may wonder whether anyone understands. Reading the words of comfort may help you as a pastoral counselor understand the variety of ways that words can be of assistance.

Safety must be the top priority when responding to someone who has experienced domestic violence. Sometimes the family home is not a safe place. One excellent resource in some communities is a transition house, or shelter, for battered women and their children. Under "Improved Shelter Maps" on the home page, you can browse a map that highlights shelters across North America; we also provide direct links to the website of those shelters that have them. Touring some of these resources with a woman who is fearful brings her one step closer to considering this as an option when she cannot go home. Being introduced to shelter contact information and the concept of a personalized safety plan will equip you as a pastoral counselor to provide the basic information a woman needs to get help from the experts.

Finally, we consider some of the lessons learned as a result of conducting our fieldwork with hundreds of pastors. In our training series "Mending Broken Hearts" (click on the "Online Training" tab), you can choose one of the lessons, such as "Mildred Jennings' Story," based on a true case from our research in which a family sought help from a pastor. After you have read the story, you can see what other professionals said about how the case unfolded. "Ask an Advocate" or "Ask a Survivor" by clicking on the appropriate category on the right side of the screen.

As you consider the real-life stories of families in crisis, you might wonder how one pastor can possibly be prepared? The good news is that pastors are one part of a loosely connected community response team, working together with others in a coordinated fashion. Teamwork lifts the load from any one pastor or counselor and ensures that no one profession bears all the responsibility for the care of a family impacted by abuse.

Having navigated the RAVE website from the perspective of a pastoral counselor, here are a few questions to consider:

- What are some of the community-based resources in my area that can help support an abused woman and her children? What help is available for men who are victims or men who are abusive?

- Do I know some of the workers in these agencies by name? Have I ever invited the director of the shelter to make a presentation in our church? Do I have brochures from the local agencies in my office?

- Are there people in our church who have a professional interest in issues of abuse, such as police, social workers or parole officers? How could I learn from their experiences in the local area? Might they identify ways that our church could be more involved in helping?

✳ ✳ ✳

We could have created other RAVE website tours as well, such as for the youth pastor or the worker in a community-based agency. As you browse the website, it will become clear that there are a multitude of resources on RAVE to help both survivors and those who walk alongside them.

YOUTH RESOURCES ON THE RAVE WEBSITE

The "Dating Game," available under the "Youth" tab, is an innovative, interactive game created with church youth, youth groups and youth leaders in mind. It highlights relationships between teens, focusing on the healthy and the unhealthy components of relationships between young men and women. It uses humor to offer a very important message: relationships can be harmful. But healthy behavior can be learned. And everyone needs assistance in promoting healthy responses to disappointment, in communicating more clearly and in ensuring that they treat others well.

The game can be played alone (on a computer at home or in an Internet café) or as part of a group function, where a group leader can access the RAVE website on a laptop connected to a data projector. In this way, all the youth can see the materials at once. Or assemble laptops in different classrooms, and have teams play the game for points.

Our website will be developing for several more years, at least until 2015. We are currently working with graduate students at three seminaries to develop Facebook pages and blogs for each of our cartoon characters. Whenever you access the "Youth" tab on the RAVE website, you will be able to see our most recent additions. And since these are updated regularly, be sure to check often.

SUMMARY

Where do I go on the RAVE website to find what I need?

Figure 1. Navigating the RAVE Website

Looking for:	Go to:	Click:
Answers to questions	"FAQ" tab	Various questions; "Ask a . . ."
Bible readings	"Resources" tab	"Selected Scripture verses that . . ."
Bible studies	"Resources" tab	"Are you looking for? . . . Bible studies"
Brochures	"Resources" tab	"Would you like to? . . . download resources"
Collaboration ideas	"Resources" tab	"Community Resources" (left column); "Learning to Build Bridges . . ."

Looking for:	Go to:	Click:
Examples of intervention	"Online Training" tab	"Mending Broken Hearts"
Innovative features (top 8)	Home Page	Click on the arrows in the "faces" boxes beside the stained glass
	Home Page	"Women's Resources" (left column); "Women's Spirituality Circle"
	"About Us" tab	"OUR Symbols" (left column); "The Significance of Stained Glass"
	Home Page	"Stained Glass Story of DV" (left column)
	"Help Now" tab	"North American Domestic Violence Shelter Locations"
	Home Page	"Violence Around the World" (left column)
	"Resources" tab	"Would you like to? . . . watch online video"
	"Youth" tab	"Dating Game"
Podcasts	"Resources" tab	"Would you like to? . . . watch online video"
Poems	"Resources" tab	"We offer . . . Stained Glass Poem"
		See also "Are you looking for? . . . sermon ideas"
Profiles of DV leaders	Home Page	"Profiles of DV Leaders" (left column)
Prayers	"Resources" tab	"Sample prayers that . . ."
Purchase books	"Resources" tab	"Would you like to? . . . purchase books"
RAVE kit materials	"Resources" tab	"Would you like to? . . . download . . . "
Referral information	"Help Now" tab	Choose a country; choose a state or "all provinces";
		click on a "pin" or dot for the closest shelter(s).

Looking for:	Go to:	Click:
Safety plan	"Resources" tab	"Would you like to? . . . download a safety plan"
Scripture verses	"Resources" tab	"Selected Scripture verses that . . ."
Sermon examples	"Resources" tab	"Are you looking for? . . . sermon ideas" (scroll down to see more sermons)
Sermon preparation	"Online Training" tab	"Useful Fast Facts"
	"Resources" tab	"Selected Scripture verses that . . ."
		"Sample prayers that . . ."
	"FAQs" tab	(Questions are listed individually.)
	Home Page	"Violence Around the World" (click on the continent; double click red dot for country information)
Statistics on woman abuse	Home Page	"Violence Around the World" (click on the continent; double click red dot for country information)
Training/lessons	"Online Training" tab	See various lessons and categories
URGENT	"Help Now" tab	Click on the directory of interest and then follow the instructions.
Voices of survivors	Home Page	"Words of Hope"
		"Women's Resources" (left column); click on "Listening to the Voices of Victims" and follow instructions
Voices of pastors	Home Page	"Words of Hope"
		"Clergy Resources" (left column); click on "Listening to the Voices of Religious Leaders" and follow instructions

Notes

Preface

[1]John Wesley, *The Journal of John Wesley: Standard Edition,* ed. Nehemiah Curnock (London: Epworth Press, 1938): 4:204.

[2]John Fletcher Hurst, "The True John Wesley" in *John Wesley the Methodist, A Plain Account of His Life and Work by a Methodist Preacher* (New York: Methodist Book Concern, 1903), chap. XX.

[3]Ibid. "I did not desert her; I did not send her away; I will not ask her to return."

[4]The members of the original International Task Force included: Winnie Bartel (United States, chair), Mary Bassali (Egypt), Esme Bower (South Africa), Janice Crouse (United States), Margaret Jacobs (Australia), Catherine Clark Kroeger (United States), Lee Eng Lee (Malaysia), Ksenija Magda (Croatia), Leela Manasseh (India), Judy Mbugua (Kenya), Gwen McVicker (Canada), Olly Mesach (Indonesia), Nancy Nason-Clark (Canada), Grace Nedelchev (Bulgaria), Sharon Payt (United States), Holly Sheldon (Singapore), Lucett Thomas (Costa Rica) and Blossom White (Jamaica).

Chapter 1: The Prevalence and Severity of Abuse Against Women

[1]We are using the masculine pronoun to refer to perpetrators or abusers and the feminine pronoun to refer to victims. While we recognize that some men are victims of husband battery and some women are perpetrators of that violence, the data from around the world reveal that the overwhelming majority of victims of spousal violence are female and the overwhelming majority of the perpetrators are male.

[2]Nason-Clark 2000c.

[3]<www.amnesty.org/en/library/asset/ASA11/008/2005/en/0e17f319-d4e6-11dd-8a23-d58a49c0d652/asa110082005en.html>. 2005. "Afghanistan: Women Still Under Attack—Systematic Failure to Protect." Amnesty International.

[4]<www.irinnews.org/Report.aspx?ReportId=72775>. 2007. "Afghanistan: Losing Hope—Women in Afghanistan." Integrated Regional Information Networks.

[5]<www.community.wa.gov.au/NR/rdonlyres/BBC41107-7341-4BDA-9051-7E963566E870/0/DCDRPTWomensReportCardUpdateApril2006.pdf>. 2006. "Women's Report Card: Measuring Women's Progress, Update 2006." Government of Western Australia, Department for Community Development.

[6]According to a 2006 information kit developed by the Government of Western Austra-

lia, Department for Community Development. For more information, see <www.the raveproject.com/mapdata/australia.html>.

[7]<www.path.org/files/EOL20_1.pdf>. 2002. Barbara Shane and Mary Ellsberg, "Violence Against Women: Effects on Reproductive Health," *Outlook* 20, no. 1 (2002): 1-8.

[8]<www.unhcr.org/refworld/country,,AMNESTY,ANNUALREPORT,BGD,,429b27 d711,0.html>. May 25, 2005. "Amnesty International Report 2005—Bangladesh." Amnesty International.

[9]<www.who.int/gender/violence/who_multicountry_study/summary_report/chapter1/ en/index6.html>. 2005. "WHO Multi-country Study on Women's Health and Domestic Violence against Women." World Health Organization.

[10]Ibid.

[11]<www.state.gov/g/drl/rls/hrrpt/2002/18238.htm>. 2002. "Cambodia." Country Reports on Human Rights Practices. U.S. Department of State, Bureau of Democracy, Human Rights, and Labor.

[12]<http://db.jhuccp.org/ics-wpd/exec/icswppro.dll?BU=http://db.jhuccp.org/ics-wpd/ exec/icswppro.dll&QF0=DocNo&QI0=144570&TN=Popline&AC=QBE_ QUERY&MR=30 percent25DL=1&&RL=1&&RF=LongRecordDisplay&DF=LongRec ordDisplay>. 1996. "Household survey on domestic violence in Cambodia." Ministry of Women's Affairs, Phnom Penh.

[13]<http://prod.library.utoronto.ca:8090/datalib/codebooks/cstdli/gss/gss18/85-224- xie2005000.pdf>. 2005. "Family Violence in Canada: A Statistical Profile, 2005." Statistics Canada.

[14]<www.statcan.gc.ca/daily-quotidien/051124/dq051124b-eng.htm>. 2004. "General Social Survey: Criminal victimization." Statistics Canada <www.statcan.gc.ca/cgibin/ imdb/p2SV.pl?Function=getSurvey&SurvId=4504&SurvVer=2&InstaId=16857&Inst aVer=3&SDDS=4504&lang=en&db=IMDB&adm=8&dis=2>. 1999. "General Social Survey—Victimization (GSS)." Statistics Canada.

[15]<www.eurowrc.org/06.contributions/1.contrib_en/25.contrib.en.htm> 2007. Lori Heise, J. Pitanguy and A. Germaine, "Violence Against Women: The Hidden Health Burden," World Bank Discussion Paper #255 (Washington, D.C.: World Bank, 1994), p. 30.

[16]<www.popline.org/docs/1332/141044.html> 1998. "The Intimate Enemy: Gender Violence and Reproductive Health." Panos Briefing No. 27.

[17]<www2.chinadaily.com.cn/china/2008-03/07/content_6515868.htm>. 2008. "Campaign to Stop Domestic Violence." *China Daily* Online, March 7, 2008.

[18]<www.chinadaily.net/china/2007-08/02/content_5447324.htm>. 2007. "Domestic Violence in Spotlight." *China Daily* Online, August 2, 2007.

[19]<www.state.gov/g/drl/rls/hrrpt/2005/61721.htm>. 2005. "Colombia" Country Reports on Human Rights Practices. U.S. Department of State, Bureau of Democracy, Human Rights, and Labor.

[20]<www.highbeam.com/doc/1P3-1005209611.html>. 2004. "Violence Against Women Act." Amnesty International.

[21]<www.stopvaw.org/sites/3f6d15f4-c12d-4515-8544-26b7a3a5a41e/uploads/CROA- TIA_VAW_FACT_SHEET_2006.pdf>. 2006. "Violence Against Women: Does the Government Care in Croatia?" Open Society Institute.

[22]<www.croatia.org/crown/articles/5927/1/E-V-DAY-Stop-violence-against-women

-and-girls.html>. 2003. "V-DAY: Stop violence against women and girls." Croatian World Network.

[23]<www.unfpa.org.eg/default.htm>. 2000. UNFPA Egypt.

[24]<www2.ohchr.org/english/bodies/cedaw/cedaws25.htm>. 2001. "Committee on the Elimination of Discrimination against Women, 25th session (2-20 July 2001)." Office of the United Nations High Commissioner for Human Rights.

[25]<www.who.int/gender/violence/who_multicountry_study/en/>. 2005. "WHO Multicountry Study on Women's Health and Domestic Violence against Women." World Health Organization.

[26] Ibid.

[27]Minna Piipspa, "Research on Violence Against Women," *Violence Against Women* 10, no. 12 (December 1, 2004), 1431-48. <www.vksv.oikeus.fi/en/Etusivu>. 1994. "A Rwandan man charged with the genocide in Rwanda in 1994." Office of the Prosecutor-General, Finland.

[28]<www.historycentral.com/nationbynation/Finland/Human.html>. 2004. "Finland." The Union of Shelter Homes. History Central.

[29]<www.dw-world.de/dw/article/0,,1334950,00.html>. 2004. "German Women Often Victims of Domestic Violence." DW-World.DE.

[30] Ibid.

[31]<http://db.jhuccp.org/ics-wpd/exec/icswppro.dll?BU=http://db.jhuccp.org/ics-wpd/ exec/icswppro.dll&QF0=DocNo&QI0=149212&TN=Popline&AC=QBE_ QUERY&MR=30 percent25DL=1&&RL=1&&RF=LongRecordDisplay&DF=LongRec ordDisplay>. 1998. "Wife-beating in rural India: a husband's right?" *Economic and Political Weekly*.

[32]R. Ramasubban and B. Singh, "Gender, Reproductive Health and Weakness Experiences of Slum Dwelling Women in Bombay, India," presented at the IUSSP Seminar on Cultural Perspectives on Reproductive Health, Rustenberg, South Africa, June 16-19, 1997, p. 24.

[33]<http://thereport.amnesty.org/en/regions/middle-east-north-africa/iran>. 2008. "Iran." Amnesty International Report 2009: State of the World's Human Rights.

[34]<www.wfafi.org/BBC-report.htm>. 2004. "Iran: Women's anti-Islamic fundamentalist radio observed on shortwave." Women's Forum Against Fundamentalism in Iran.

[35]<www.unhcr.org/refworld/publisher,AMNESTY,,IRL,40b5a1f78,0.html>. 2004. "Amnesty International Report 2004—Ireland." Amnesty International.

[36]<http://emergency-medicine.jwatch.org/cgi/content/citation/2002/327/10>. 2002. "Domestic Violence in Ireland: Don't Ask, Don't Tell." Journal Watch Emergency Medicine.

[37]<www.yadsarah.org/index.asp?id=131&newsid=472>. 2007. "Yad Sarah Family Center: Undoing Domestic Violence." Yad Sarah Family Center.

[38]<www.1202.org.il/English/template/default.asp?siteID=1&maincat=5&catId=11&pa geId=107&parentId=25>. 2005. "Breaking the Silence: Rape Victim Cycles Across Israel to Lay Childhood Ghosts to Rest." The Association of Rape Crisis Centers in Israel.

[39]<http://freeofviolence.org/jamaica.htm>. 1997. "Jamaica." United Nations Inter-Agency Campaign on Women's Human Rights in Latin America and the Caribbean.

[40] Ibid.

[41]<www.unhcr.org/refworld/type,ANNUALREPORT,AMNESTY,KEN,429b27e820,0

.html>. 2005. "Amnesty International Report 2005—Kenya." Amnesty International.

[42]<www.unicef.org/infobycountry/kenya_35433.html>. 2006. "Education and awareness make progress against female genital cutting in Kenya." UNICEF.

[43]<www.wao.org.my/Documents/Annual%20Reports/WAO%20ANNUAL%20REPORT%202006.final.pdf>. 2006. "WAO Annual Report 2006." Women's Aid Organisation.

[44]<www.wao.org.my/Documents/Annual%20Reports/Annual%20Report%202007_21 May2008.pdf>. 2007. "WAO Annual Report 2007." Women's Aid Organisation.

[45]<www.unhcr.org/refworld/topic,463af2212,469f2e812,3df4be7214,0.html>. 2002. "Mexico: Guerrilla or paramilitary activity in the municipality of La Trinitaria, Chiapas, including references to kidnapping, forced recruitment and other crimes against the population, particularly those of Mayan descent, by guerrillas or paramilitary groups." Immigration and Refugee Board of Canada.

[46]<www.ncbi.nlm.nih.gov/pubmed/15176573>. 2004. "Prevalence and determinants of male partner violence against Mexican women: a population-based study." Centro de Investigación en Salud Poblacional, Mexico.

[47]<www2.ohchr.org/english/bodies/CRC/docs/study/responses/Netherlands.pdf>. 2004. "United Nations Study on Violence against Children: Response to questionnaire received from the Government of the Kingdom of the Netherlands." United Nations.

[48]<www.coe.int/T/E/Human_Rights/Equality/PDF_EG-SEM-MV_2003_Proceedings.pdf>. 2003. "Measures dealing with men perpetrators of domestic violence." Council of Europe.

[49]<www.nzfvc.org.nz/PublicationDetails.aspx?publication=13120>. 2005. "Domestic violence statistics: what can they tell us?" New Zealand Family Violence Clearinghouse.

[50]<www.2shine.org.nz/index.php?section=28>. 2006. "Facts about domestic violence." SHINE (Safer Homes in NZ Every Day).

[51]Ellsberg et al., "The Reality of Battered Women in Nicaragua."

[52]<http://new.vawnet.org/category/Documents.php?docid=1283>. 2004. "Profiling Domestic Violence: A Multi-Country Study." VAWnet.

[53]<www.state.gov/g/drl/rls/hrrpt/2006/78751.htm>. 2006. "Nigeria." U.S. Department of State, Bureau of Democracy, Human Rights, and Labor.

[54]<http://new.vawnet.org/category/Documents.php?docid=1283>. 2004. "Profiling Domestic Violence: A Multi-Country Study." VAWnet.

[55]<www.amnesty.org/en/library/asset/EUR36/001/2009/en/106889e0-5876-4350-a124-91ad9ca8098e/eur360012009en.html>. 2006. "Norway: Submission to the UN Universal Periodic Review: Sixth session of the UPR Working Group of the Human Rights Council, November-December 2009." Amnesty International.

[56]<http://assembly.coe.int/main.asp?Link=/documents/adoptedtext/ta02/erec1582.htm>. 2002. "Domestic violence against women." Council of Europe, Parliamentary Assembly.

[57]<www.unhcr.org/refworld/publisher,AMNESTY,,PRY,46558edce5,0.html>. 2007. "Amnesty International Report 2007—Paraguay." Amnesty International.

[58]Ibid.

[59]<www.who.int/mediacentre/news/releases/2005/pr62/en/index.html>. 2005. "Landmark Study on Domestic Violence: WHO report finds domestic violence is widespread and has serious impact on health." World Health Organization.

[60]<www.who.int/gender/violence/who_multicountry_study/en/>. 2005. "WHO Multi-

country Study on Women's Health and Domestic Violence against Women." World Health Organization.

[61]<www.omct.org/pdf/Prev_Torture/2003/stateviolence_philippines_03_eng.pdf>. 2000. "State violence in the Philippines: An alternative report to the United Nations Human Rights Committee." PNP Surveys.

[62]Ibid.

[63]<www.tendenciaspr.com/ingles/violence.html>. 2007. "State violence in Puerto Rico."

[64]Ibid.

[65]<www.unhcr.org/refworld/country,,FREEHOU,,RUS,,487ca25327a0,0.html>. 2008. "Freedom in the World 2008—Russia." UNHCR Refworld.

[66]<www.amnesty.org/en/library/asset/EUR46/056/2005/en/dom-EUR460562005en. html>. 2008. "Russian Federation: Nowhere to turn to: Violence against women in the family." Amnesty International.

[67]<www.sscnet.ucla.edu/polisci/wgape/papers/7_Gonzalez.pdf>. 2004. "Domestic Violence and Household Decision-making: Evidence from East Africa." Department of Economics, University of California, Berkeley.

[68]<www.popline.org/docs/1727/311690.html>. 2006. "Rwanda Demographic and Health Survey, 2005." Institut National de la Statistique.

[69]<www.state.gov/g/drl/rls/hrrpt/2006/78758.htm>. 2006. "South Africa." U.S Department of State, Bureau of Democracy, Human Rights, and Labor.

[70]<www.mrc.ac.za/gender/nodemocracy.pdf>. 1999. "'I Do Not Believe in Democracy in the Home': Men's Relationships with and Abuse of Women." CERSA (Women's Health) Medical Research Council.

[71]<www.unhcr.org/refworld/publisher,AMNESTY,,ESP,483e27b155,0.html>. 2008. "Amnesty International Report 2008—Spain." Amnesty International.

[72]Ibid.

[73]<www.eurowrc.org/06.contributions/1.contrib_en/28.contrib.en.htm>. 1999. "Male violence: the economic costs—A methodological review." Council of Europe.

[74]<www.swissinfo.ch/eng/index.html?siteSect=105&sid=4488274>. 2003. "More women seek shelter from domestic violence." Swiss Info.

[75]<www.hrw.org/legacy/reports/2000/tanzania/>. 2000. *Seeking Protection: Addressing Sexual and Domestic Violence in Tanzania's Refugee Camps.* Human Rights Watch.

[76]<www.who.int/gender/violence/multicountry/en/print.html>. 2005. WHO Multi-Country Study on Women's Health and Domestic Violence Against Women.

[77]<www.unhcr.org/refworld/type,QUERYRESPONSE,,THA,47d6547b23,0.html>. 2007. "Thailand: Domestic violence; state protection and resources available to victims of domestic abuse." Immigration and Refugee Board of Canada.

[78]<www.womenthai.org/eng/voice01.htm>. 2003. "Voices of Thai Women." The Foundation for Women.

[79]<http://archive.amnesty.org/report2007/eng/Regions/Europe-and-Central-Asia/ Turkey/default.htm>. 2007. "Turkey." Amnesty International.

[80]<www.omct.org/pdf/VAW/Publications/2003/Eng_2003_09_Turkey.pdf>. 2003. "Violence against Women in Turkey: A Report to the Committee against Torture." World Organisation Against Torture.

[81]<http://endabuse.org/content/features/detail/999/>. 2005. "The World Health Report 2005." Family Violence Prevention Fund.

[82]<www.scielosp.org/scielo.php?pid=S0042-96862003000100011&script=sci_arttext>.

2003. "Domestic violence in rural Uganda: evidence from a community-based study." Bulletin of the World Health Organization.

[83]<www.refuge.org.uk/page_l1-2_l2-162_l3-175_.htm>. 2002. "Domestic violence—the facts." U.K. Home Office.

[84]<www.data-archive.ac.uk/findingData/snDescription.asp?sn=5059>. 2002. "British Crime Survey, 2002-2003." British Crime Survey Series.

[85]<www.crimereduction.homeoffice.gov.uk/domesticviolence/domesticviolence066. htm>. 2007. "National Domestic Violence Delivery Plan: Annual Progress Report 2006/07." U.K. Home Office.

[86]<http://bjs.ojp.usdoj.gov/content/intimate/ipv.cfm>. Shannan Catalano, "Intimate Partner Violence in the United States," Bureau of Justice Statistics, 2007.

[87]<www.cdc.gov/violenceprevention/intimatepartnerviolence/consequences.html>. 2004. "Intimate Partner Violence: Consequences." U.S. Centers for Disease Control and Prevention.

[88]<www.ncjrs.gov/pdffiles1/nij/grants/182435.pdf>. 1997. "Police Use of Domestic Violence Information Systems, Final Report." U.S. Department of Justice.

[89]<www.unifem.org/afghanistan/docs/pubs/08/evaw_primary%20database%20report_EN.pdf>. 2006. "Violence Against Women: Primary Database." United Nations Development Fund for Women.

[90]Ibid.

[91]<www.undg.org/archive_docs/7622-Bangladesh_CCA.pdf>. 2005. "Common Country Assessment of Bangladesh." United Nations.

[92]<www.searo.who.int/LinkFiles/Reproductive_Health_Profile_Chapter7ver3-up_Amin.pdf>. 2002. "Approaches in Reproductive Health." Chap. 7 in *Reproductive Health Profile*. World Health Organization.

[93]<www.who.int/gender/violence/who_multicountry_study/en/>. 2005. "WHO Multicountry Study on Women's Health and Domestic Violence against Women." World Health Organization.

[94]<www.state.gov/g./drl/rls/hrrpt/2002/18238.htm>. 2002. "Cambodia." U.S. Department of State, Bureau of Democracy, Human Rights, and Labor.

[95]<www.state.gov/g/drl/rls/hrrpt/2005/61720.htm>. 2005. "Chile." U.S. Department of State, Bureau of Democracy, Human Rights, and Labor.

[96]<www.unicef-irc.org/publications/pdf/digest6e.pdf>. 2000. "Domestic Violence: Against Women and Girls." UNICEF.

[97]<http://db.jhuccp.org/ics-wpd/exec/icswppro.dll?BU=http://db.jhuccp.org/ics-wpd/exec/icswppro.dll&QF0=DocNo&QI0=276062&TN=Popline&AC=QBE_QUERY&MR=30percent25DL=1&&RL=1&&RF=LongRecordDisplay&DF=LongRecord Display>. 2004. "Intimate partner violence in China: National prevalence, risk factors and associated health problems." International Family Planning Perspectives.

[98]<www.state.gov/g/drl/rls/hrrpt/2005/61721.htm>. 2005. "Colombia." U.S. Department of State, Bureau of Democracy, Human Rights, and Labor.

[99]<www.rapeis.org/activism/humanrights/colombiaarticle.html>. 2003. "Colombia: 'Scarred bodies, hidden crimes': Sexual violence against women in the armed conflict." Amnesty International.

[100]<www.croatia.org/crownarticles/5927/1/E-V-DAY-Stop-violence-against-women-and-girls.html>. 2003. "V-DAY: Stop violence against women and girls." Croatian World Network.

[101]Ibid.

[102]<www2.irbcisr.gc.ca/en/research/rir/?action=record.viewrec&gotorec=449378>. 2003. "Egypt: Domestic violence; whether there is state protection for the victims; existence of women's groups, shelters, or hot-lines." 2003 survey by the Center for Egyptian Women's Legal Affairs. Immigration Refugee Board.

[103]<www.measuredhs.com/pubs/pub_details.cfm?Filename=FR176.pdf&id=586>. 2005. "Egypt: DHS [Demographic and Health Survey] 2005—Final Report." Demographic and Health Surveys.

[104]<www.who.int/gender/violence/who_multicountry_study/en/>. 2005. "WHO Multicountry Study on Women's Health and Domestic Violence against Women." World Health Organization.

[105]Ibid.

[106]<http://books.google.com/books?id=s9_EWPshR4QC&pg=PA125&lpg=PA125&dq=Teuvo+Peltoniemi,+domestic+violence,+finland&source=bl&ots=1lriznu5Y1&sig=nIFm5IUyILk6zOkJ8glQcUlRxQ0&hl=en&ei=pqNpStnzJtyBtgfJu_nECw&sa=X&oi=book_result&ct=result&resnum=2>. Teuvo Peltoniemi, "Cooperation between the Police and Social Care in the Treatment of Alcohol and Family Violence Problems in Finland," in *Drug and Alcohol Use: Issues and Factors* (New York: Plenum Press, 1989).

[107]<http://vaw.sagepub.com/cgi/reprint/8/7/873>. 2004. "Complexity of Patterns of Violence Against Women in Heterosexual Partnerships," in Minna Piispa, *Violence Against Women 2002*.

[108]<www.dw-world.de/dw/article/0,,1792343,00.html>. 2005. "Fighting Violence Against Women." DW-World.DE.

[109]<www.dw-world.de/dw/article/0,,1334950,00.html>. 2004. "German Women Often Victims of Domestic Violence." DW-World.DE.

[110]<www.vedamsbooks.com/no38662.htm>. 1997. Lalit Latta, *Women Development in India: A Statistical Profile.*

[111]Radhika Ramasubban and Bhanwar Singh. "'Ashaktapana' (Weakness) and Reproductive Health in a Slum Population in Mumbai, India," in *Cultural Perspectives in Reproductive Health*, ed. Carla M. Obermeyer (Oxford: Oxford University Press, 1998).

[112]<www.wfafi.org/Press-ReleaseNov8.htm>. 2004. "Mullahs! Beware of the Radio Voice of Women Against Fundamentalism in Iran." Women's Forum Against Fundamentalism in Iran.

[113]<www.iom.ch/jahia/webdav/shared/shared/mainsite/policy_and_research/un/58/A_58_12_supp_en.pdf>. 2002. "Report of the United Nations High Commissioner for Refugees, 2002." United Nations General Assembly.

[114]<http://emergency-medicine.jwatch.org/cgi/content/citation/2002/327/10>. 2002. "Domestic Violence in Ireland: Don't Ask, Don't Tell." Journal Watch Emergency Medicine.

[115]<www.drugsandalcohol.ie/11501/1/Courts_service_AR_2006.pdf>. 2006. "Courts Service [Ireland]: Annual Report 2006." National Documentation Centre on Drug Abuse.

[116]<www.no2violence.co.il/Articles_eng.htm>. 1992. "L.O. Combat Violence Against Women." Women's Aid Centers.

[117]<www.yadsarah.org/index.asp?id=131&newsid=472>. 2007. "Undoing Domestic Violence." Yad Sarah Family Center.

[118]<www.who.int/gender/violence/who_multicountry_study/en/>. 2005. "WHO Multi-

country Study on Women's Health and Domestic Violence against Women." World
Health Organization.

[119]<http://new.vawnet.org/category/Documents.php?docid=584>. 2000. "Domestic Violence Against Women and Girls." UNICEF.

[120]<www.state.gov/g/drl/rls/hrrpt/2005/61615.htm>. 2005. "Malaysia." U.S. Department of State. Bureau of Democracy, Human Rights, and Labor.

[121]<www.state.gov/g/drl/rls/hrrpt/2001/wha/8320.htm>. 2001. "Mexico." U.S. Department of State. Bureau of Democracy, Human Rights, and Labor.

[122]<www2.irbcisr.gc.ca/en/research/ndp/ref/index_e.htm?docid=91&cid=0&sec=CH02>. 2003. "Mexico: Domestic Violence and Other Issues Related to the Status of Women." Immigration and Refugee Board of Canada.

[123]<www.who.int/whr/2002/en/>. 2002. "The World Health Report 2002—Reducing Risks, Promoting Healthy Life." World Health Organization.

[124]<www.state.gov/g/drl/rls/hrrpt/2006/78830.htm>. 2006. "The Netherlands." U.S. Department of State. Bureau of Democracy, Human Rights, and Labor.

[125]<www.nzfvc.org.nz/>. 2005. New Zealand Family Violence Clearinghouse.

[126]<www.unicef.org/violencestudy/3.%20World%20Report%20on%20Violence%20against%20Children.pdf>. 2006. "Violence against children in the home and family." UNICEF.

[127]<http://jech.bmj.com/cgi/content/full/55/8/547>. Mary Ellsberg and Rodolfo Pena, "Women's Strategic Responses to Violence in Nicaragua," *Journal of Epidemiology and Community Health* 55, no. 8 (1996): 547-55.

[128]<http://new.vawnet.org/category/Documents.php?docid=1283>. 2004. "Profiling Domestic Violence: A Multi-Country Study." VAWnet.

[129]<www.child.alberta.ca/secure/public/wcpfv/tuesday/miriam_menkiti.pdf>. 2005. "Domestic Violence Against Women—A Story of Community Prevention Strategies from Two States in Nigeria: Enugu and Ondo," presented at the World Conference on Prevention of Family Violence, October 23-26, 2005, Banff, Canada.

[130]<www.state.gov/g/drl/rls/hrrpt/2006/78751.htm>. 2006. "Nigeria." U.S. Department of State. Bureau of Democracy, Human Rights, and Labor.

[131]<https://no.amnesty.org/web2.nsf/pages/8A4B756E42DCE15DC125710300567A3C>. 2004. Amnesty International Norway.

[132]<http://sjp.sagepub.com/cgi/content/refs/36/2/161>. 2004. "Partner violence and health: Results from the first national study on violence against women in Norway." Statistics Norway.

[133]<http://webapps01.un.org/vawdatabase/searchDetail.action?measureId=23843&baseHREF=country&baseHREFId=1025>. 2004. "National Survey on Sexual and Reproductive Health 2004: Paraguay." United Nations General Secretary's Database Violence Against Women.

[134]<www.who.int/gender/violence/who_multicountry_study/en/>. 2005. "WHO Multi-country Study on Women's Health and Domestic Violence against Women." World Health Organization.

[135]Ibid.

[136]<www.state.gov/g/drl/rls/hrrpt/2001/eap/8371.htm>. 2000. "Philippines." U.S. Department of State. Bureau of Democracy, Human Rights, and Labor.

[137]Ibid.

[138]<www.amnesty.org/en/region/russia/report-2008>. 2008. "Russian Federation: Am-

nesty International Report 2008." Amnesty International.

[139]Ibid.

[140]<http://db.jhuccp.org/ics-wpd/exec/icswppro.dll?BU=http://db.jhuccp.org/ics-wpd/exec/icswppro.dll&QF0=DocNo&QI0=311690&TN=Popline&AC=QBE_QUERY&MR=30percent25DL=1&&RL=1&&RF=LongRecordDisplay&DF=Long RecordDisplay>. 2006. "Rwanda Demographic and Health Survey, 2005." Institut National de la Statistique.

[141]<www.state.gov/g/drl/rls/hrrpt/2006/78789.htm>. 2006. "Samoa." U.S. Department of State. Bureau of Democracy, Human Rights, and Labor.

[142]Ibid.

[143]<www.mrc.ac.za/gender/violence.pdf>. 1999. "'He Must Give Me Money, He Mustn't Beat Me': Violence against women in three South African Provinces." CERSA (Women's Health) Medical Research Council.

[144]S. Mathews et al. 2004.

[145]<http://archive.amnesty.org/report2008/eng/regions/europe-and-central-asia/spain.html>. 2008. "Amnesty International Report 2008: State of the World's Human Rights." Amnesty International.

[146]<http://ipsnews.net/news.asp?idnews=42397>. 2007. "Spain: Fight Against Domestic Violence Only Strong on Paper." Inter Press Service News Agency.

[147]<www.nmun-berlin.de/index.php?id=263>. 2007. "United Nations Development Fund for Women." The National Model United Nations, Berlin.

[148]<www.ch.ch/private/00093/00096/00537/00539/index.html?lang=en>. 2005. "Projects and Financial Aid." Swiss Federal Office for Gender Equality.

[149]<www.who.int/gender/violence/who_multicountry_study/en/>. 2005. "WHO Multi-country Study on Women's Health and Domestic Violence against Women." World Health Organization.

[150]<www.womenthai.org/eng/voice01.htm>. 2003. "Voices of Thai Women." The Foundation for Women.

[151]Ibid.

[152]<www.omct.org/pdf/VAW/Publications/2003/Eng_2003_09_Turkey.pdf>. 2003. "Violence against Women in Turkey: A Report to the Committee against Torture." World Organisation Against Torture.

[153]Ibid.

[154]<www.state.gov/g/drl/rls/hrrpt/2006/78763.htm>. 2006. "Uganda." U.S. Department of State. Bureau of Democracy, Human Rights, and Labor.

[155]<www.amnestyusa.org/women/pdf/rapeinwartime.pdf>. 2005. "Rape as a Tool of War: A Fact Sheet." Amnesty International.

[156]<http://assembly.coe.int/Main.asp?link=/Documents/AdoptedText/ta02/EREC1582.htm>. 2002. "Domestic violence against women." Council of Europe. Parliamentary Assembly.

[157]<www.nspcc.org.uk/Inform/policyandpublicaffairs/policysummaries/DomesticViolence2_wdf63297.pdf>. 1998. "NSPCC Domestic Violence Campaign Briefing 2." National Society for the Prevention of Cruelty to Children (U.K.).

[158]<www.data-archive.ac.uk/findingData/snDescription.asp?sn=6066>. 2007. "British Crime Survey, 2007-2008." UK Data Archive.

[159]<www.homeoffice.gov.uk/rds/pdfs04/hors276.pdf>. 2004. "Domestic violence, sexual assault and stalking: Findings from the British Crime Survey." U.K. Home Office.

[160]<www.bbc.co.uk/pressoffice/pressreleases/stories/2003/01_january/17/hitting_home_facts.pdf>. 2000. "Fact File: Statistics." BBC.

[161]<www.womensaid.org.uk/domestic-violence-articles.asp?section=00010001002200410001&itemid=1280>. 2004. "Statistics: how common is domestic violence?" Women's Aid.

[162]H. Waters, A. Hyder, Y. Rajkotia, S. Basu, J. A. Rehwinkel and A. Butchart, "The Economic Dimensions of Interpersonal Violence," Department of Injuries and Violence Prevention (Geneva: World Health Organization 2004), p. 21.

[163]United States Senate Judiciary Committee, Violence Against Women (Washington, D.C.: Government Printing Office, 1992).

[164]<www.path.org/files/GBV_rvaw_complete.pdf>. 2005. Mary Ellsberg and Lori Heise, Researching Violence Against Women: A Practical Guide for Researchers and Activists (Geneva: World Health Organization and Program for Appropriate Technology in Health, 2005).

[165]<www.hrw.org/en/reports/2006/11/06/question-security>. 2006. "A Question of Security: Violence against Palestinian Women and Girls." Human Rights Watch.

[166]World Health Organization, "Violence Against Women Information Pack: A Priority Health Issue," 1997 <http://whqlibdoc.who.int/hq/1997/WHO_FRHWHD_97.8.pdf>.

[167]Heise 1993.

[168]See Nason-Clark 1998a for a discussion of the impact of Roman Catholic priests' sexual violation on the life of the parish.

[169]<www.cetim.ch/en/documents/Annex5-WG-Report-2005_000.pdf>. 2005. "Economic, Social and Cultural Rights." United Nations Commission on Human Rights.

[170]<www.un.org/events/women/violence/2008/sg_message.shtml>. 2008. "Message of the Secretary-General on the International Day for the Elimination of Violence against Women: 25 November 2008."

[171]World Health Organization, "Violence Against Women Information Pack," 1997 <http://whqlibdoc.who.int/hq/1997/WHO_FRH_WHD_97.8.pdf>.

[172]Female genital mutilation (FGM) is a form of violence against a girl child that affects her life as an adult woman. It is a traditional cultural practice meant to ensure the self-respect of the girl and her family and to increase her marriage opportunities. According to the World Health Organization ("Violence Against Women Information Pack"), FGM constitutes "all procedures that involve partial or total removal of the external female genitalia or other injury to the female genital organs whether for cultural or any other non-therapeutic reasons" (p. 14). See also <www.prb.org/Publications/Datasheets/2008/fgm2008.aspx>. 2008. "Female Genital Mutilation/Cutting: Data and Trends." Population Reference Bureau.

[173]In a World Health Organization, "Violence Against Women in Situations of Armed Conflict and Displacement" (1997), it is argued that son preference can lead to physical violence against daughters, higher rates of abortion of female fetuses and the practice of female infanticide. <www.who.int/gender/violence/v7.pdf>.

[174]Cited in World Health Organization, "Violence Against Women Information Pack," 1997, <http://whqlibdoc.who.int/hq/1997/WHO_FRH_WHD_97.8.pdf>.

[175]Sent directly to Nancy Nason-Clark by the woman on whose life this story is based.

[176]Told to Nancy Nason-Clark after this woman read some of Nancy's published work.

[177]Giesbrecht and Sevcik 2000; Winkelmann 2004.

[178]Miles 2000.

179Horton, Wilkins and Wright 1988.
180The number of evangelical clergy participating in this project was 343, representing a response rate of 70 percent of those clergy contacted.
181Nason-Clark 1997.
182Brownridge 2003; Kiyoshk 2003; Menjivar and Salcido 2002; Potter 2007; Raj and Silverman 2002; Sokoloff and Dupont 2005.
183Boehm et al. 1999; Tarrezz Nash 2006; Senter and Caldwell 2002.
184Horton and Williamson 1988.
185Bowker 1988.
186Moran et al. 2005.
187Beaman and Nason-Clark 1997; Nason-Clark 1996.
188Nason-Clark 1997; 1998b.
189Nason-Clark 1999; Nason-Clark and Kroeger 2004.
190Beaman and Nason-Clark, 1997; Nason-Clark 1995.
191Nason-Clark and Kroeger 2004; Nason-Clark 2005, 2009.
192Nason-Clark 1996, 2000a, 2008.
193Nason-Clark 2004; Nason-Clark et al. 2003; Fisher-Townsend et al. 2008.
194Based on stories told to Leela Manasseh, Women's Commission representative from India on the World Evangelical Fellowship and sent to Nancy Nason-Clark by email.
195Information supplied by Leela Manasseh.
196Ibid.
197Straus, Gelles and Steinmetz 1980.
198Barling and Rosenbaum 1986.
199Goldstein and Rosenbaum 1985.
200O'Leary and Curley 1986.
201Goodwin 1985; O'Leary and Curley 1986.
202Jaffe et al. 1986; see also Statistics Canada 1993.
203See Nason-Clark 1997, chap. 1.
204Ptacek 1988. See also Fisher-Townsend et al. 2008.
205Ptacek 1988, 249-50.
206Abusive men's expectations are often arbitrary and unspoken, so that a wife feels as if she is walking on eggshells, never sure what is required of her.
207Nason-Clark, Murphy, Fisher-Townsend and Ruff 2003; Fisher-Townsend et al. 2008.
208Stacey, Hazlewood and Shupe 1994; Hirschel and Buzawa 2002.
209Walker 1988.
210Bennett 1995; quote on p. 760.
211Statistics Canada 1993; Straus, Gelles and Steinmetz 1980; Bennett 1995.
212Gelles 1985; Gelles and Straus 1979.
213<www.opdv.state.ny.us/whatisdv/about_dv/nyresponse/nysdv.pdf>.
214Griffin and Maples 1997.
215Martin 1981; see also Stirling et al. 2004; Nason-Clark and Kroeger 2004.
216Gelles 1985; Sullivan and Rumptz 1994; Martin 1981.
217Martin 1981; Walker 1984.
218See the articles in Timmins 1995; Horton and Williamson 1988; Gaddis 1996.
219For discussions of the needs of the religious woman, see Nason-Clark 1999; Kroeger and Beck 1998.

[220]Nason-Clark 1997; see also 1998a.
[221]Knickmeyer et al. 2003.

Chapter 2: Beginning to Respond
[1]Based on clergy interview 396; portions of this story were told in Nason-Clark and Kroeger, 2004.
[2]Based on a presentation by Julie Owens at a PASCH conference in California in 2006.
[3]<www.un.org/womenwatch/daw/vaw/launch/english/v.a.w-consequenceE-use.pdf>. 2006. "Ending Violence Against Women: From Words to Action." U.N. Secretary-General.
[4]<www.aafp.org/online/en/home/policy/policies/v/violencepubhealth.html>. 2006. "Violence as a Public Health Concern." American Academy of Family Physicians.
[5]<www.aacn.nche.edu/publications/positions/violence.htm>. 1999. "Violence as a Public Health Problem." American Association of Colleges of Nursing, Position Statement.
[6]<www.surgeongeneral.gov/news/speeches/violence08062003.htm>. 2003. "Family Violence as a Public Health Issue. U.S. Department of Health and Human Services, Office of the Surgeon General.
[7]Quoted in Nason-Clark 1988b:57.
[8]Quoted in Nason-Clark 1995:123.
[9]Based on a story that emerged from our focus group research; discussed further in Nason-Clark 2000b.
[10]Clergy interview 373, quoted in Nason-Clark 1997:xii.
[11]Clergy interview 376, quoted in Nason-Clark 2000a.
[12]This story appears in Nason-Clark 1997.
[13]Nason-Clark 1998a.

Chapter 3: Growing in Compassion
[1]Based on clergy interview 350, with text in italics quoted verbatim from the interview transcript.
[2]Discussed more fully in Nason-Clark 1997.
[3]This story appears in Nason-Clark 1997:38-39.
[4]Quoted in Nason-Clark 1998:62.
[5]Based on a survivor's account told to Nason-Clark in the northeastern United States.
[6]Langley 1983.
[7]See Nason-Clark 1995; 1996; 1997; 1998; 1999.
[8]Beaman 1992; Fisher-Townsend et al. 2008; Fortune 1988; Ptacek 1988.
[9]Galbraith 2009.
[10]See Alsdurf and Alsdurf 1988; Bowker 1988.
[11]Dobash and Dobash 1979; Walker 1988; Timmins 1995.
[12]Schüssler Fiorenza and Copeland 1994; Brown and Bohn 1989. See also Horton and Williamson 1988; Bussert 1986; Clarke 1986 for early attempts to sound a wake-up call to churches.
[13]Some limited data are available in Alsdurf and Alsdurf 1988 and Bowker 1988, but they are based on rather limited research samples.
[14]See Nason-Clark 1997, chap. 4.

[15]A large proportion of Canadian clergy have reported that they feel ill-equipped to deal with the issues surrounding wife abuse and other forms of family violence and indicate high interest in further training related to these matters (Nason-Clark 1996; 1999).

[16]For a fuller discussion of wife abuse, consult DeKeseredy and MacLeod 1999; Martin 1981.

[17]For a fuller discussion of the impact of religious belief on violence, see Clarke 1986; Strom 1986; McDill and McDill 1991; Horton and Williamson 1988.

[18]See Beaman and Nason-Clark 1999; Fortune 1991; Beaman and Nason-Clark 1997.

[19]For a fuller discussion of shelters, see Timmins 1995; G. Walker 1990.

Chapter 4: Steeple to Shelter

[1]Karen is a composite character based on years of fieldwork with shelters in various locations in Canada, the United States and abroad. Our knowledge of the issues surrounding shelter staff has been supplemented by speaking engagements with, and for, those working within the shelter movement for twenty years. At the beginning of our research program, we conducted a small study employing telephone interviews with shelter staff in various locations in eastern Canada; an honor student under me (Nason-Clark's) supervision was engaged in research involving boards of directors of shelters.

[2]This story is based on the practices of a community church in Calgary, Alberta; the quilts are donated to the Sheriff King YWCA facility.

[3]See Whipple 1987; Holden, Watts and Brookshire 1991.

[4]See Beaman-Hall and Nason-Clark 1997; Pagelow and Johnson 1988.

[5]For more information on PASCH (Peace and Safety in the Christian Home), consult <www.peaceandsafety.com>. or refer to Catherine Clark Kroeger, Nancy Nason-Clark and Barbara Fisher-Townsend, *Beyond Abuse in the Christian Home: Raising Voices for Change* (Eugene, Ore.: Wipf and Stock, 2008).

[6]Nason-Clark 1997.

[7]Nason-Clark 2000b.

[8]Comments made during focus group interviews, reported more fully in Nason-Clark 1998:60.

[9]Statistics Canada 1993.

[10]Thorne-Finch 1992; McLeod 1987; G. Walker 1990.

[11]This in part explains why shelters do not advertise their addresses to the public; they want to reduce the risk that an abusive man will come to the transitional house, seeking retaliation.

[12]The length of stay allowed at most shelters is thirty to ninety days maximum. In some communities, second-stage housing is available for women after they have left a transitional house, usually for twelve months or a maximum of two years.

[13]See Smalley 1996, 1998; Dobson 1995, 1996.

[14]See Brown and Bohn 1989; Copeland 1994; Morris 1998; Strom 1986; Fortune 1988, 1991; McDill and McDill 1991; Nason-Clark 1997.

Chapter 5: Searching the Scriptures

[1]J. L. Grady, *25 Tough Questions About Women and the Church* (Lake Mary, Fla.: Charisma House, 2003), p. 2.

[2]Office of the [Wesleyan Church] General Secretary, *Standing Firm: The Wesleyan Church Speaks on Contemporary Issues* (Indianapolis: Wesleyan Publishing House. 2000), pp. 9-10.

[3]Jacqueline C Campbell, ed., *Assessing Dangerousness: Violence by Batterers and Child Abusers*, 2nd. ed. (New York: Stringer Publishing, 2007).

[4]As reported in a handout of the Family Safety Project of Caritas Holy Family Hospital. (See www.usdoj.gov.)

[5]Michele Penta, Children Who Witness Violence (presentation given at the Caritas Holy Family Hospital's Family Safety Project, Methuen, Mass., April 2009).

[6]Presidential Task Force on Violence and the Family, "Report of the American Psychological Association," Washington, D.C., 1996.

[7]Michele Penta, Children Who Witness Violence (material presented at the Certified Batterer Intervention Program, certified by the state of Massachusetts, at Caritas Holy Family Hospital and Medical Center, Methuen, Mass., April 3, 10 and 17, 2009).

[8]Ibid.

[9]Gerhardt 2000, 100.

[10]Sheila Y. Moore, "Adolescent boys are the underserved victims of domestic violence," *Boston Globe*, December 26, 1999, E7.

Chapter 6: Man and Woman

[1]Frederick William Danker, ed., *The Greek-English Lexicon of the New Testament and Other Early Christian Literature* (Chicago: University of Chicago Press, 2000), s.v. "harpax."

[2]Story told to Catherine Kroeger.

[3]Story told to Kroeger.

Chapter 7: Does the Suffering of an Abused Woman Bring Salvation to Her Husband?

[1]Story told to Catherine Kroeger.

[2]Based on a story told to Kroeger after a lecture by a popular woman speaker.

[3]For the latter, Polybius *Histories* 3.36.6-7; 18.15.40; for *hypotassō* as "to bring under the influence of," see Moulton 1970.

[4]Justin Martyr 2 *Apology* 2.1-9.

Chapter 8: A Concern for the Christian Family?

[1]Story told to Catherine Kroeger by the child's mother.

[2]David Hempton "Evangelical Enchantment and Disenchantment," *HDS Bulletin*, Winter 2008, pp. 50-51.

[3]Disclosed to Kroeger by a student.

[4]Based on a personal conversation with Kroeger.

[5]B. A. Robinson, "Divorce and Remarriage: U.S. Divorce Rates for Various Faith Groups, Age Groups, & Geographic Areas," Ontario Consultants on Religious Tolerance site, April 27, 2000 <www.religioustolerance.org/chr_dira.htm>.

Chapter 9: Repentance and Forgiveness

[1]Disclosed by the victim to Catherine Kroeger.

[2]Told to Catherine Kroeger by a therapist in a private conversation.

[3]Personal story told to Catherine Kroeger by the victim.

[4]Disclosed by the victim to Catherine Kroeger.

[5]Marie Fortune, "Preaching Forgiveness?" in John S. McClure and Nancy J. Ramsay, eds., *Telling the Truth: Preaching about Sexual and Domestic Violence* (Cleveland: United Church Press, 1998), p. 56.

[6]Disclosed by the victim to Catherine Kroeger.

Chapter 10: Issues of Abuse and Authority

[1]Susan Milton, "Community of Jesus Implicated in 1990s Abuse Probe," *Cape Cod Times,* September 20, 2007, A12.

[2]Dr. Ganson Purcell Jr., board member of the Jeanine Geiger Crisis Center, in a letter to the editor of the *Boston Globe,* July 22, 2009.

[3]Other instances of reversal may be found in Genesis 21:12; Judges 4:4–5:31; 1 Samuel 25:1-44; 2 Samuel 20:14-22; 21:7-14; 1 Kings 1:11-40.

Chapter 11: Good News for and About Abusers

[1]Based on research conducted by Nancy Nason-Clark and Barbara Fisher-Townsend; names and details have been changed to protect confidentiality. See Nason-Clark and Fisher-Townsend 2009.

[2]Fisher-Townsend et al. 2008.

[3]Ptacek 1988; Scott and Wolfe 2000.

[4]According to Dr. Elizabeth Gerhardt, the focus of treatment for the perpetrator should be on his abusive behavior and on the safety of the victim.

[5]Based on the victim's story told to Catherine Kroeger.

[6]For other injunctions to avoid the company of the violent, see Proverbs 1:10-16; 16:29.

[7]Adams 1994, 92.

[8]"This really couldn't happen to me," *Cape Cod Times,* April 11, 2007, p. 12.

[9]Patricia A. Levesh, "Letter to the Editor," *Boston Globe,* sec. A, p. 8.

[10]Brochure prepared by Gerhardt.

Chapter 12: The Biblical Option of Divorce

[1]Personal conversation by telephone between the therapist and Catherine Kroeger.

[2]According to the research of Nancy Nason-Clark (1997, 1998c), pastors want to be involved in any decision regarding the timetable of the possibility of divorce. In this way, clergy feel they are able to judge for themselves whether reconciliation is possible.

[3]Prentiss Findlay, "Couple Had Happy Beginnings Here," *Post and Courier,* April 2, 2008.

[4]As explained on their website <www.theduluthmodel.org>, the Duluth Model is recognized nationally and internationally as the leading tool to help communities eliminate violence in the lives of women and children. The model seeks to eliminate domestic violence through written procedures, policies and protocols governing intervention and prosecution of criminal domestic assault cases. The Duluth Model was the first to outline multidisciplinary procedures to protect and advocate for victims. Information about a faith-based version of this domestic abuse intervention is available at Changing Men, Changing Lives, P.O. Box 161213, Duluth, MN 55816.

[5]Told by a survivor to Catherine Kroeger.

Chapter 13: What Can Church Folk Do?

[1]Anderson and Saunders 2003; Burke, Gielen, McDonnell, O'Campo and Maman 2001;

Griffing et al. 2002; Landenburger 1998; Wuest and Merritt-Gray 1999.

[2]Adrian Walker, "After Abuse, A Life Renewed," *Boston Globe,* October 13, 2009, B1.

Chapter 14: Taking Action

[1]The development of the RAVE Project was made possible by a five-year development grant from the Lilly Endowment to Nancy Nason-Clark. When completed, it will be maintained by the University of New Brunswick, where Nancy has taught for the past twenty-five years. A team of highly competent graduate students, post-doctoral fellows and IT personnel have participated in the project, housed at the university, as well as teams of domestic violence advocates, criminal justice workers, therapists and religious leaders from four additional location sites: Charlotte, North Carolina; Eugene, Oregon; Columbia, Missouri; and Calgary, Alberta.

[2]Produced by the Day of Discovery, in Grand Rapids, Michigan, this four-part documentary was first aired as a television series in the fall of 2007.

References

Abu-Nasr, Donna. 2000. Honor Crimes: In Some Cultures, the Price of a Woman's Honor Is Blood. *Cape Cod Times,* July 2, 2000, C1.

Adams, Carol J. 1994. *Woman-Battering.* Creative Pastoral Care and Counseling Series. Minneapolis: Fortress.

Agger, Inger. 1994. *The Blue Room: Trauma and Testimony Among Refugee Women—A Psycho-social Exploration.* Trans. Mary Bille. London: Zed.

Alsdurf, James, and Phyllis Alsdurf. 1988. Wife Abuse and Scripture. In *Abuse and Religion: When Praying Isn't Enough,* ed. A. Horton and J. Williamson, pp. 221-28. Lexington, Mass: Heath.

Alvarado-Zaldivar, G., J. Salvador-Moysén, S. Estrada-Martinez and A. Terrones González. 1998. Prevalencia de violencia domestica en la ciudad de Durango. *Salud pública de Mexico* 40, no. 6:481-86.

American Medical Association. 1992. Diagnosis and Treatment Guidelines on Domestic Violence. March. Typescript.

American Medical Association Council on Scientific Affairs. 1992. Violence Against Women: Relevance for Medical Practitioners. *Journal of the American Medical Association* 267, no. 23.

Bachman, Ronet, and L. E. Saltzman. 1995. *Violence Against Women: Estimates from the Redesigned National Crime Victimization Survey.* NCJ-154348. Washington, D.C.: U.S. Department of Justice, Bureau of Justice Statistics.

Balch, David. 1981. *Let Wives Be Submissive: The Domestic Code in First Peter.* Atlanta: Scholars Press.

Baleta, A. 1999. Studies Reveal the Extent of Domestic Violence in South Africa. *Lancet* 14, no. 354:580.

Bancroft, L. 2002. *Why Does He Do That? Inside the Minds of Angry and Controlling Men.* New York: Berkeley Publishing Group.

Barling, J., and A. Rosenbaum, 1986. Work Stressors and Wife Abuse. *Journal of Applied Psychology* 71:346-48.

Beaman, Lori G. 1992. Negotiating the Options: How a Program for Men Who Batter Negotiates Its Identity in a Network of Community Agencies. MA thesis, University of New Brunswick.

Beaman, Lori G., and Nancy Nason-Clark. 1999. Evangelical Women as Activists: Their Response to Violence Against Women. In *Shared Beliefs, Different Lives: Women's Identities in Evangelical Context*, pp. 111-32. St. Louis: Chalice.

———. 1997. Partners or Protagonists: Exploring the Relationship Between the Transition House Movement and Conservative Churches. *Affilia: Journal of Women and Social Work* 12, no. 2:176-96.

Bennett, L. W. 1995. Substance Abuse and the Domestic Assault of Women. *Social Work* 40:760-61.

Bettencourt, B. Ann, and Norman Miller. 1996. Gender Differences in Aggression as a Function of Provocation: a Meta-analysis. *Psychological Bulletin* 119, no. 3:422-47.

Bewley, S., and Gillian Mezey. 1997. Domestic Violence and Pregnancy. *British Medical Journal* 314:1295.

Blanc, Ann K., et al. 1996. *Negotiating Reproductive Outcomes in Uganda*. Kampala: Institute of Statistics and Applied Economics.

Boehm, R., J. Golec, R. Krahn and D. Smyth. 1999. *Lifelines: Culture, Spirituality and Family Violence. Understanding the Cultural and Spiritual Needs of Women Who Have Experienced Abuse*. Edmonton, Alb.: The University of Alberta Press.

Bohannon, Judy R., David A. Doser and S. Eugene Lindley. 1995. Using Couple Data to Determine Domestic Violence Rates: An Attempt to Replicate Previous Work. *Violence and Victims* 10, no. 2:133-41.

Bowker, Lee. 1982. Battered Women and the Clergy: An Evaluation. *Journal of Pastoral Care* 36:226-34.

———. 1988. Religious Leaders and Their Victims: Services Delivered to One Thousand Battered Women by the Clergy. In *Abuse and Religion: When Praying Isn't Enough*, ed. A. Horton and J. Williamson, pp. 229-34. Lexington, Mass.: Heath.

Bradley, Christine. 1988. Wife-Beating in Papua New Guinea: Is It a Problem? *Papua New Guinea Medical Journal* 3, no. 1:257-68.

Briggs, David. 1992. Catholic Bishops Condemn Wife Abuse. *Boston Globe*, October 30, 1992.

Brinkerhoff, Merlin B., and Eugen Lupri. 1988. Interspousal Violence. *Canadian Journal of Sociology* 13, no. 4:407-34.

British Home Office Research and Planning Unit. 1996. *British Crime Survey.*

Brown, Joanne, and Carol Bohn, eds. 1989. *Christianity, Patriarchy and Abuse: A Feminist Critique.* New York: Pilgrim.

Brown, R. 1996. Violence in America: The Status Today. American Medical Association, June 1996. Typescript.

Browning, James, and Donald Dutton. 1986. Assessment of Wife Assault with the Conflict Tactics Scale: Using Couple Data to Quantify the Differential Reporting Effect. *Journal of Marriage and the Family* 48:375-79.

Brownridge, D. A. 2003. Male Partner Violence Against Aboriginal Women in Canada: An Empirical Analysis. *Journal of Interpersonal Violence* 18, no. 1: 65-83.

Brush, L. 1990. Violent Acts and Injurious Outcomes in Married Couples: Methodological Issues in the National Survey of Family and Households. *Gender and Society* 4, no. 1:56-67.

Burbank, Victoria K. 1987. Female Aggression in Cross-cultural Perspective. *Behavior Science Research* 2, no. 1:70-100.

Bussert, J. M. K. 1986. *Battered Women: From a Theology of Suffering to an Ethic of Empowerment.* New York: Lutheran Church of America, Division for Mission in North America.

Buttell, F. P. 2001. Moral Development Among Court-Ordered Batterers: Evaluating the Impact of Treatment. *Research on Social Work Practice* 11, no. 1: 93-107.

Cantos, Arthur L., Peter H. Neidig and K. Daniel O'Leary. 1994. Injuries of Women and Men in a Treatment Program for Domestic Violence. *Journal of Family Violence* 9, no. 2:113-24.

Carlson, Bonnie E. 1984. Children's Observations of Interparental Violence. In *Battered Women and Their Families: Intervention Strategies and Treatment Programs,* ed. Albert R. Roberts, pp. 147-67. New York: Springer.

Carrillo, R. 1992. *Battered Dreams: Violence Against Women as an Obstacle to Development.* New York: United Nations Fund for Women.

Centro Paraguayo de Estudios de Población. 1996. *Encuestra nacional de demografía y salud reproductiva, 1995-1996.*

Christian Reformed Church Committee to Study Physical, Emotional and Sexual Abuse. 1992. Report 30. In *The Agenda for Synod 1992 of the Chris-*

tian Reformed Church in North America, pp. 313-58. Grand Rapids: CRC Publications.

Clarke, Rita-Lou. 1986. *Pastoral Care of Battered Women.* Philadelphia: Westminster Press.

Clinkin, C. 1994. Rape and Sexual Abuse of Women in International Law. *European Journal of International Law* 326:23-28.

Colombia Demographic Health Surveys III. 1995. *Encuesta national de demografta ydalud, 1995.* Bogotá: Profamilia.

Commonwealth Secretariat 1992. *Confronting Violence: A Manual for Commonwealth Action.* London: Women and Development Programme, Commonwealth Secretariat.

Cook, Rebecca J., ed. 1994. *Human Rights of Women National and International Perspectives.* Philadelphia: University of Pennsylvania Press.

Copeland, Mary Shawn. 1994. Reflections. In *Violence Against Women,* ed. Elisabeth Schüssler Fiorenza and M. S. Copeland, pp. 119-22. London: SCM Press.

Cosgrove, Katie. No Man Has the Right. 1996. In *Women in a Violent World: Feminist Analyses and Resistance Across Europe,* ed. Chris Corrin. Edinburgh: Edinburgh University Press.

Dan, Alice J., ed. 1994. *Reframing Women's Health: Multi-disciplinary Research and Practice.* Thousand Oaks, Calif.: Sage.

Davies, Miranda, ed. 1994. *Women and Violence: Realities and Responses Worldwide.* London: Zed.

DeKeseredy, Walter S. 1992. In Defense of Self-Defense: Demystifying Female Violence Against Male Intimates. In *Debates in Canadian Society,* ed. R. Hinch, pp. 245-52. Toronto: Nelson.

———. 1995. Enhancing the Quality of Survey Data on Woman Abuse. *Violence Against Women* 1, no. 2:158-73.

DeKeseredy, Walter S., and Brian D. Maclean. 1990. Researching Woman Abuse in Canada: A Realistic Critique of the Conflict Tactics Scale. *Canadian Review of Social Policy* 25:19-27.

DeKeseredy, Walter S., and Linda MacLeod. 1998. *Woman Abuse: A Sociological Story.* Toronto: Harcourt Brace.

DeKeseredy, Walter S., et al. 1997. The Meanings and Motives for Women's Use of Violence in Canadian College Dating Relationships: Results from a National Survey. *Sociological Spectrum* 17:199-222.

Demographic and Health Surveys. 1994. Domestic Violence and Rape. In *Na-*

tional Safe Motherhood Survey, 1993. Calverton, Md.: Macro International.

Departamento de Salud y Escuela de Salud Pública and Centers for Disease Control and Prevention. 1998. *Encuesto de dalud reproductii'a 1995-1996: Resumen de loi hallazgoi.* San Juan: Universidad de Puerto Rico/CDC.

Deyessa, N., et al. 1998. Magnitude, Type and Outcomes of Physical Violence Against Married Women in Butajira Southern Ethiopia. *Ethiopian Medical Journal* 36:83-92.

Dobash, R. P., and R. E. Dobash. 1979. *Violence Against Wives: A Case Against the Patriarchy.* New York: Free Press.

———. 1983. Patterns of Violence in Scotland. In *International Perspectives on Family Violence,* ed. R. Gelles and C. Cornell. Lexington, Mass.: Lexington.

———. 1995. Domestic Violence: The Northern Ireland Response. In *Women and Violence,* ed. M. Davies. London: Zed.

Dobash, R. P., et al. 1998. Separate and Intersecting Realities: A Comparison of Men's and Women's Accounts of Violence Against Women. *Journal of Violence Against Women* 4, no. 4:382-414.

Dobson, James C. 1995. *Straight Talk: What Men Need to Know; What Women Should Understand.* Dallas: Word.

———. 1996. *Love Must Be Tough: New Hope for Families in Crisis.* Dallas: Word.

Dutton, Donald. G., and Kenneth J. Hemphill. 1992. Patterns of Socially Desirable Responding Among Perpetrators and Victims of Wife Assault. *Violence and Victims* 7, no. 1:29-39.

Ellsberg, Mary Carroll. 1997. *Candies in Hell: Domestic Violence Against Women in Nicaragua.* Umea, Sweden: Department of Epidemiology and Public Health, University of Umea.

Ellsberg, Mary Carroll, et al. 1996. *Confites en el infierno: Prevalencia y características de la violencia conyugal hacia las mujeres en Nicaragua.* Managua: Asociación de Mujeres Profesionales por la Democracia en el Desarrollo.

Ellsberg, Mary, et al. 1996. *The Reality of Battered Women in Nicaragua.* Umea, Sweden: University of Umea.

Elman, R., and M. Eduards. 1991. Unprotected by the Swedish Welfare State: A Survey of Battered Women and the Assistance They Received. *Women's Studies International Forum* 14, no. 5:413-21.

El-Zanaty, F., et al. 1996. *Egypt Demographic and Health Surveys III.* Cairo: National Population Council.

Falik, Marilyn M., and Karen Scott Collins, eds. 1996. *Women's Health: The Commonwealth Fund Survey*. Baltimore, Md.: Johns Hopkins University Press.

Family Violence Prevention Fund. 1993. Men Beating Women: Ending Domestic Violence—A Qualitative and Quantitative Study of Public Attitudes on Violence Against Women. New York: EDK Associates.

Federal Bureau of Investigation. 1988. Supplement Homicide Report from the Uniform Crime Reports and a Bureau of Justice Statistics Study. Washington, D.C., Annual Report.

———. 1992. Uniform Crime Reports: Crime for the United States. Washington, D.C., Annual Report.

Fennell, Caroline. 1993. Criminal Law and the Criminal Justice System: Woman as Victim. In *Gender and Law in Ireland*, ed. A. Connelly. Dublin: Oak Tree.

Finkelhor, David, et al., eds. 1983. *The Dark Side of Families: Current Family Violence Research*. Beverly Hills, Calif.: Sage.

Fisher-Townsend, B., et al. 2008. I am Not Violent: Men's Experience in Group. In *Beyond Abuse in the Christian Home: Raising Voices for Change*, ed. C. Kroeger, N. Nason-Clark and B. Fisher-Townsend, pp. 78-99. Eugene, Ore.: Wipf and Stock.

Foley, M. 1995. "Who Is in Control?" Changing Responses to Women Who Have Been Raped and Sexually Abused. In *Women, Violence and Male Power: Feminist Activism, Research and Practice*, ed. Marianne Hester, Liz Kelly and Jill Radford. Milton Keynes, England: Open University Press.

Fortune, Marie. 1987. *Keeping the Faith: Questions and Answers for the Abused Woman*. San Francisco: Harper.

———. 1988. Reporting Child Abuse: An Ethical Mandate for Ministry. In *Abuse and Religion: When Praying Isn't Enough*, ed. A. Horton and J. Williamson, pp. 189-98. Lexington, Mass.: Heath.

———. 1991. *Violence in the Family: A Workshop Curriculum for Clergy and Other Helpers*. Cleveland: Pilgrim.

———. 1998. Preaching Forgiveness? In *Telling the Truth: Preaching about Sexual and Domestic Violence*, ed. John S. McClure and Nancy J. Ramsay, pp. 49-57. Cleveland: United Church Press.

Gaddis, Patricia Riddle. 1996. *Battered but Not Broken: Help for Abused Wives and Their Church Families*. Valley Forge, Penn.: Judson.

Galbraith, Joanne. 2009. A Healing Voice: Exploring the Response of Protestant Clergy Women to Women Who Are Victims of Intimate Partner Violence. MA thesis, University of New Brunswick.

Gelles, Richard J. 1985. Family Violence. *Annual Review of Sociology* 11:347-67.

Gelles, Richard J., and Murray A. Straus. 1979. Violence in the American Family. *Journal of Social Issues* 35:15-39.

Gelles, Richard J., and Donileen R. Loseke, eds. 1993. *Current Controversies on Family Violence*. Newbury Park, Calif.: Sage.

Gerhardt, Elizabeth L. 2000. Martin Luther's Theology of the Cross: Cause or Cure of Domestic Violence? Th.D. diss., Boston University.

Giesbrecht, N., and I. Sevcik. 2000. The Process of Rebuilding and Recovery Among Abused Women in the Conservative Evangelical Subculture. *Journal of Family Violence* 15:229-48.

Gill, M., and Leslie M. Tutty. 1997. Sexual Identity Issues for Male Survivors of Childhood Sexual Abuse: A Qualitative Study. *Journal of Child Sexual Abuse* 6, no. 3:31-47.

Gillioz, L., et al. 1996. *Domination masculine et violences envers les femmes dans la famille en Suisse*. Typescript. Geneva.

Gillioz, L., et al. 1997. *Domination et violences envers les femmes dans la couple*. Lausanne: Editions Payot.

Goldstein, D., and A. Rosenbaum. 1985. An Evaluation of the Self-Esteem of Maritally Violent Men. *Family Relations* 34:425-28.

Gonzales de Olarte, E., et al. 1997. *Poverty and Domestic Violence Against Women in Metropolitan Lima*. Washington, D.C.: Inter-American Development Bank.

Goodwin, J. 1985. Family Violence: Principles of Intervention and Prevention. *Hospital and Community Psychiatry* 36:1074-79.

Grandin, Elaine, and Eugen Lupri. 1997. Intimate Violence in Canada and the United States: A Cross-national Comparison. *Journal of Family Violence* 12, no. 4:417-43.

Griffin, J., and M. F. Maples. 1997. The Battered Committed Christian Woman: The Value Difference. *Counseling and Values* 41:117-127.

Guiliani, M. 1991. Battered Women. *New Directions for Women* 20, no. 2:4.

Haj-Yahia, Muhammad M. 1997. The First National Survey of Abuse and Battering Against Arab Women from Israel: Preliminary Results. Typescript.

———. 1998. *The Incidence of Wife-Abuse and Battering and Some Sociodemographic Correlates as Revealed in Two National Surveys in Palestinian Society.*

Ramallah, Palestinian Authority: Besir Center for Research and Development.

Hamby, S. L., Valerie C. Pondexter and Bernadette Gray-Little. 1996. Four Measures of Partner Violence: Construct Similarity and Classification Differences. *Journal of Marriage and the Family* 58:127-39.

Heise, Lori. 1993. Violence Against Women: The Hidden Health Burden. *World Health Statistical Quarterly* 46, no. 1:78-85.

Heise, Lori, Jacqueline Pitanguy and Adrienne Germain. 1994. *Violence Against Women: The Hidden Health Burden*. World Bank Discussion Paper 255. Washington, D.C.: World Bank.

Heise, Lori, et al. 1994. Violence Against Women: A Neglected Public Health Issue in Less Developed Countries. *Social Science and Medicine* 39, no. 4:1165-79.

Hirschel, D., and E. S. Buzawa. 2002. Understanding the Context of Dual Arrest with Directions for Future Research. *Violence Against Women* 8, no. 12: 1449-73.

Hoffman, Kristi, et al. 1994. Physical Wife Abuse in a Non-Western Society: An Integrated Theoretical Approach. *Journal of Marriage and the Family* 56:131-46.

Holden, Janice Miner, R. E. Watts and W. Brookshire. 1991. Beliefs of Professional Counselors and Clergy About Depressive Religious Ideation. *Counseling and Values* 35:93-103.

Holtmann, Catherine. 2009. Heart, Mind and Soul: Catholic Women and Social Justice. M.A. thesis, University of New Brunswick.

Horton, Anne, Melany Wilkins, and Wendy Wright. 1988. Women Who Ended Abuse: What Religious Leaders and Religion Did for These Victims. In *Abuse and Religion: When Praying Isn't Enough*, ed. A. Horton and J. Williamson, pp. 235-46. Lexington, Mass.: Heath.

Horton, Anne, and Judith Williamson, eds. 1988. *Abuse and Religion: When Praying Isn't Enough*. Lexington, Mass.: Heath.

Ilkkaracan, Pinar, and Women for Women's Human Rights. 1988. Exploring the Context of Women's Sexuality in Eastern Turkey. *Reproductive Health Matters* 6, no. 12:66-75.

———. 1997. Domestic Violence and Family Life as Experienced by Turkish Immigrant Women in Germany. Report 3. Istanbul: Women for Women's Human Rights.

Jacobson, N. S., et al. 1994. Affect, Verbal Content and Psychophysiology in the Arguments of Couples with a Violent Husband. *Journal of Consulting and Clinical Psychology* 62, no. 5:982-88.

Jaffe, Peter, et al. 1986. Similarities in Behavioral and Social Maladjustment Among Child Victims and Witnesses to Family Violence. *American Journal of Orthopsychiatry* 56, no. 1:142-46.

Jejeebhoy, Shireen, and Rebecca J. Cook. 1997. State Accountability for Wife-Beating: The Indian Challenge. *Lancet* 349 (supp.): sl10-sl12.

Jewkes, R., et al. 1999. "He Must Give Me Money, He Mustn't Beat Me": Violence Against Women in Three South African Provinces. Pretoria: Medical Research Council. Typescript.

Johnson, Michael P. 1995. Patriarchal Terrorism and Common Couple Violence: Two Forms of Violence Against Women. *Journal of Marriage and the Family* 57:283-94.

Jurevic, Linda S. 1996. Between a Rock and a Hard Place: Women Victims of Domestic Violence and the Western Australian Criminal Injuries Compensation Act. *Murdoch University Electronic Journal of Law* 3, no. 2 (July).

Kerr, J., ed. 1994. *Calling for Change: International Strategies to End Violence Against Women*. The Hague: Development Cooperation Information Department, Ministry of Foreign Affairs.

Khodyreva, Natalia. 1996. Sexism and Sexual Abuse in Russia. In *Women in a Violent World: Feminist Analyses and Resistance Across "Europe,"* ed. Chris Corrin. Edinburgh: Edinburgh University Press.

Kim, K., and Y. Cho. 1992. Epidemiological Survey of Spousal Abuse in Korea. In *Intimate Violence: Interdisciplinary Perspectives*, ed. Emiio Viano. Washington, D.C.: Hemisphere.

Kiyoshk, R. 2003. Integrating Spirituality and Domestic Violence Treatment: Treatment of Aboriginal Men. *Journal of Aggression, Maltreatment & Trauma* 71, no. 1/2:237-256.

Knickmeyer, N., et al. 2003. Responding to Mixed Messages and Double Binds: Religious Oriented Coping Strategies of Christian Battered Women. *Journal of Religion and Abuse* 5, no. 2:29-54.

Koss, Mary P., et al. 1991. Deleterious Effects of Criminal Victimization on Women's Health and Medical Utilization. *Archives of Internal Medicine* 15, no. 1:342-47.

Kroeger, Catherine Clark, and James Beck, eds. 1996. *Women, Abuse and the Bible: How Scripture Can Be Used to Hurt or to Heal*. Grand Rapids: Baker.

Kroeger, Catherine Clark, and James Beck, eds. 1998. *Healing the Hurting: Giv-*

ing Hope and Help to Abused Women. Grand Rapids: Baker.

Kroeger, Catherine Clark, Nancy Nason-Clark and Barbara Fisher-Townsend, eds. 2008. Beyond Abuse in the Christian Home: Raising Voices for Change. Eugene, Ore.: Wipf & Stock.

Langhinrichsen-Rohling, Jennifer, Peter Neidig and George Thorn. 1995. Violent Marriages: Gender Differences in Level of Current Violence and Past Abuse. Journal of Family Violence 10, no. 2:159-76.

Langley, Myrtle. 1983. Equal Woman: A Christian Feminist Perspective. Basingstoke, U.K.: Marshall, Morgan & Scott.

Larrain, Soledad. 1993. Estudio de frecuencia de la violencia intrafamiliar y la condición de la mujer en Chile. Santiago: Pan American Health Organisation.

Larrain-Heiremans, S. 1993. Violencia familiar y la situacion de la mujer en Chile. Typescript.

Latin American and Caribbean Women's Health Network. 1996. The Right to Live Without Violence: The Women's Health Collection. Santiago: Women's Health Network.

Leonard, M. 1993. Rape: Myths and Reality. In Irish Women's Studies Reader, ed. Alibhe Smyth. Dublin: Attic.

Leung, W. C., et al. 1999. The Prevalence of Domestic Violence Against Pregnant Women in a Chinese Community. International Journal of Gynecology and Obstetrics 6, no. 1:23-30.

Lieberman Research. 1995. Domestic Violence Advertising Campaign Tracking Survey: Wave III, November 1995. San Francisco: The Advertising Council and Family Violence Prevention Fund. Typescript.

Lloyd, Marion. 2000. To Prevent Dowry-Related Slayings, Women Urge India to Revamp Laws. Boston Globe, June 23, 2000, p. 2.

Louis, M-V. 1994. Sexual Harassment at Work in France: What Stakes for Feminists? In Women and Violence: Realities and Responses Worldwide, ed. Miranda Davies. London: Zed.

Lundgren, Eva. 1994. "I Am Endowed with All the Power in Heaven and on Earth": When Men Become Men Through "Christian" Abuse. Studia Theologica: Scandinavian Journal of Theology 48, no. 1.

Lung, C. T., and D. Daro. 1996. Current Trends in Child Abuse Reporting Fatalities: The Results of the 1995 Annual Fifty State Survey. Chicago: National Committee to Prevent Child Abuse.

Macmullen, Ramsay. 1984. Christianizing the Roman Empire A.D. 100-400. New Haven, Conn.: Yale University Press.

Mama, Amina. 1989. Violence Against Black Women: Gender, Race and State Response. *Feminist Review* 32:30-48.

———. 1990. A Hidden Struggle: Black Women and Violence. *Spare Rib* 209 (February): 8-11.

———. 1993. Woman Abuse in London's Black Communities. In *Inside Babylon: The Caribbean Diaspora in Britain,* ed. W. James and C. Harris. London: Verso.

Marin, L., H. Zia and E. Soler, eds. 1998. *Ending Domestic Violence: Report from the Global Frontlines.* San Francisco: Family Violence Prevention Fund.

Martin, Del. 1981. *Battered Wives.* San Francisco: New Glide.

Mathews, S., et al. 2004. "'Every six hours a woman is killed by her intimate partner': A national study of female homicide in South Africa." MRC Policy Brief, no. 5. Medical Research Council, Cape Town, June 2004.

Maynard, Mary, and Jan Winn. 1993. Violence Towards Women. In *Introducing Women's Studies,* ed. Diane Richardson and Victoria Robinson. London: Macmillan.

Mazza, D., et al. 1996. Physical, Sexual and Emotional Violence Against Women: A General Practice-Based Prevalence Study. *Medical Journal of Australia* 164, no. 1:14-17.

McDill, S. R., and Linda McDill. 1991. *Shattered and Broken: Wife Abuse in the Christian Community: Guidelines for Hope and Healing.* Old Tappan, N.J.: Revell.

McFarlane, Judith, et al. 1991. Assessing for Abuse: Self-Report Versus Nurse Interview. *Public Health Nursing* 8, no. 4:245-50.

McLeod, Linda. 1987. *Battered but Not Beaten: Preventing Wife Battering in Canada.* Ottawa: Canadian Advisory Council on the Status of Women.

Menjivar, C., and O. Salcido. 2002. Immigrant Women and Domestic Violence: Common Experiences in Different Countries. *Gender & Society* 16, no. 6:898-920.

Mezey, G. C., and S. Bewley. 1997. Domestic Violence and Pregnancy. *British Medical Journal* (British Medical Association) 314, no. 7090:1295.

Michalski, J. H. 2004. Making Sociological Sense Out of Trends in Intimate Partner Violence—The Social Structure of Violence Against Women. *Violence Against Women* 10, no. 6:652-75.

Miles, Al. 2000. *Domestic Violence: What Every Pastor Needs to Know.* Minneapolis: Augsburg Fortress.

Miller, G. 1989. Violence by and Against America's Children. *Journal of Juvenile Justice Digest* 17, no. 12:6.

Mirrlees-Black, Catriona, Pat Mayhew and Andrew Percy. 1996. The 1996 British Crime Survey, England and Wales. *Home Office Statistical Bulletin* 19, no. 96.

Mooney, J. 1993. *The Hidden Figure: Domestic Violence in North London.* London: School of Sociology and Social Policy, Middlesex University.

Moore, Sheila Y. 1999. Adolescent Boys Are the Underserved Victims of Domestic Violence. *Boston Globe,* December 26, 1999, E7.

Moran, M., et al. 2005. A Study of Pastoral Care, Referral and Consultation Practices Among Clergy in Four Settings in the New York City Area. *Pastoral Psychology* 53, no. 3:255-66.

Morley, Rebecca. 1993. Recent Responses to Domestic Violence Against Women: A Feminist Critique. In *Social Policy Review 5: The Evolving State of Welfare,* ed. R. Page and J. Baldock. Canterbury: Social Policy Association.

Morris, R. 1988. *Ending Violence Against Families: A Training Program for Pastoral Care Workers.* Toronto: United Church of Canada.

Morrison, Andrew, and Maria Beatring Orlando. 1997. *The Socio-economic Impact of Domestic Violence Against Women in Chile and Nicaragua.* Washington, D.C.: Inter-American Development Bank.

Morse, Barbara J. 1995. Beyond the Conflict Tactics Scale: Assessing Differences in Partner Violence. *Violence and Victims* 10, no. 4:251-72.

Moulton, Harold. 1970. *Analytical Greek Lexicon.* Grand Rapids: Zondervan.

Mullen, P., et al. 1988. Impact of Sexual and Physical Abuse on Women's Mental Health. *Lancet* 1:841-45.

Myers, J. A. 1994. Advocates Versus Researchers—A False Dichotomy? A Feminist, Social Constructionist Response to Jacobson. *Family Process* 33:87-91.

Narayana, G. 1996. Family Violence, Sex and Reproductive Health Behavior Among Men in Uttar Pradesh, India. Paper presented at the annual meeting of the National Council on International Health, Arlington, Va., June 1996.

Nason-Clark, Nancy. 1995. Conservative Protestants and Violence Against Women: Exploring the Rhetoric and the Response. In *Sex, Lies and Sanctity: Deviance and Religion in Contemporary America,* ed. Mary Jo Neitz and Marion Goldman. Greenwich, Conn.: JAI, pp.109-30.

———. 1996. Religion and Violence Against Women: Exploring the Rhetoric and the Response of Evangelical Churches in Canada. *Social Compass* 46, no. 4:515-36.

———. 1997. *The Battered Wife: How Christians Confront Family Violence.* Louisville, Ky.: Westminster John Knox.

———. 1998a. Abuses of Clergy Trust: Exploring the Impact on Female Congregants' Faith and Practice. In *Wolves Among the Fold*, ed. Anson Shupe, pp. 85-100. New York: Rutgers University Press.

———. 1998b. Canadian Evangelical Church Women and Responses to Family Violence. In *Religion in a Changing World: Comparative Studies in Sociology*, ed. Madeleine Cousineau. Westport, Conn.: Greenwood.

———. 1998c. The Evangelical Family Is Sacred . . . but Is It Safe? In *Healing the Hurting: Giving Hope and Help to Abused Women*, ed. Catherine Clark Kroeger and James R. Beck. Grand Rapids: Baker.

———. 1999. Shattered Silence or Holy Hush: Emerging Definitions of Violence Against Women. *Journal of Family Ministry* 13, no. 1:39-56.

———. 2000a. Defining violence in religious contexts. In *Bad Pastors: Clergy Malfeasance in America*, ed. Anson Shupe. Albany: New York University Press, 2000.

———. 2000b. Religion, Violence and Social Welfare. In *Religion and Social Policy for the Twenty-first Century*, ed. P. Nesbitt. Walnut Creek, Calif.: AltaMira.

———. 2001. Woman Abuse and Faith Communities: Religion, Violence and the Provision of Social Welfare. In *Religion and Social Policy*, ed. P. Nesbitt, pp. 128-45. Walnut Creek, Calif.: Rowman & Littlefield.

———. 2004. When Terror Strikes at Home: The Interface Between Religion and Domestic Violence. *Journal for the Scientific Study of Religion* 42, no. 3:303-10.

———. 2005. Linking Research and Social Action: Violence, Religion and the Family. *Review of Religious Research* 46, no. 3:221-34.

———. 2008. When Terror Strikes in the Christian Home. In *Beyond Abuse in the Christian Home: Raising Voices for Change*, ed. C. Kroeger, N. Nason-Clark and B. Fisher-Townsend, pp. 167-83. Eugene, Ore.: Wipf and Stock.

———. 2009. Christianity and the Experience of Domestic Violence: What does faith have to do with it? *Journal of Social Work and Christianity*, forthcoming.

Nason-Clark, N., et al. 2003. An Overview of the Characteristics of the Clients at a Faith-Based Batterers' Intervention Program. *Journal of Religion and Abuse* 5, no. 4:51-72.

Nason-Clark, Nancy, and Catherine Clark Kroeger. 2004. *Refuge from Abuse: Hope and Healing for Abused Religious Women.* Downers Grove: InterVarsity Press.

Nason-Clark, Nancy, et al. 2009. The RAVE Project: Developing Web-Based Religious Resources for Social Action on Domestic Violence. *Critical Social Work* 10, no. 1:1-11.

National Health and Social Survey. In *Sex in America: A Definitive Survey,* ed. R. T. Micheal et al., pp. 40-44. New York: National Academic Press.

National Violence Against Women Survey. 1998. Washington, D.C.: National Institute of Justice.

Nelson, Erin, and Cathy Zimmerman. 1996. *Household Survey on Domestic Violence in Cambodia.* Phnom Penh: Cambodia Ministry of Women's Affairs, Project Against Domestic Violence.

Nordquist, J. 1998. *Violence Against Women—International Aspects: A Bibliography.* Contemporary Social Issues: Bibliographic Series 49. Santa Cruz, Calif.: Reference and Research Services.

Odujinrin, O. 1993. Wife Battering in Nigeria. *International Journal of Gynecology and Obstetrics* 41:159-64.

O'Leary, K. D., and A. D. Curley. 1986. Assertion and Family Violence: Correlates of Spouse Abuse. *Journal of Marital and Family Therapy* 12:281-89.

O'Leary, K. D., et al. 1989. Prevalence and Stability of Physical Aggression Between Spouses: A Longitudinal Analysis. *Journal of Consulting and Clinical Psychology* 57, no. 2:263-68.

Pagelow, M. D., and P. Johnson. 1988. Abuse in the American Family: The Role of Religion. In *Abuse and Religion: When Praying Isn't Enough,* ed. A. Horton and J. Williamson, pp. 1-12. Lexington, Mass.: Heath.

Peled, I., P. G. Jaffe and J. L. Edleson, eds. 1995. *Ending the Cycle of Violence: Community Responses to Children of Battered Women.* Thousand Oaks, Calif.: Sage.

Peters, J. S., and Andrea Wolper, eds. 1995. *Women's Rights, Human Rights: International Feminist Perspectives.* New York: Routledge.

Plichta, S. B., et al. 1992. The Effects of Woman Abuse on Health Care Utilization and Health Status: A Literature Review. *Women's Health Issues* 2, no. 3:154-61.

———. 1996. Violence and Gynaecologic Health in Women <50 years old. *American Journal of Obstetrics and Gynecology* 174:903-7.

Potter, H. 2007. Battered Black Women's Use of Religious Services and Spirituality for Assistance in Leaving Abusive Relationships. *Violence Against Women* 13, no. 3:262-84.

ProFamilia. 1990. *Encuesta de prevalencia, demografia y salud* (Demographic and Health Survey). Bogotá: Profamilia.

Ptacek, James. 1988. How Men Who Batter Rationalize Their Behavior. In *Abuse and Religion: When Praying Isn't Enough,* ed. A. Horton and J. Williamson, pp. 247-58. Lexington, Mass.: Heath.

Radford, Jill, and Elizabeth Stanko. 1995. Violence Against Women and Children: The Contradictions of Crime Control Under Patriarchy. In *Women, Violence and Male Power: Feminist Activism, Research and Practice,* ed. Marianne Hester, Liz Kelly, and Jill Redford, pp. 65-80. Milton Keynes, England: Open University Press. First published in *The Politics of Crime Control,* ed. Kevin Stenson and David Cowell. London: Sage, 1991.

Raikes, Alanagh. 1990. *Pregnancy, Birthing and Family Planning in Kenya— Changing Patterns of Behaviour: A Health Utilisation Study in Kissi District.* Copenhagen: Centre for Development Research.

Raj, A., and J. Silverman. 2002. Violence Against Immigrant Women: The Roles of Culture, Context, and Legal Immigrant Status on Intimate Partner Violence. *Violence Against Women* 8, no. 3:367-98.

Ramasubban, Radhika, and Bhanwar Singh. 1997. *Gender, Reproductive Health and Weakness Experiences of Slum Dwelling Women in Bombay, India.* IUSSP Seminar on Cultural Perspectives on Reproductive Health, Rustenberg, South Africa, June 16-19, 1997, p. 24.

―――. 1998. "Ashaktapana" (Weakness) and Reproductive Health in a Slum Population in Mumbai, India. In *Cultural Perspectives in Reproductive Health,* ed. Carla M. Obermeyer. Oxford: Oxford University Press.

Ramirez Rodriguez, Juan Carlos, et al. 1996. *Una espada de doble filo: La salud reproductiva y la violencia doméstica contra la mujer.* Presentation to Seminario Salud Reproductiva en America Latina y el Caribe, Brazil.

Randall, Margaret, and L. Haskell. 1995. Sexual Violence in Women's Lives: Findings from the Women's Safety Project, a Community-Based Survey. *Violence Against Women* 1, no. 1:6-31.

Rodgers, K. 1994. Wife Assault: The Findings of a National Survey. *Juristat Service Bulletin of the Canadian Centre for Justice Statistics* 14, no. 9:1-22.

Rodríguez, J., and P. Becerra. 1997. *Que tan serio es el problema de la violencia doméstica contra la mujer? Algunos datos para la discusión.* Paper presented at the Congreso Nacional de Investigación en Salud Pública, Brazil. March 1997.

Römkens, Renée. 1997. Prevalence of Wife Abuse in the Netherlands: Combining Quantitative and Qualitative Methods in Survey Research. *Journal of Interpersonal Violence* 12, no. 1:99-125.

Rothenberg, Karen H., et al. 1995. Domestic Violence and Partner Notification: Implications for Treatment and Counseling of Women with HIV. *Journal of the American Medical Women's Association* 50, no. 3:87-93.

Rothery, M., L. Tutty and G. Weaver. 1999. Tough Choices: Women, Abusive Partners and the Ecology of Decision-Making. *Canadian Journal of Community Mental Health* 18:5-18.

Rotunda, R. J., G. Williamson and M. Penfold. 2004. Clergy Response to Domestic Violence: A Preliminary Survey of Clergy Members, Victims and Batterers. *Pastoral Psychology* 52, no. 4:353-365.

Saltzman, L. 1995. Violence Against Women Estimated from the Redesigned Survey. National Crime Victimization Survey, U.S. Department of Justice, Bureau of Justice Statistics, August monthly report, 1995.

Saunders, Daniel G. 1986. When Battered Women Use Violence: Husband-Abuse or Self-Defense? *Victims and Violence* 1, no. 1:47-60.

Schafer, J., Raul Caetano and Catherine L. Clark. 1998. Rates of Intimate Partner Violence in the United States. *American Journal of Public Health* 88, no. 11:1702-4.

Schei, Berit, and L. S. Bakketeig. 1989. Gynaecological Impact of Sexual and Physical Abuse by Spouse: A Study of a Random Sample of Norwegian Women. *British Journal of Obstetrics and Gynaecology* 96:1379-83.

Schuler, Sidney Ruth, et al. 1996. Credit Programs, Patriarchy and Men's Violence Against Women in Rural Bangladesh. *Social Science and Medicine* 43, no. 12:1729-42.

Schüssler Fiorenza, Elisabeth, and M. S. Copeland, eds. 1994. *Violence Against Women*. London: SCM Press.

Schwartz, M. D. 1987. Gender and Injury in Spousal Assault. *Sociological Focus* 20, no. 1:61-75.

Seager, Joni. 1997. *The State of Women in the World Atlas*. New ed. London: Penguin.

Senter, K. E., and K. Caldwell. 2002. Spirituality and the Maintenance of Change: A Phenomenological Study of Women Who Leave Abusive Relationships. *Contemporary Family Therapy* 24, no. 4:543-56.

Sexwale, B. 1994. Violence Against Women: Experiences of South African Domestic Workers. In *The Dynamic of "Race" and Gender: Some Feminist Inter-*

ventions, ed. Haleh Afshar and Mary Maynard. Bristol, Penn.: Taylor & Francis.

Shaw, M. 1996. The Survey of Federally Sentenced Women, as cited in *The Arbour Report*. Ottawa: Correctional Services of Canada.

Shelly, L. 1987. Inter-personal Violence in the USSR. *Violence, Aggression and Terrorism* 1, no. 2:41-67.

Shiroma, M. 1996. *Salud reproductiva y violencia contra la mujer: Un análisis desde la perspectiva de género*. Nuevo León: Asociación Mexicana de Población, Consejo Estatal de Población, Colegio de México.

Siddiqui, Hannana. 1996. Domestic Violence in Asian Communities: The Experience of Southall Black Sisters. In *Women in a Violent World: Feminist Analyses and Resistance Across "Europe,"* ed. Chris Corrin. Edinburgh: Edinburgh University Press.

Siklova, J., and J. Hradilkova. 1994. Women and Violence in Post-Communist Czechoslovakia. In *Women and Violence*, ed. Miranda Davies. London: Zed.

Smalley, Gary. 1988. *Hidden Keys of a Loving, Lasting Marriage*. Grand Rapids: Zondervan.

———. 1996. *Making Love Last Forever*. Dallas: Word.

Smyth, Ailbhe. 1996. Seeing Red: Men's Violence Against Women in Ireland. In *Women in a Violent World: Feminist Analyses and Resistance Across "Europe,"* ed. Chris Corrin. Edinburgh: Edinburgh University Press.

Sokoloff, N. J., and I. Dupont. 2005. Domestic Violence at the Intersections of Race, Class and Gender. *Violence Against Women* 11, no. 1:38-64.

South Africa Department of Health. 1999. *South Africa Demographic and Health Survey, 1998: Preliminary Report*. Calverton, Md.: Macro International.

Spijkerboer, Thomas. 1994. *Women and Refugee Status: Beyond the Public/Private Distinction*. The Hague: Emancipation Council.

Stacey, William, Lonnie Hazlewood and Anson Shupe. 1994. *The Violent Couple*. New York: Praeger.

Stacey, William L., and Anson Shupe. 1983. *The Family Secret*. Boston: Beacon.

Stanko, B. 1995. The Struggle over Common Sense: Feminism, Violence and Confronting the Backlash. In *Proceedings of the Fifth Symposium on Violence and Aggression*, ed. B. Gillis and G. James, pp. 156-72. Saskatoon: University of Saskatchewan Press.

Stark, Evan, and Anne Flitcraft. 1982. Medical Therapy as Repression: The Case of Battered Women. *Health and Medicine*, Summer-Fall 1982, pp. 29-32.

Statistics Canada. 1993. The Violence Against Women Survey. *The Daily,* November 18, 1993.

Stirling, M. L., et al., eds. 2004. *Woman Abuse: Partnering for Change.* Toronto: University of Toronto Press.

Straus, Murray A., and Richard J. Gelles. 1986. Societal Change and Change in Family Violence from 1975 to 1985 as Revealed by Two National Surveys. *Journal of Marriage and the Family* 48:465-79.

———, eds. 1990. *Physical Violence in American Families: Risk Factors and Adaptations to Violence in 8,145 Families.* New Brunswick, N.J.: Transaction.

Straus, Murray A., Richard J. Gelles and Susan K. Steinmetz. 1980. *Behind Closed Doors: Violence in the American Family.* Garden City, N.Y.: Doubleday/Anchor.

Strom, Kay Marshall. 1986. *In the Name of Submission.* Portland, Ore.: Multnomah Press.

Sullivan, C. M., and M. H. Rumptz. 1994. Adjustment and Needs of African-American Women Who Utilized a Domestic Violence Shelter. *Violence and Victims* 9:275- 86.

Swiss, S., and J. Giller. 1993. Rape as a Crime of War: A Medical Perspective. *Journal of the American Medical Association* 270:612-15.

Szinovacz, Maximiliane E., and Lance C. Egley. 1995. Comparing One-Partner and Couple Data on Sensitive Marital Behaviors: The Case of Marital Violence. *Journal of Marriage and the Family* 57:1995-2020.

Tarrezz Nash, Shondrah. 2006. Changing of the Gods: Abused Christian Wives and Their Hermeneutic Revision of Gender, Power, and Spousal Conduct. *Qualitative Sociology* 29:195-209.

Terris, Christy. 1996. Cares, Conflict and Counselling: A Study of Evangelical Youth and Their Youth Pastors. M.A. thesis, University of New Brunswick.

Thorne-Finch, Ron. 1992. *Ending the Silence: The Origins and Treatment of Male Violence Against Women.* Toronto: University of Toronto Press.

Timmins, Leslie. 1995. *Listening to the Thunder: Advocates Talk About the Battered Women's Movement.* Vancouver: Women's Research Centre.

Trainor, C. 1999. Canada's Shelters for Abused Women. *Juristat Bulletin of the Canadian Centre for Justice Statistics* 19, no. 6.

Tutty, Leslie M. 1998. "Mental Health Issues of Abused Women: The Perceptions of Shelter Workers. *Canadian Journal of Community Mental Health* 17:79-102.

United Nations. 1989. *Violence Against Women in the Family.* New York: United Nations.

––––––. 1994a. Declaration on the Elimination of Violence Against Women. Resolution No. A/Res/48/104. New York: United Nations, February 23.

––––––. 1994b. Preliminary Report of the Special Rapporteur on Violence Against Women, Its Causes and Consequences in Accordance with Commission on Human Rights Resolution 1994/45. Document E/CN.4/1995/42. New York: Economic and Social Council, Commission on Human Rights.

––––––. 1994c. *Strategies for Confronting Domestic Violence: A Resource Manual.* New York: United Nations.

––––––. 1995. The World's Women 1995: Trends and Statistics. *Social Statistics and Indicators,* series K, no. 12.

––––––. 1996. Report of the Special Rapporteur on Violence Against Women, Its Causes and Consequences, in Accordance with Commission on Human Rights Resolution 1995/85. Document E/CN.4/1996/53. New York: Economic and Social Council, Commission on Human Rights.

––––––. 1997. Report of the Special Rapporteur on Violence Against Women, Its Causes and Its Consequences. Document E/CN.4/1997/47. New York: Economic and Social Council, Commission on Human Rights.

––––––. 1998. Status of Women Commission Hears Call for Elaboration of Legally Binding International Instrument on Violence Against Women. Status of Women press release, March 5, 1998.

United States Department of Justice. 1993. National Crime Victimization Survey, 1973-92. Washington, D.C.: Bureau of Justice Statistics.

––––––. 1995. National Crime Victimization Survey, 1992-93. Washington, D.C.: Bureau of Justice Statistics, August 1995.

––––––. 1998. Prevalence, Incidence and Consequences of Violence Against Women: Findings from the National Violence Against Women Survey. Washington, D.C.: Department of Justice.

van der Straten, A. 1995. Couple Communication, Sexual Coercion and HIV Risk Reduction in Kigali, Rwanda. *AIDS* 9, no. 8:935-44.

Vivian, D., and Jennifer Langhinrichsen-Rohling. 1994. Are Bi-directionally-Violent Couples Mutually Victimized? A Gender-Sensitive Comparison. *Violence and Victims* 9, no. 2:107-24.

Walker, Gillian. 1984. *The Battered Woman Syndrome.* New York: Springer.

––––––. 1990. *Family Violence and the Women's Movement: The Conceptual Politics of Struggle.* Toronto: University of Toronto Press.

Walker, Lenore. 1988. Spouse Abuse: A Basic Profile. In *Abuse and Religion: When Praying Isn't Enough,* ed. Anne Horton and Judith Williamson, pp. 13-20. Lexington, Mass.: Heath.

Ware, K. N., H. N. Levitt and G. Bayer. 2003. May God Help You: Faith Leaders' Perspective of Intimate Partner Violence Within Their Communities. *Journal of Religion and Abuse* 5, no. 2:55-82.

Watts, C., M. Ndlovu and E. Keogh. 1997. *The Magnitude and Health Consequences of Violence Against Women in Zimbabwe: Musasa Project Report, 1997.* Geneva: World Health Organization.

Whipple, Vicky. 1987. Counseling Battered Women from Fundamentalist Churches. *Journal for Marital and Family Therapy* 13, no. 3:251-58.

White, J. W., and Robin M. Kowalski. 1994. Deconstructing the Myth of the Nonaggressive Woman. *Psychology of Women Quarterly* 18: 487-508.

Widom, C. S. 1992. *The Cycle of Violence.* Washington, D.C.: National Institute of Justice.

———. 1996. *The Cycle of Violence Revisited.* Washington, D.C.: National Institute of Justice.

Wilson, M., and Martin Daly. 1993. Spousal Homicide Risk and Estrangement. *Victims and Violence* 8, no. 1:3-16.

———. 1994. Spousal Homicide. *Juristat Bulletin of the Canadian Centre for Justice Statistics* 14, no. 8:1-15.

Winkelmann, C. 2004. *The Language of Battered Women: A Rhetorical Analysis of Personal Theologies.* Albany, N.Y.: State University of New York Press.

World Association for Christian Communication. 1998. *Action: News from the World Association for Christian Communication* 204, March 1998.

World Bank. 1993. *World Development Report 1993: Investing in Health.* New York: Oxford University Press.

World Health Organization. 1994. *Violence Against Women.* Geneva: WHO.

———. 1996. Female Genital Mutilation. Document WHO/FRH/WHD/96.26. Geneva: WHO.

Wulf, D. 1994. *Refugee Women and Reproductive Health: Reassessing Priorities.* New York: Women's Commission for Refugee Women and Children.

Yarbrough, D. N., and P. W. Blanton. 2000. Socio-demographic Indicators of Intervention Program Completion with the Male Court-Referred Perpetrators of Partner Abuse. *Journal of Criminal Justice* 28, no. 6:517-26.

Zabelina, T. 1996. Sexual Violence Towards Women. In *Gender, Generation and Identity in Contemporary Russia,* ed. H. Pilkington. London: Routledge.

Zapata, B. C., et al. 1992. The Influence of Social and Political Violence on the Risk of Pregnancy Complications. *American Journal of Public Health* 82, no. 5:685-90.

Zwi, A., and A. Ugalde, 1989. Towards an Epidemiology of Political Violence in the Third World. *Social Science and Medicine* 28, no. 7:649-57.

DATE DUE
